WALKING EASY

in the

ITALIAN AND FRENCH ALPS

Chet and Carolee Lipton

The Globe Pequot Press

Guilford, Connecticut

To Barbara, Arnie, Dustin, Sue, and Steve—
the next generation of *Easy Walkers*

Maps and page design: Lisa Reneson
Photographs and pen and pencil illustrations: Chet Lipton

ISBN 0-7627-2232-0

Manufactured in the United States of America
First Edition/First Printing

CONTENTS

ACKNOWLEDGMENTS   IV

BECOMING AN EASY WALKER   V

    Dressing for the Trail—From Boots to Backpack • Pack Light and Right • Currency and Credit Cards • For Your Information • Rules of the Road

ITALY   1

    Timing Is Everything • Arriving in Italy by Airplane • Italy by Train • Italy by Car • Italy by Bus • Comfortable Inns and Hotels • Regional Food Specialties • Where to Eat and Drink

Selva/Wolkenstein (Gardena Valley)   11
Cortina d'Ampezzo   29
Merano/Meran   48
Alleghe   65
Vigo di Fassa   79
Venice   95

FRANCE   101

    Timing Is Everything • Arriving in France by Airplane • France by Train • France by Car • France by Bus • France Up and Down • Comfortable Inns and Hotels • Regional Food Specialties • Where to Eat and Drink

Chamonix   112
Megève   136
Morzine   151
Méribel   159
Les Arcs/Bourg-Saint-Maurice   177
Embrun   193
Paris Expressed   211

Indexes   221
About the Author   227

ACKNOWLEDGMENTS

A special thank you to Marion Fourestier, French Government Tourist Office, New York; A. J. Lazarus Associates, Public Relations Rail Europe; Auto France, Inc., Ramsey, N.J.; and Gianni Milani, Cortina Radio, Cortina d'Ampezzo.

A special *grazie* to the helpful personnel at the Tourist Offices in Alleghe, Cortina d'Ampezzo, Merano, Selva, and Vigo di Fassa.

Another *merci* goes to the Tourist Offices in Les Arcs/Bourg-Saint-Maurice, Chamonix, Embrun, Megève, Méribel, and Morzine.

We also wish to thank the hotel owners and staffs for providing the authors with local village history, general background information, and helpful hints about their best walking trails.

BECOMING AN *EASY WALKER*

Walking Easy in the Italian and French Alps, like its predecessors in the *Walking Easy* series of hiking guides, is written for active adults and young families who enjoy walking, prefer the exhilarating outdoors, and have the need to fulfill a quest for discovery. This is a how-to book, filled with carefully detailed day walks, based out of charming alpine villages and towns. It also provides sight-seeing excursions for lazier days, including special itineraries for Venice, Bolzano, Paris, and Annecy; suggestions for comfortable accommodations; and helpful hints to benefit the recreational walker.

Each section in this guide book is devoted to a particularly beautiful village or mountain area and includes a brief description of its location, access by auto or public transportation, and excursions to nearby points of interest. We recommend that *Easy Walkers* spend five days to a week in each base village from which the area walks can be conveniently accessed. Every walk is preceded by an overview, followed by directions on how to arrive at the start of the walk from the base village. Many walks begin with a mountain railway or thrilling cable-car ride, while others are gentle walks through the forest or around a tranquil lake. Some are above the tree line along balcony trails, while others descend through alpine meadows—all within the capability and range of most active adults, planned to give *Easy Walkers* maximum visual pleasure. Every activity described in the following chapters has been experienced by the authors, joining travelers of all ages who walk on the intricate and fascinating network of Italian and French alpine hiking trails.

The walks are graded into three classifications: **gentle**—low-level walks with few ascents and descents, through valleys, around lakes, and along rivers; **comfortable**—walks with ascents and descents over mixed terrain; **more challenging**—walks that involve longer, more challenging ascents and descents on narrower, rockier trails.

Most walks can be accomplished in two to five hours by walkers of any age in good health. In addition to many "easy-guide" maps, you'll also find a recommended easy-to-follow hiking map (or maps) listed at the beginning of each village's Walks section. These, and other maps, can be purchased at a local Tourist Information office or newspaper/magazine store. While a map is a necessity, you may find it fun to also carry a small compass to check directions and a pedometer to keep track of walking distances.

The walking time listed before each walk is time spent *actually walking.* It does *not* include time spent for lunch, resting, photography, scenery breaks, sight-seeing, and transportation. This additional time is left to the discretion of each *Easy Walker*, so that an average day with a three-hour walk usually begins at 9:00 or 10:00 A.M., and can end back at your hotel in late afternoon.

The Alps have hundreds of miles of trails, most well signed and easily followed. As in our other *Walking Easy* guidebooks, the paths in the Italian and French Alps were chosen for their beauty, accessibility, walking time, and ease of use. But be warned: *Not* all the hikes are easy. Many will joyously challenge your capabilities with ascents and descents over rocky terrain. However, it's not uncommon for people of all ages to be steadily wending their way along favorite trails. Walking is not just for the young, it's also for the young at heart. The Italians and French have created a wonderful alpine trail system, and it's the best way to see the magnificent countryside. Walkers are welcome almost everywhere in their hiking boots and daypacks.

Dressing for the Trail—
From Boots to Backpack

Walking Easy clothing should ideally be lightweight and layerable. All clothing is not suitable for all types of walking: climate, altitude, and time of day during the alpine hiking season are points to consider. You must make a decision each day, taking those factors into consideration. It's not necessary to bring a dress or sport jacket on this walking vacation. However, a classic mix of slacks layered with shirts and sweaters is appropriate for dinner or sightseeing.

Hiking Boots: The most important item for a satisfactory *Walking Easy* experience is a good pair of broken-in, medium-weight hiking boots, preferably waterproof. These can be above or below the ankle, with the higher ones providing more support on rocky or steep trails. Do *not* wear sneakers or sneakers that look like hiking boots. They do not provide the support and traction needed. Remember, inexpensive hiking boots may not have the same level of construction as costlier boots—durability, water-proofing, foot stability, and overall quality. All boots will probably feel good when the trail is level and smooth, but remember the ascents, descents, rocks, and rain!

Socks: Experts tell us that socks worn closest to the skin should *not* be made of cotton. Cotton absorbs perspiration and holds it, possibly producing friction leading to blisters. A lightweight undersock made of a "hydrophobic" or water-hating synthetic will wick sweat away from your feet and keep them dry. Whether you prefer to wear one or two pair of socks, *when purchasing hiking boots, make sure to wear the type of socks you'll wear on the trail.*

Outerwear: A Polartec-type jacket is essential for walking and sightseeing in the high Alps. These lightweight but warm fleece jackets are easily put into backpacks when not needed. Rain protection is best provided by a good quality waterproof poncho with a snap-down back to fit over a backpack or by a waterproof jacket. Don't let rain cancel your walking plans.

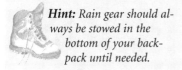

Hint: *Rain gear should always be stowed in the bottom of your backpack until needed.*

Hats: A hat with a brim provides protection from sun as well as rain and should always be worn.

Pants: We prefer the new, lightweight synthetic pants—great for hiking in cooler temperatures. Some alpine walkers wear jeans—an acceptable choice if they are not skintight and do not restrict movement. Walking shorts should also be considered in warmer weather, preferably worn with high socks (protection against brambles and bushes) that can be rolled down if necessary.

Sweaters: A medium-weight sweater is essential for cool evenings in the mountains.

Sweatshirts: Medium-weight sweatshirts can be layered over short- or long-sleeved knit shirts for hiking.

Shirts: While many people prefer 100 percent natural fibers for comfort, a polyester blend shirt might be used for ease of laundering, as it dries overnight. Short-sleeved knit shirts, along with long-sleeved knits and turtlenecks, are essential for layering under sweaters and sweatshirts, both for day and evening wear.

Backpack: Each *Easy Walker* should carry a lightweight, nylon backpack with wide, extra-heavy, adjustable foam shoulder straps. Roomy, outside zipper compartments (three to four if possible) are necessary to organize day-backpacking essentials, i.e., camera equipment, lunch, water, sunscreen, binoculars, emergency roll of toilet tissue, rain gear, jacket, etc.

Waist Pack: Use a well-made, comfortable waist pack to carry money, traveler's checks, passport, etc. *No pocketbook is necessary on a walking vacation.* Hands should be left free for a walking stick and/or camera.

Walking Stick: We strongly recommend a walking stick with a pointed, metal tip for *all Easy Walkers*. These sticks are indispensable aids to balance when walking downhill or on rocky terrain. They come in many sizes and styles and can be purchased in the United States or at village sporting goods stores in the Alps. The latest walking stick innovation looks like a telescoping aluminum ski pole. It fits into your backpack when not in use. We think this item is a "must."

Pack Light and Right

1. Keep luggage small, lightweight and expandable, even when using luggage with wheels.

2. Wear your hiking boots for overseas and intercity travel—they can be heavy and bulky to carry or pack. Remove them on the plane, perhaps changing to a pair of lightweight slippers you've put into your backpack.

3. On the plane, wear comfortable slacks, knit shirt, and an unlined jacket, along with your waist pack and hiking boots. A lightweight warm-up suit can be a good alternative. The jacket can be worn when it's too warm for your insulated jacket.

4. Every *Easy Walker* should use his/her backpack as carry-on luggage. When traveling, your backpack should include the following:

All drugs and toiletries, with prescriptions in a separate zippered pouch for easy accessibility. Bring more than an adequate supply of prescription drugs in case you are delayed in returning home, plus prescriptions for medications using their generic name, in case a local doctor must write a new one. Carry over the counter medications to relieve diarrhea, sunburn, constipation, indigestion, colds and allergies, cuts and bruises, etc. If you wear glasses, carry a spare pair and a copy of your prescription.

For the plane, a change of socks, underwear, and shirt, rolled into a plastic bag, just in case.

Waterproof outerwear, always left in the bottom of your backpack till needed.

Reading material and, of course, your *Walking Easy* guidebook.

Roll of toilet paper in a plastic bag.

Polartec-type jacket.

Slippers for the plane and later use.

Incidentals, such as binoculars, compass, whistle, pedometer, tiny flashlight, pocket knife, plastic bags, small sewing kit, sunglasses, travel alarm, small address book or preprinted labels, small packs of tissues, and "handiwipes."

Photographic equipment, unless carried separately.

Currency and Credit Cards

In early 2002 the euro replaced the currency of Austria, Belgium, Finland, *France*, Germany, Greece, Ireland, *Italy*, Luxembourg, the Netherlands, Portugal, and Spain. The Italian lira and the French franc became a remembrance of things past.

Hint: *Keep a record of charge card numbers and telephone numbers for reporting a lost or stolen card separately from your credit cards.*

Most retail stores, hotels, and restaurants accept credit cards; while mountain inns, *refuges*, or *rifugi* do not. Determine if your hotels accept credit cards before leaving home. You might wish to take American traveler's checks to exchange for euros, or consider the use of an ATM machine for cash.

MasterCard and Visa are widely accepted, while American Express cards may have some limitations. Charging can work in your favor because of the card's rate of exchange advantage.

For Your Information

Tourist Information Offices: These offices, designated in Italy and France by an "i," are a valuable friend to the hiker. They're found on the main street of even the smallest village and near the train station in larger towns. The personnel are usually multilingual and can help with everything from maps to local information.

Metric Measurements: Italy and France operate on the metric system. To convert kilometers to miles, multiply the number of kilometers by .62; to convert meters to feet, multiply the number of meters by 3.281; to convert liters to U.S. gallons, multiply the number of liters by .26; to convert kilograms to pounds, multiply the kilograms by 2.2; to convert Celsius to Fahrenheit degrees, multiply Celsius degrees by 9, divide by 5, and add 32.

Electricity: In Italy and France, electricity is measured in alternating current, with 220 voltage. Bring a converter to adjust voltage to 110 volts and plug adaptors for electrical outlets.

Calling from the United States: To call Italy or France from the United States, first dial the international access number (011) followed by the country code (33 for France and 39 for Italy), followed by the number as it appears in this book.

Rules of the Road

1. Plan your route by checking this book and local hiking maps before beginning each walk. Always carry a local hiking map with you.

2. Ask about local weather conditions and adjust the day's activities accordingly.

3. Tell someone about your planned route, either a friend or one of the hotel staff.

4. Take your time, especially at higher altitudes.

5. *Never* leave the marked trail.

6. Turning back is not a disgrace if you feel the trail is too difficult or the weather looks threatening. Return on the same path or check available public transportation.

7. Make sure your hiking shoes are in good shape and your backpack holds the needed items, plus lunch and a snack in case you are delayed. *Always* carry bottled water in your backpack. Longer and more strenuous hikes require more water—figure on at least one liter per person per hike.

8. In case of accident, stay calm and send for help. If this is not possible, use the standard alpine distress signal with your whistle. Make six signals, spaced evenly within one minute, pause for one minute, then repeat until your signal has been answered.

9. Don't litter. Take out what you bring in and carry plastic bags in your backpack for this purpose.

10. Alpine gates work in wondrous ways—some are turnstiles, some have spring-attached hooks, some feature sliding boards, and others are meant to be ducked under or stepped over. Whichever the case, be sure you leave the gate the way you approached it—closed.

11. Appreciate the beauty of the wildflowers but don't pick them.

12. Always check current timetables when using public transportation.

13. Sunscreen and sunglasses are very important at high altitudes, especially on glacier walks.

The purpose of any walking trip is to have fun. So take a hike—you can do it! Just tuck a copy of *Walking Easy in the Italian and French Alps* in a pocket, and you're on your way!

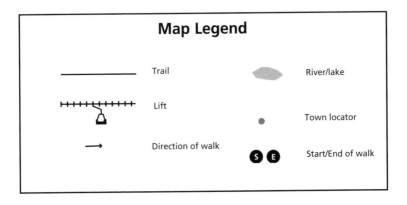

Map Legend

———————	Trail		River/lake
⊢⊢⊢⊢⊢⊢⊢⊢⊢⊢	Lift	•	Town locator
→	Direction of walk	**S** **E**	Start/End of walk

ITALY

Lake Geneva

Merano/Meran ❖   ❖ Selva/Wolkenstein

Cortina d'Ampezzo

Vigo di Fassa ❖   ❖ Alleghe

Milan ❖

Venice ❖

Padua ❖

ADRIATIC SEA

LIGURIAN SEA

⭐ Rome

TYRRHENIAN SEA

ITALY

The Italian Alps range is a vast band of enormous peaks, encompassing the dramatic shadings and ever-changing hues of the awe-inspiring Dolomites and the lush, green meadows of the Südtirol. Walking trails in the Italian Alps match the high quality of those in the neighboring alpine countries of Switzerland, France, and Austria. These trail systems are supported by helpful local Tourist Offices, along with friendly villagers and hotelkeepers, anxious to share the wonders of their mountains with hikers from around the world. In summer, most tourists flock to the popular destinations of Florence, Rome, and Venice—too few taking the opportunity to experience the overwhelming natural beauty of the Italian Alps, to taste the local cuisine in remote villages, or to share in the Ladino and Südtirolean cultures.

The Südtirol/Alto Adige or South Tyrol of northern Italy (near the Swiss and Austrian borders) has much to offer *Easy Walkers* who are interested in the customs of this unusual area, part of Austria until it was ceded to Italy over eighty years ago. Not one, but three languages are spoken: Ladin, an ancient Rhaeto-Romance language; German, a result of the Südtirol's Austrian heritage; and Italian. This is the reason for multilingual names and signs, such as Selva/Wolkenstein, Vipitano/Sterzing, Chiusa/Klausen, and Ortesei/St. Ulrich/Urtejei. The high altitude of the Südtirol is attractive to visitors, with 85 percent of its total area over 3300 ft. (1000 m.), ensuring cool summer evenings. The landscape appeals to those who want a wide variety of walking experiences—trails through the boundless orchards and terraced vineyards around Merano, to high alpine hamlets and remote dairy farms above Vigo di Fassa, to glacial lakes and tall pine forests above Cortina d'Ampezzo, and to steep slopes under snow-capped peaks towering over Selva. From the Mediterranean climate and palm trees in elegant Merano to the high, jagged Dolomite peaks at the Sella Pass, the Südtirol/Alto Adige in Italy's northern mountains has an abundance of well-signed, diverse walking trails to thrill *Easy Walkers*.

The base villages chosen in Italy are Alleghe, Cortina d'Ampezzo, Merano, Selva, and Vigo di Fassa. All beckon you to discover the varied delights of *Walking Easy* in the Italian Alps. As a bonus for *Easy Walkers*, a short walking tour of romantic Venice is included, only a two- to three-hour ride from many Italian alpine areas. Additional sightseeing opportunities are explored, including a visit to the "Ice Man" museum in Bolzano.

The Dolomites, Europe's most dramatic and spectacular mountain range, lie within the Südtirol of northeastern Italy, and are composed of over fourteen different mountain chains, separated by high passes, valleys, and rivers, with at least one 10,000-foot (3050-meter) peak in each massif. They differ from mountains in other alpine regions because of the composition of their rock. An ancient sea has been transformed by time, ice, and water into peaks and ridges that have been frequently photographed, painted, explored, and described. These are the majestic, pale mountains with unforgettable names—Cinque Torri and Tre Cime near Cortina d'Ampezzo, the wall of Civetta towering over Alleghe, the mighty Sassolungo across from Selva, and Catanaccio/Rosengarten working its magic spell above Vigo di Fassa—all are locations of *Walking Easy* hikes.

The marks of history are everywhere in the Italian Alps. Eighty of the 350 Gothic-style castles, fortresses, manor houses, and monasteries in the Südtirol, dating from the twelfth and thirteenth centuries, are still inhabited, and several of the walks in this guidebook take you through their gates to evoke memories of knights in shining armor and bygone eras. It's enlightening to visit a museum in a large city with artifacts presented behind glass cases, but entering a castle or church at the place where it was erected 600 years ago is a very personal experience. *Easy Walkers* can do it all, especially in the Italian Alps, where you will walk in these impressive mountains and touch a little bit of history along the way.

Winter sports are the basis of many thriving northern Italian economies, and fabulous summer hiking possibilities attract walkers from around the world to many of the same villages, keeping the hotels filled during the shorter summer season. Strategically placed lifts bring outdoor enthusiasts to the beginning of pleasant day-hikes through pine and larch forests on well-marked trails. *Ristorantes* and *rifugi* are everywhere, with their owners anxious to prepare local specialties from recipes that have been a part of their family tradition for generations. Enjoy!

Timing Is Everything

The villages in the Dolomites are usually warmer and have less annual rainfall than northern alpine areas in Switzerland and Austria. Hiking season here can begin at the end of June and last through mid-September. Mid-June to early August features pleasant days and cool nights, with little rain. The days become warmer in August, with late afternoon showers not uncommon. However, September is usually clear and pleasant.

If you have a choice of selecting the timing of your walking vacation in the Italian Alps, the end of June and the month of July are superior—there are fewer tourists and a cooler climate—ideal for walking. July features brilliant explosions of wildflowers throughout the mountains and valleys. While the cities are crowded with European summer vacationers, the serenity of hundreds of miles of shaded forest and high alpine trails is hardly ever shattered by too many walkers. Although the trails are usually uncrowded, remember that in August almost all of Italy goes on vacation, especially around the August 15th national holiday of *Ferragosto*. Vacationing Italians descend upon the roads and the trains—don't leave home without reservations! Hotels are also more expensive in August; try to avoid this month in the Italian Alps! However, whichever month you choose, the Italian Alps will provide an exhilarating vacation.

Arriving in Italy by Airplane

The Venice airport is only two to three hours by car from many of our favorite alpine villages. From Milan, it takes about five hours' driving time to reach the general area of the Alps; from Munich, a little less, picking up the Brenner Pass south near Innsbruck, Austria. Rental cars are available at all airports.

 Hint: *Some lifts do not open until July 1, and others may close the first week in September. Always check with the Tourist Office in the base villages to be sure lifts are running and plan your walking trip accordingly.*

Italy by Train

The Italian rail system is run by **Ferrovie Italiene dello Stato (FS).** Seven types of trains make up the rail service:

1. **Eurostar:** Super fast trains, making few stops. They require a supplement that includes seat reservations.
2. **ETR 500 Pendelino:** Similar to the fast French TGV. There is a supplementary charge for these trains, and a seat reservation is necessary and must be made at least five hours in advance.
3. **Eurocity:** Links Italian cities with major European cities.
4. **Intercity:** Fast, first-class trains between major cities and towns, with a supplementary charge.

5. Expresso: Long distance trains with first- and second-class cars, stopping only at main stations.

6. Diretto: First- and second-class cars, stopping at most stations.

7. Locale: Slow, short-distance trains, most second-class only, with basic comforts and stopping at all stations along the route.

Many European and Italian cities have convenient train service into larger towns and cities bordering the Italian Alps. Major railroad lines run

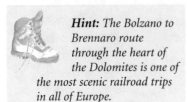

Hint: The Bolzano to Brennaro route through the heart of the Dolomites is one of the most scenic railroad trips in all of Europe.

north and south over the Brenner Pass and connect Italy with Austria and Germany. The main railroad stations in the Dolomites are at Bolzano, Trento, and Bressanone, with smaller connecting lines going into Ora, Chiusa, and Mezzocorona. Zurich, Switzerland, is connected by train to the Italian Alps through a change of train at Innsbruck, Austria.

Discount Train Travel in Italy

Italian Flex Rail Card: You can pick the days you'd like to travel by train to meet your own schedule. This pass includes the following:

1. Choice of three pass durations: any four days unlimited train travel in one month; any eight days unlimited train travel in one month; or any twelve days unlimited train travel in one month.

2. Choice of first- or second-class train travel.

Hint: For information or ordering Italian rail passes, call Rail Europe at (800) 4–EURAIL, or look for them at www.raileurope.com.

Italian Rail 'n Drive Pass: The Rail 'n Drive Pass gives you complete flexibility with the train and your own rental car.

Senior Discount Pass: This Italian railroad senior card, the Carte Argent, is valid for one year and provides a 30 percent discount on trains. It can be bought at major Italian railroad stations, and the cost is about $20 in euros.

Here are some Italian words that may be useful at the train station:

arrivi - arrival

biglietto - ticket

binario - track

di prima classe - first class

di seconda classe - second class

gabinetti per signore (or *donne*) - ladies room

orario ferroviario - timetable

partenza - departure

piattaforma - platform

prenotazione posti - seat reservation

stazione ferroviaro - railroad station

ufficio bagagli - baggage checkroom

ufficio biglietto - ticket office

uomini - men's room

uscita - exit

Italy by Car

If you are going to be in Italy for an extended period of time or traveling between villages, you'll probably be more comfortable using a car.

For those who require a car for less than seventeen days, most major car rental agencies are represented in Italy, and you can save on car rentals by making arrangements at home. Check to see whether your own auto insurance covers damage to a rental car overseas. Your credit card company may include CDW (collision damage waiver) if you charge the car rental to the credit card. You should also make sure that insurance for theft of the car is included. Confirm these facts with your credit card company and your insurance company before making your rental car reservations.

Hint: *If you are planning a trip to Europe for seventeen days or longer and prefer to travel by car, there is an interesting cost-saving Vacation Plan offered by Auto France. A new Peugeot is delivered to your airport or city of choice, and all insurance is included. There is no VAT (value added tax) and no maximum age restrictions. Check their Web site at www.auto-france.com and for further details call Auto France (800) 572–9655.*

You'll need a valid driver's license from your home country. An International Driver's License, available with two passport photos and $10 from the AAA in the United States, is a viable and readily understandable additional piece of identification when driving.

Gasoline is expensive in Europe. Unleaded gas in Italy is called *benzina piombo*, leaded gas is *benzina*, and diesel is *gasolio*. Many stations close for lunch, and few stay open late at night, except on the *autostrade*.

You'll drive on various types of roads during your stay in Italy. Among these are *autostrade* or toll highways and *superstrade* or free expressways. All are signed and numbered. *Raccordo* are connecting expressways, and a *strade statali* is a state highway with an "S" or "SS" number. It may be a single-lane road in each direction. In Italy, you drive on the right and pass on the left, just as you do in the United States. Remember though, that the speed limits may be different from what you are used to: 130 km/h (80 mph) on the *autostrade*, 90 km/h (55 mph) on main and local roads, and 50 km/h (30 mph) in cities and towns. You should also keep in mind that many Europeans drive over these stated speed limits. Stay to the right and use your rearview mirror often.

Road maps are sold at Italian newsstands and bookstores, and in the United States, many bookstores carry Michelin Map #988, *Italy*. Of course, other maps cover specific regions in more depth. An excellent road map of alpine Europe, especially if you are driving from one country to another, is *Alpen/The Alps*, published by Freytag & Berndt. The Automobile Club D'Italia publishes a map of "Südtirol/Dolomiten Italien." Write to *Azienda per la Promozione Turistica del Trentino*, Via Sighele, 3, 38100 Trento, Italy, and ask them to send you an excellent map called "Trentino Itineraries and Road Map."

Hint: Directions and turns are not always clearly marked on country roads, so stay alert.

The A22 *autostrada*, running north to south through the Brenner Pass, connects Austria and Germany with the Dolomites and alpine Italy. There are many exits from A22 leading into the mountains. All local roads leading into the Südtirol and/or the Dolomites are winding, and you usually drive up and over high passes through the mountains. Adjust your driving times accordingly.

Hint: Horn blowing is forbidden in most towns, and the large Zona di Silenzio *signs* are your indication.

A key point to remember is that Italian roadside emergency service is only a phone call away: call 116 in case of a breakdown.

Italy by Bus

Italy's bus network, although extensive, may not be as comprehensive as that of some other European countries. However, regional bus companies are sometimes the only means, other than car, of getting to out-of-the-way places, especially in the mountainous regions of the Italian Alps. Bus information is available at the local Tourist Office.

> **Hint:** *The local bus transportation in Selva and Merano is a big plus—use it to get to the start of hikes. Their service is excellent, and you can leave your car parked at the hotel. In Alleghe and Vigo, a car is a necessity for most hiking and sightseeing. In Cortina, we'd rather take a car, but bus service to the beginning and at the end of many hikes is available.*

Comfortable Inns and Hotels

Accommodations in Italy range from world-class, deluxe hotels to comfortable rooms in rural farmhouses. The quality of a hotel (*albergo*) and its prices can be judged by the number of stars awarded to it: five stars denotes deluxe; four stars, first-class; three stars, superior; two stars, standard; and one star, minimum. For comfort, quality of food, price, and convenience, we prefer to recommend three- or four-star hotels with half-board dining (breakfast and dinner) included. (Please see the Favorite *Walking Easy* Hotels section in each base village chapter.) Smaller guesthouses or *pensioni* are also available. They are less formal than hotels and usually less expensive. Rental apartments are a viable alternative to hotels. There are also other, less traditional accommodations available. Farm holidays have become increasingly popular. Many castles, convents, and palaces in the Südtirol have been converted into hotels. Italy also has camping sites, many of them in the Italian Alps. You might write to the Tourist Office in each area you are interested in and ask if accommodations other than traditional hotels are available.

Regional Food Specialties

Cuisine in Italian alpine areas can be a combination of Italian, Austrian, and Ladino specialities, depending on which village you are visiting. In the southern area of the Alps, the food will be distinctly Italian, but as you travel north into the Südtirol, the accent is definitely more Tyrolean, Germanic, and in certain valleys, Ladino. Expect to find Venetian-influenced, typically Italian dishes in Alleghe, and heartier, Tyrolean specialties in Selva.

Some of the more popular Südtirolean dishes are *krapfen*, a round, fried doughnut filled with jam; *knödlsuppe*, a clear soup with large bread dumplings; *wienerschnitzel*, breaded and sauteed veal cutlet; *spaetzli*, small dumplings; and, of course, *apfelstrudel*, a winner in any language. Typical Italian dishes can range from *risotto con funghi*, a creamy rice with mushrooms, to *patate fritte* (french fries), to the varied pastas we all know and love. Italian cheeses come in a grand variety. Fresh cheeses include mascarpone, mozzarella, and ricotta; mild cheeses are fontina, provolone dolce, scamorza; sharp cheeses can be asiago, gorgonzola, pecorino, and provolone piccante.

Beverages

Wine: The production of wine in the Trentino-Alto Adige is influenced by the proximity of the Südtirol to Austria, and white wine predominates. The Riesling, sauvignon, Sylvaner, pinot grigio, and Gewürtztraminer are excellent. The southern end of the Italian Alps or Trentino area produces a red cabernet and Teroldego.

Hint: Red = rosso, *white* = bianco, *rosé* = rosato, *dry* = secco *or* asciutto, *sweet* = dolce, *and bubbly* = spumanti.

Beer: Beer brewed in Italy is usually lighter than German beer, and many companies with familiar German names brew their beer in Italy specially formulated to the Italian taste. When in Italy, you should specify Italian beer, or you'll be served more expensive imported beer.

Liqueur: You can order almond-flavored amaretto, herb-flavored Galliano or Strega, cherry-flavored maraschino, or anise-flavored sambucca, which is traditionally served with coffee beans in the glass. Campari is the most famous aperitif, bright red and bitter from its herbs, usually served with ice and club soda. Grappa has a high alcohol content and is made just after the wine has been pressed. Drunk before or after dinner, it is considered to be an acquired taste.

Coffee: Enjoying coffee is an important part of Italian life. Italians normally drink *espresso*, very strong, black coffee, served in small cups. Strong coffee with foaming hot milk and a sprinkling of grated chocolate is *cappuccino*. *Caffè latte* is a large cup of coffee with hot milk, usually drunk at breakfast. A double measure of *espresso* is called *caffè doppio*. Extra-strong coffee is *caffè ristretto,* while a weak black coffee is *caffè alto* or *lungo. Caffè macchiato* is black coffee with a dash of milk, while *latte macchiato* is the opposite, a glass of milk with a dash of coffee. *Caffè montata* is coffee with whipped cream, and *caffè corretto* is served with brandy or *grappa* in it.

Mineral Water: Called *acqua minerale*, it comes carbonated (*frizzante* or *gassata*) or without bubbles (*naturale* or *senza gas*).

Where to Eat and Drink

Hotels: Three- and four-star Italian hotels in the Alps usually offer a buffet breakfast (more lavish in the Südtirol), and a four-course meal for dinner, if you take half-board. *Note: Hotel food in Italy is uniformly excellent, and* Easy Walkers *can take advantage of lower costs by booking hotel reservations with dinner.* A typical breakfast consists of juice, rolls, bread, butter, jam, cold cereal—perhaps cold meat, cheese, yogurt, and a hot beverage. Dinner can consist of a first course or *primo piatto* of pasta or soup, a second course with meat, fish or poultry, and vegetables, followed by salad and dessert (*dolci*) or fruit (*frutta*). Unlike France, the cheese course is usually eliminated in the Italian Alps, unless you are staying in a four- or five-star hotel. Most diners prefer to take their after-dinner coffee later at an outdoor cafe or in the hotel sitting room.

Restaurants: Check out a restaurant's *menu turistico*, usually including three courses, and often a quarter liter of wine or mineral water, as well as bread, cover charge, and tip (although you should leave a small, extra tip). The fixed price, or *prezzo fisso*, menu, is probably lower in price than the tourist menu, but it doesn't include wine, bread, cover charge, and tip—you'll be billed for all of these—and it usually isn't as good a buy.

> **Hint:** *A small bread and a cover charge* (pane e caperto) *is added in most Italian restaurants. The tip* (servizio compreso) *is usually included in the bill, but since it's only 10 to 15 percent, it's customary to leave something extra if the service was satisfactory.*

Picnicking: When planning a day of walking, we recommend taking a picnic lunch in your backpack. The bakery or *panificio* will astound you with its choice of bread and rolls, and you can select a local cheese and/or sliced cooked meat in the grocery (*drogheria*). Fresh fruit completes a healthy and inexpensive meal. Mustard can be bought in reusable squeeze tubes. Mineral water, juice, and soda are available in plastic bottles or cans.

Once you've hiked in northern Italy and discovered the warmth of its people and the quality of its trails, you'll return time and time again to *Walk Easy* in the Italian Alps.

SELVA/WOLKENSTEIN

(GARDENA VALLEY)

The picturesque, *Walking Easy* base village of Selva/Wolkenstein is nestled on the side of a sunny green meadow in the Val Gardena (Gardena Valley) between the majestic peaks and imposing rock formations of the "pale mountains" or Dolomites. The rocky giants of Stevia, Sella, and Sassolungo tower above Selva, while the two forest areas of Dantercepies and Ciampinoi act as buffer zones between village, meadow, and mountain.

Val Gardena includes the neighboring villages of Selva/Wolkenstein, Santa Cristina, and the cosmopolitan Ortisei/St. Ulrich. Selva, at 5128 ft. (1563 m.) at one end of the valley, is the entrance into the tranquil, un-spoiled glacial valley of Vallunga/Langental and the high, twisting Sella and Gardena Passes. Two major lifts operate during the summer in Selva, both used during *Easy Walker* excursions and hikes. The Ciampanoi gondola will take you to the start of hikes to Sassolungo, Passo Sella, and Monte Pana. The Dantercepies lift takes walkers up for a hike to Passo Gardena and the meadows and forests surrounding Selva.

Charming Santa Cristina, with its old town center and many farms sit-uated on the steep sides of Mont Pic, is between Selva and Ortisei and has two major summer lifts taking thousands of day-hikers to the impressive Col Raiser plateau on one side of the valley and to Monte Pana on the other side. Signed valley walking paths connect Selva and Santa Cristina to Ortisei, the major commercial and cultural center of the Val Gardena, with its beau-tiful seventeenth-century church, carefully maintained walking streets, col-orfully decorated buildings, fascinating shops filled with local handcrafts, and wood-carving workshops. Ortisei lifts include a cable car that rises to the Alpe di Siusi/Seiser Alm, at 6562 ft. (2005 m.), a particularly beautiful plateau and Europe's largest alp. A double cable lift rises to 8203 ft. (2500 m.) for viewing of the Dolomites to the north and east, and the Raschötz chairlift provides other mountain perspectives and is the start of many area hikes.

The earliest road through this enchanting valley was built in 1856 and brought geologists, biologists, and mountaineers, soon followed by tourists and hikers. The valley was part of Austria at the time, but in 1919 its province was separated from Austria and incorporated into Italy, the reason for the double and sometimes triple town names and culture—Italian, German, and Ladino. Many of the place names, including those of rivers and mountains, provide evidence that the entire Dolomite area supported settlements well before the time of Christ. However, about 15 B.C. the various peoples of the Central Alps, all speaking different languages and belonging to different races, were forcibly united into a new Roman province called Rhaetia. There was a period of colonization by Rome, with an influx of soldiers, merchants, officials, and new settlers who introduced Latin into the area. This language was modified by the original inhabitants who wove it into their existing language structure, and thus the Ladin language of the Val Gardena evolved over many centuries. Today's Ladins speak this Rhaeto-Roman dialect, one of the world's oldest languages, based on Latin with traces of Catalonian, Provençal, and French, and the old expressions are kept alive in local legends and songs. In Selva/Wolkenstein, population 2300, a large percentage of the local population still speak Ladino, and children study the language in school, along with Italian and German.

Early inhabitants of the Gardena Valley were poor mountain farmers, and at the beginning of the seventeenth century, when the art of wood-carving developed, it was a turning point in their harsh lives. The first wood-carving school in the Val Gardena was set up in Ortisei in 1872. Creative wood carving continues to be a major commercial and cultural force in the valley, with skills handed down from father to son over generations.

The entire valley gears up for walkers from all over the world, offering frequent local bus service, well-maintained and well-marked trails, unparalleled views of the surrounding Dolomites, and a large variety of hotels providing quality accommodations at all levels. The inhabitants of the Gardena/Gröden Valley try to maintain their ancient language, their beautiful costumes, and their Ladino names for traditional alpine food, such as doughnuts (*crafuncins da ula vërda*), dumplings (*bales de furmenton*), or barley soup with smoked pork and dumplings (*panicia cun cërn sfumiëda y bales*). The area's inhabitants still tell stories of a land of mythical creatures—dwarfs, gnomes and elves, earth-shattering giants, and princes—who created edelweiss from moonbeams. Enjoy the enchanting atmosphere of Selva and the Val Gardena.

Hint: *Try to visit the Val Gardena during July and the beginning of September—August can be hectic, the countryside and hotels filled with happy Italian families.*

Transportation

By Plane - The international airport at Munich is 186 miles (300 km) from Selva, as is the airport in Milan. From the airports, there are train and then bus connections through Bolzano/Bozen and Bressanone/Brixen. (See By Bus.) Car rentals are available at all airports.

By Train - The closest train stations to Selva are at Bolzano/Bozen and Bressanone/Brixen. There you can transfer to the SAD bus or take a taxi for the trip to Selva.

By Car - From the north, take *autostrada* A22 and exit at Ponte Gardena/Waidbrucke. Follow the signs to 242 east and the Val Gardena. You'll pass through Ortisei/St. Ulrich and S. Cristina before arriving in Selva. From the south, take *autostrada* A22 and also exit at Ponte Gardena/Waidbrucke, taking 242 east into Selva.

From the east and Cortina d'Ampezzo, use 48 west from Cortina over Passo Falzarego, 6907 ft. (2105 m.), and Passo Pordoi, 7510 ft. (2289 m.), picking up 242 west to Selva over the Passo Sella, at 7363 ft. (2244 m.).

By Bus - There is "SAD" bus service (*Servizi Autobus Dolomiti/ Südtiroler Autobus Dienst*) from Bolzano and Bressanone to Selva and excellent local area bus SAD bus connections. *Note: Check bus schedules on the Internet at www.sad.it.*

Favorite *Walking Easy* Hotel

Hotel Malleier
Three-Star; Owner - Elmar Torggler
39048 Selva/Gardena
Tel: 04 71 79 52 96, **Fax:** 04 71 79 43 64
E-mail: info@malleier.com
Internet: www.malleier.com

The chalet-style Hotel Malleier, situated on a quiet street above the village of Selva, offers wonderful views of the Sella mountain group and Sassolungo from its rooms and the sunny garden patio. Elmar Torggler has owned the hotel for over thirty years and, with his brother ensconced in the kitchen as chef, has made the Malleier a family hotel with many satisfied return guests. The hotel has been recently remodeled, and its comfortable bedrooms have modern, private facilities; balconies; and down comforters to sink into on cool mountain evenings.

The buffet breakfasts set the standard for the day, and dinners reflect the local cuisine—a mixture of northern Italian and Austrian specialties—with dishes ranging from polenta to schnitzel to pasta. There is also a salad bar plus a fresh vegetable buffet.

In the evening, the public rooms are usually filled with guests playing cards, reading, talking, and discussing the next day's activities. The hotel is away from the hustle and bustle of Selva's main street, but it is close to lifts, buses, shopping, and walking trails. Mr. Torggler assures us that *Easy Walkers* will be welcomed warmly at any time, but especially during those less-hectic months of July and September and the last weeks in June—in August, all of Italy is on vacation.

Lifts in and around Selva

Dantercepies - These gondolas rise to 7710 ft. (2350 m.) and provide superb views of the Sella group, Sassalungo, and into the Passo Sella/Grödner Joch. (See Walk #3.)

 Ciampinoi - This gondola rises to 7481 ft. (2280 m.). Like other lifts in the Selva area, views from the top station are extraordinary. (See Walks #1 and #2.)

 Col Raiser - Outside of Selva in Plan da Tieja above Santa Christina, this gondola rises to 6890 ft. (2100 m.) on grassy alps with sensational views of Sassalungo. (See Walks #5, #7, and #8.)

 Directions: Leave from the western end of Selva, walking on the highest auto road toward Santa Cristina and Plan da Tieja, a forty-minute walk. Follow the sign up to the right to the Col Raiser lift station.

Lifts in Ortisei

Alpe di Siusi - This lift links Ortisei with the slopes on the Alpe di Siusi/Seiser Alm—alpine meadows drenched in summer with colorful fields of flowers—Europe's largest mountain pasture. Alpe di Siusi was developed as a major center for hikers in the 1970s. (See Walk #4.)

 Seceda - The lift rises to 8039 ft. (2450 m.) and provides excellent closeup views of the nearby Dolomites and panoramas of the Val Gardena. (See Walks #7 and #8.)

 Raschötz - This chairlift rises to 6913 ft. (2107 m.). (See Walk #6.)

 Directions: By car - Take the main road northwest through Santa Cristina into Ortisei. By SAD bus - Bus service in the morning and afternoon between Selva and Ortisei is quite frequent. Check current bus schedules.

Excursions

The Selva Tourist Office is located on the main street, via Meisules.
Fax: 04 71 79 42 45
E-mail: selva@val-gardena.com
Internet: www.val-gardena.com

1. **Selva -** The **Parish Church of S. Maria** was originally built in 1878 in neo-Gothic style and has been refurbished. The bell tower was built in 1678, and its original chapel was renovated in the sixteenth, seventeenth, and eighteenth centuries. The **Chapel of the Victims of the Mountain,** a small chapel with a carved wooden *Pietà*, is located in the local cemetery behind the parish church in Selva. Inside is a bronze book dedicated to those who died on the mountains surrounding Selva.

    The ruins of thirteenth-century **Castle Wolkenstein** can be found at the entrance to the Vallunga/Langental, clinging to a high rock wall. It was acquired by Randolph von Villanders, who then called himself "von Wolkenstein," and who founded the mighty dynasty of the counts of Wolkenstein. The castle was ruined in 1525 and never restored. The path to the castle from the Vallunga/Langental road is short, but steep.

2. **Ortisei/St. Ulrich -** With a population of about 5000, Ortisei is the largest village in the Val Gardena. Take advantage of its charming main street and piazza, with chic boutiques, restaurants, and cafes. Visit the Baroque **parish church,** built in the late eighteenth century and dedicated to the "Three Kings" and St. Ulrich, bishop and patron saint of the village. Beautifully carved pews date from 1888, and the many ornately carved wood sculptures are the work of local turn-of-the-twentieth-century wood-carvers. The **Chapel of Remembrance,** situated near the parish church, has one of the oldest bells in the world hanging in its little facade tower. The chapel commemorates the dead of the world wars, but the bell was found in the fields by a farmer, and it originally hung in the medieval castle of Stetteneck, no longer in existence.

    Congress Hall and Permanent Exhibition of Gardenese Handicrafts is located in the church. On the ground floor is a permanent exhibit of local artisans—original work of wood-carvers as well as mass-production workshops—giving visitors a clear picture of the wood-carver's art. On the ground floor of the Congress Hall is the Ortisei Tourist Information Office. The lovely little **Church of St. Anthony** was built between 1673 and 1676 and is located across from the bus stop. Its steep shingle roof and onion dome make it a favorite of photographers. The **Gardena Folk Museum** offers valuable insights into the culture of the Gardena Valley and includes handicrafts, folk culture, minerals and fossils, flora and fauna, paintings, and a documentation of the valley's 300-year-old art of wood carving.

3. Bolzano/Bozen - See Merano section, Excursion #4.

Directions: By car - Take the main road northwest through Ortisei, following signs into Bolzano. By bus - A morning bus from Selva arrives in Bolzano in about eighty minutes.

4. Bressanone/Brixen - The South Tyrol's oldest and largest city with a population of about 16,000, Bressanone is 22 miles (35 km) northwest of Selva. Its Old Town is small and easy to walk, with narrow alleys, lanes of arcades, patrician homes, stately churches, and crumbling bridges, all dating from the Middle Ages. The **cathedral (duomo)** was built in the thirteenth century and remodeled in the eighteenth century with Baroque interiors. The **cloisters** were rebuilt after a fire in 1174; they contain fine frescoes painted between 1390 and 1509. The eleventh-century **Chapel of St. John the Baptist (Baptistry San Giovanni Battista)** is at the southern end of the cloisters. The **cathedral treasury** can be reached from the cloisters and contains sacred robes and shrines. Walk to the late Renaissance **Palace of the Prince-Bishops (Palazzo Vescovile)** in the southwestern corner of the Old Town, over a bridge crossing a moat.

You'll enjoy this small, charming city, lying where the Rienz River flows into the Eisack River, and where the distinctive character of the Südtirol/Alto Adige/South Tyrol first becomes apparent.

Directions: By car - Take main road 242 northwest out of Selva, picking up 12 north, and following signs into Bressanone/Brixen. By bus - You can leave Selva in the morning, arriving at Bressanone/Brixen in about seventy minutes.

5. Corvara - At 5145 ft. (1568 m.), with a population of only 700, Corvara lies below the towering Sasso Songher and is the largest of the Tyrolean villages in the Val Badia/Gadertal region of the Südtirol. This area is steeped in the Ladino culture and is quieter and less crowded than many other South Tyrol resorts. Corvara is situated on a valley floor at the base of the Pralongia Plateau, with many shops and hotels close to the small, central piazza. The Col Alto lift rises from Corvara to the plateau and an excellent view of the surrounding mountains.

Directions: Drive over the Passo Gardena/Grödner Joch to Corvara.

6. **Ponte Gardena/Waidbruck** - *Easy Walkers* can visit **Castle Trostburg** in Ponte Gardena, at the entrance to the Val Gardena, and only 12 miles (19 km) from Selva. This ancient castle is at the valley entrance, high above Ponte Gardena/Waidbruck, and dates from the twelfth century. It contains a superb Gothic room with a richly decorated, raftered ceiling. The library, one of the most famous of its time, and the banquet hall are also worth seeing. Trostburg is unmatched by any other South Tyrol castle in its wealth and range of architectural details. Access is by a path from Ponte Gardena, about a thirty-minute uphill walk. Guided tours are given daily except Monday.

Directions: By car - Take the main road from Selva, through Ortisei, following signs to Ponte Gardena, northeast of Bolzano. By bus - A morning bus from Selva arrives in less than one hour.

7. **Puez-Geisler Park -** The 22,758 acres (9400 hectares) of this park in the Dolomites includes the villages of Selva and Santa Christina. Note the spectacular contrast between the immense slopes of valleys and meadows and the sudden, almost vertical rise of the dolomite rocks. Inside the park, the Vallunga/Langental is the only example in the Dolomite region of an unspoiled, glacial valley. At the Vallunga's entrance are the ruins of Castle Wolkenstein on the Stevia rock wall, surrounded by high rocks that rise majestically from the valley's meadows. (See Walk #9.) The park, with its huge pine forests, gently rolling meadows, quaint villages, and farmhouses, is a peaceful, natural environment with spectacular scenery for all to enjoy.

8. **Venice -** See the Venice chapter.

Directions: Drive out of Selva on main road 242 southeast over the Sella Pass to 42 east, picking up 51 south. North of Belluno on autostrada A27 south, follow signs to Venice. You'll go over a long causeway and arrive at a busy and confusing area, the Piazza Roma, a dead end for car traffic. On your right is a pair of large garages where you can park your car, but there can be a long line of cars trying to get into these garages if you don't arrive by 9:00 A.M. Walk from the garage across the top of Piazza Roma to the Grand Canal piers and take the large, inexpensive public water bus or vaporetto to San Marco.

9. Merano/Meran - See the Merano chapter.
    Directions: Drive on the main road to Ortisei, following directions to Bolzano, where you will pick up the new expressway into Merano.

10. Cortina d'Ampezzo - See the Cortina d'Ampezzo chapter.
    Directions: Take the main road over Passo Sella and drive over the Passo Pordoi and Passo Falzarego into Cortina.

11. SAD Bus Tours - Prices and current timetables are available at the Tourist Office for bus trips to the following destinations: **Venice, Cortina, Lago di Carezza/Karersee, Lake Garda, Merano/Lago Caldaro, Innsbruck, Salzburg, Munich,** and **Neuschwanstein Castle.**

Selva/Wolkenstein Walks

Recommended Map:
    ❖ Tabacco—Gröden/Val Gardena, Seiser Alm/Alpe di Siusi

Walk #1

Selva Lift to Ciampinoi, Walk to Rifugio Comici to Rifugio Passo Sella to Plan de Gralba to Selva
Walking Easy Time: 3½ to 4 hours
Rating: Comfortable

Easy Walkers should plan the better part of the day for today's popular walk. Although the actual walking time is three and one-half hours, there will be many opportunities to stop and enjoy the remarkable panorama. If you begin your walk from Ciampinoi by 10:00 A.M., you should be back in Selva by late afternoon.

You'll take the gondola in Selva to Ciampinoi, at 7395 ft. (2254 m.), and the walk will proceed in the direction of Rifugio Comici, at 7064 ft. (2153 m.). Here, you'll be rewarded with close-up views of the east wall of Sassolungo, rising to 10,437 ft. (3181 m.). Your destination is now Rifugio Passo Sella, at 7153 ft. (2180 m.).

The return to Selva is on a descending trail through the hamlet of Plan de Gralba, at 5870 ft. (1789 m.), continuing down to Selva, at 5118 ft. (1560 m.). This hike is considered "comfortable," as most of the walking is not difficult, with ascents and descents at a reasonable rate. There are many options for good food at the *rifugi*, but a picnic on the meadow at the Passo Sellajoch may be the best option.

Lift at Passo Sella, Selva

Directions: The Ciampinoi lift station is on the main street of Selva. Purchase a one-way ticket to the top station for the ten-minute gondola ride.

Start: The hike begins at Ciampinoi. Walk toward the impressive Sassolungo massif in front of you and follow the signs RIF. COMICI and PASSO SELLA JOCH. After about ten minutes of walking around the mountain, follow the trail as it descends to the valley below, bringing you to the foot of Sassolungo.

The path forks, the left trail being the short way to Plan de Gralba, but *Easy Walkers* will continue ahead toward the right to Rifugio Comici. The well-beaten trail splits again—continue to the left in the direction of the *rifugio*. After a comfortable forty-minute walk, you'll reach the sun-terrace of Rifugio Comici before continuing on to the Sella Pass.

When ready, walk directly through the sun-terrace, exiting on to a rocky trail blazed in red and white, signed PASSO SELLAJOCH 526. This path traverses open meadows with herds of friendly cows and jagged peaks edging the sky. In the last fifteen minutes before you reach Passo Sella, the trail becomes more rocky as it ascends. You should reach the *rifugio* at the top of the Sella Pass after about two hours of hiking from Ciampinoi.

The walk to Selva returns on trail #657 to Plan de Gralba, descending through the valley, not very far from the twisting auto road up on the right. From Rifugio Passo Sella, walk down the auto road against the traffic flow, and about five minutes below the *rifugio*, a sign directs you left on trail

#657. Turn left on to a small, unpaved road, and when the split rail fence ends on the right, turn right on to a path that may be *unmarked*. After a few hundred yards, the path will be blazed #657. Follow it all the way down to Plan de Gralba, at 5870 ft. (1789 m.), with some nice restaurants and their sun-terraces.

Walk through Plan de Gralba on a small country road past two closed lifts on your left. After the second lift, make a left turn over a little bridge, and after a few hundred feet, turn right on an *unmarked*, wide, descending gravel path (actually a ski trail), leading to the small hamlet of Fungeia. Continue walking into Selva.

Walk #2

Selva Lift to Ciampinoi, Walk to Monte Pana
Walking Easy Time: 3 hours
Rating: Comfortable

Easy Walkers have another walking option from the top station at Ciampinoi. As in Walk #1, you'll hike in the direction of the Rifugio Comici. But this time, before reaching the *rifugio*, you'll turn to the right toward Monte Pana, walking underneath the impressive Sassolungo on your left. At Monte Pana, you'll take the lift down to Santa Cristina to catch the bus back to Selva.

Directions: See Walk #1.

Start: At the top station, walk toward the Sassolungo massif in front of you and follow the sign RIF COMICI. After about ten minutes of walking around the mountain, follow the trail as it descends to the valley below. Just after the path forks, take the trail to the right toward Monte Pana on #526-528, with the Sassolungo mountain on your left. After a while, take #528, which splits off to your right, descending to Monte Pana. Here you have the option of taking the small lift down to S. Cristina and the bus to Selva or continuing the hike down to the main street and the bus return to Selva.

Walk #3

Selva Lift to Dantercepies, Walk to Rifugio Clark to Passo Gardena to Plan to Selva
Walking Easy Time: 3½ hours
Rating: Comfortable

The walk from Dantercepies to Passo Gardena is filled with views of craggy, dolomitic peaks on both sides of the pass, and the path travels along the edge of Naturpark Puez-Geisler. The hypnotic face of Sassolungo dominates the panorama on the return hike.

Walkers and climbers seem to be everywhere on well-marked paths, rolling easily through meadows and scrambling up and down rocky mountain trails. Plan a full day for this walk, as you'll want to spend time watching climbers ascending the craggy peaks of the mountains and another hour or more for resting, photography, lunch, and scenery viewing.

From trails winding along the mountain, walkers can see the twisting auto road snaking through the pass from Selva to Colfusco. However, today's itinerary is for *Easy Walkers* to take the trail to Passo Gardena and then descend through the beautiful valley and forest to the hamlet of Plan and a pleasant *spazierweg* to Selva.

Although this hike is considered comfortable, there is a half-hour rocky descent that is not dangerous, but requires some care—downhill walking can bring stress to the knees.

Directions: Check your Selva village map and walk up to the Dantercepies Lift Station. Buy a one-way ticket to the top and take the continuously moving gondola for the ten-minute ride to 7540 ft. (2298 m.). Walkers can view the Passo Gardena/Grödner Joch down on the right and climbers scrambling up jagged peaks to the left.

Start: From the lift, follow the sign RIFUGIO CLARK down steps to the left, reaching the sun-terrace of this tiny restaurant in only fifteen minutes. Just past the restaurant, path #2 goes up to the left in the direction of Rifugio Puez, at 8121 ft. (2475 m.), but this climb is not on today's agenda. Instead, walk to the right under the ski lift, following the signs FORCELLES and then COLFUSCO, over a little grassy path, and on to a narrow, rocky, descending trail. This trail is somewhat steep and descends in a half-hour from 7290 to 6890 ft. (2222 to 2100 m.) through a scrubby pine forest. It does take some care going down.

The trail meets the Passo Gardena path. Turn right, following the sign PASSO GARDENA, the high point for auto traffic through the pass, at 6969 ft. (2124 m.). The trail winds to a barn and tiny farmhouse. Turn right and walk past the little house to a narrow mountain path on your left. Turn left and follow this trail, ending at a souvenir stand on the main road at the pass. Turn right and walk on the road to the second group of buildings and the Rifugio Passo Gardena on the left (which serves some delicious Austrian specialties: *kaiserschmarrn, knoedlsuppe,* and *bratwurst).*

Continue walking on the road past the restaurant, and after a few minutes, on the right you'll see the sign SELVA #654. Turn right on this path, descending gently through serene, grassy meadows; passing old barns; leading into a more steeply descending forest path. Watch for signs to Selva on blazed trail #654. This trail ends at an auto road.

Follow the sign to Selva around to the right of the road, down to the hamlet of Plan, again meeting the auto road. Turn right and walk down the road for a few minutes. Enter a parking area on the right, next to a sports field, and look for the sign to the left reading PASSEGGIATA/SPAZIERWEG. This is a little paved path above the auto road that is down on the left. Stay on this paved path until it ends in Selva.

Walk #4

Ortisei Lift to Alpe di Siusi/Seiser Alm, Walk to Saltria to Santa Cristina through the Jëndertal
Walking Easy Time: 3½ hours
Rating: Comfortable

Today's hike crosses Europe's largest alp (meadowland), framed by the western wall of Sassolungo and other dramatic Dolomite peaks of the Südtirol. Try to take this special hike on a clear day, when every mountain appears to be finely etched against a brilliant blue sky. You'll take the bus from Selva to Ortisei, traveling through S. Cristina (passing the bus stop you'll use to return to Selva at the conclusion of today's hike). Ortisei is the major village in the Val Gardena, with brightly painted shops and hotels, churches, and museums, hosting lifts that take summer walkers up to mountains on both sides of the valley. However, today you'll take the Alpe di Siusi cable car to 6578 ft. (2005 m.) and walk through one of the most picturesque alps in Europe.

It will take about ninety minutes to descend through the Alpe di Siusi/Seiser Alm to the auto road at Saltria at 5597 ft. (1706 m.). The hike continues through the natural wilderness and deep gorge of the Jëndertal to S. Cristina, at 4685 ft. (1428 m.), and a short bus ride to Selva.

Directions: Take one of the frequent SAD buses from Selva (across from the Ciampinoi lift on the main street) to Ortisei. After leaving the bus, walk across the river on a small bridge and turn right. After the five-minute walk to the cable car station, purchase a one-way ticket to the top.

Start: As you exit the cable car, follow the sign to the left to SALTRIA #9, on a well-graded path. The path descends easily to the four-star Hotel Sonne and proceeds on an unsigned, grassy path in front of the hotel. Walk through the tranquil Alpe di Siusi/Seiser Alm to Saltria at 5597 ft. (1706 m.). Although this part of the hike takes about ninety minutes, you might wish to spend some time on the trail absorbing the beauty of this tranquil setting with its panorama of Sassolungo and Sciliar. At Saltria, there is a hotel restaurant and meadow benches for picnicking.

When ready, face away from the hotel and turn left and then right, following the sign JËNDERTAL, on a small mountain road passing in front of the Brunelle Hotel. This path is blazed #8/3a as you pass an old farmhouse, where you can buy milk and honey. At the first intersection, cross the river on the little bridge to the right. This comfortable path continues through the forest, with the river on your left, and rises to another intersection with a conveniently placed bench. Follow the sign down to the left to S. Cristina and Ortisei. You are now walking on a well-defined path, descending through the natural, unspoiled wilderness of the Jëndertal above the river as it runs rapidly through its narrow gorge to S. Cristina. Exit this path onto a small, paved auto road with views of S. Cristina down to the right. From the road, turn right and take the signed S. Cristina hillside path descending *very* steeply through the meadows to the auto road. Turn right and quickly left, walking up and around on the small road directly to the main auto road in front of you. At the road, proceed to the bus stop, with frequent service posted to Selva.

Walk #5:

Selva to Plan da Tieja, Col Raiser Lift, Walk to Gamsblut to St. Jakob to Ortisei/St. Ulrich

Walking Easy Time: 3½ hours

Rating: Comfortable

Today's hike brings *Easy Walkers* from Selva, through the Val Gardena by

Dantercepies, Selva

way of Col Raiser, to the village of Ortisei/St. Ulrich. Plan the better part of a day for today's hike, as you will first take a forty-minute walk up to the Col Raiser lift in the village of Plan da Tieja above Santa Cristina. Then, you'll take the gondola up to Col Raiser and walk around and down the mountain to Ortisei, stopping at the ancient church above St. Jakob, and finally returning to Selva by bus.

The top station at Col Raiser, at 6890 ft. (1430 m.), sits in the midst of a grassy plain, surrounded by the Dolomites, with exciting views of Sassalungo. The walk continues to Ortisei by way of a mountain road, through meadows and forest, with an optional stop above St. Jakob to visit the church. Paths are well-marked and well-engineered. There is a restaurant with a large sun-terrace at the top station of Col Raiser and another restaurant at Gamsblut.

Start: Leave from the western end of Selva, walking on the highest auto road, signed toward S. Cristina, for the forty-minute walk to Plan da Tieja, where you follow the sign up to the right to the Col Raiser lift station. Purchase a one-way ticket and take the continuously moving gondola for the ten-minute ride to Col Raiser.

The Col Raiser restaurant sits in the middle of a tranquil, grassy alp, and views from this point are sensational. There are several hikes from Col Raiser to *rifugi* in the area, but today *Easy Walkers* will leave Col Raiser by following the sign (at the far side of the sun-terrace as you enter it), marked GAMSBULT and ST. JAKOB on #4. The narrow path leaves from the side of the terrace, descending somewhat steeply at first to the restaurant at Gamsblut, at 6405 ft. (1952 m.), on path #4. After passing the restaurant, walk on path #4 into the forest, on the jeep road, down and around the mountain, following signs to the church at St. Jakob.

To view the church, you'll have to leave the trail and walk to the right at a signed intersection to visit the chapel at 5135 ft. (1565 m.), sitting above the little hamlet of St. Jakob. This church is the oldest in the valley and dates back to the mid-thirteenth century. Its original Romanesque interior was added to, and the present church dates back to the Gothic period, with both Gothic and Baroque interior decoration. Many of the sculptures are excellent local copies, with originals in the Gardena Folk Museum in Ortisei. Descend through the larch trees overlooking the village of St. Jakob and rejoin the trail into the village of Ortisei, where you catch the bus back to Selva at the main square.

Walk #6

Ortisei Chairlift to Raschötz, Walk to Rifugio Brogles to Mid-Station Seceda Lift

Walking Easy Time: 3½ hours
Rating: Comfortable

The walk today begins and ends at Ortisei, involving the chairlift to Raschötz, with a top station at 6890 ft. (2100 m.), and a walk on a continuously ascending and descending path on Seceda's upper plains. You'll travel to Rifugio Brogles, at 6710 ft. (2045 m.), on the back side of Seceda, with fabulous views of the Odle/Geisler Range and its highest peak, Sas Rigais, at 9925 ft. (3025 m.). The walk continues to a high point of 7071 ft. (2155 m.), and then winds down through meadow and forest to the Seceda cable car mid-station for the descent to Ortisei and the bus return to Selva.

Directions: Take one of the frequent morning buses to Ortisei. Follow signs to Raschötz and purchase a one-way ticket to the top.

Start: There are several walks from the top station of this chairlift, all clearly signed. Today, follow the signs to #35 in a northerly direction to Rifugio Brogles, at 6710 ft. (2045 m.). This trail is well defined and offers sensational views of the surrounding mountains.

After a rest and perhaps lunch at the *rifugio*, follow path #3, climbing a bit at first, then descending to 5545 ft. (1690 m.) at the middle station of the Seceda cable car. Purchase a one-way ticket down to Ortisei and catch the return bus to Selva.

Walk #7

Ortisei Lift to Seceda, Walk to Col Raiser via the "Restaurant Route"
Walking Easy Time: 1½ to 2 hours
Rating: Comfortable

Easy Walkers will walk on scenic paths to sample local specialities during today's lighthearted hike, and descend from the top station of the Seceda lift along the "Restaurant Route" to the top station of the Col Raiser lift—enjoying the food on sun-terraces of little mountain restaurants, the rolling green alps, and the surrounding Dolomites. The walk from Seceda to Col Raiser is only ninety minutes of pleasant, downhill walking, but the experience can be extended for as long as you wish, depending on how much time you spend eating and taking in the sun and the views at each rustic *ristorante*.

There are several options at Col Raiser for those who wish to hike further. Or, it's possible to take the Col Raiser gondola down to Plan de Tieja, continuing into S. Cristina on the *passeggiata* before returning to Selva by bus. Another option is to take the trail down the mountain and through the meadow and forest to St. Jakob and Ortisei, if you have not taken Walk #5. A third option is to continue the hike to the Regensbergerhütte, then walk down to Juac and Selva.

Directions: Take a morning bus from Selva to Ortisei. Walk up the pedestrian street toward the large church, where you follow walking signs to the Seceda lift. Purchase a one-way ticket to the top station at 8058 ft. (2456 m.), transferring at the mid-station to the waiting cable car.

Start: There are a variety of *ristoranti* and *rifugi* on this hike, with the possibility of putting a few pounds on today rather than taking them off, considering the local specialties served at these mountain restaurants. After exiting the lift at Seceda, walk to the right, facing the Seceda mountain range, following signs to Sofie, Mastlé, Daniel, and Rifugio Fermeda Hütte. Walk first to Ristorante Sofie, at 7914 ft. (2412 m.), continuing down to the right on #6, and making a left turn at the intersection to Ristorante Mastlé, at 7494 ft. (2284 m.). Proceed to Ristorante Daniel, at 7310 ft. (2228 m.), under one of the Seceda ski lifts, then descend further to Rifugio Fermeda, at 6926 ft. (2111 m.). *Note: Plan a lunch and/or snack stop at any of the mentioned restaurants—they all serve delicious, local food.*

After the Rifugio Fermeda, you have three options:

1. At the intersection just past Rifugio Fermeda, walk on path #2 in the direction of the lift station at Col Raiser, at 6913 ft. (2107 m.), for the descent by gondola to Plan da Tieja. Exiting the lift station, walk down the hill on the road and turn right, following the signs to S. Cristina to catch one of the frequent buses to Selva.

2. For those who don't mind some additional downhill walking, there is an option on trail #2 that can be exercised just before reaching the Col Raiser gondola. Continue ahead on #2 to the Rifugio Firenze/Regensburgerhütte, at 6683 ft. (2037 m.), following jeep trail #3 down to Juac, at 6244 ft. (1903 m.). Remain on #3 and descend all the way into Selva.

3. Or, take the path back to Ortisei by way of St. Jakob if it's still early and you haven't taken Walk #5.

Walk #8

Ortisei Lift to Seceda, Walk to Col Raiser with Optional Walk to Regensburgerhütte/Rifugio Firenze
Walking Easy Time: 2 to 3½ hours
Rating: Comfortable

Another hike down to Col Raiser from Seceda rises gently from the Seceda lift station toward the Odle Geisler peaks on a trail with magnificent panoramic views.

Directions: Follow Directions in Walk #7 to the Seceda lift.

Start: At the top Seceda station, do *not* turn down the trail toward Sophie as in the Restaurant Walk. Walk ahead on #1 and #2A on your map, toward the high mountain ridge ahead. The open trail ascends gently on #2A, eventually turning right on #1, down toward the mountain restaurant at Troier, 7154 ft. (2271 m.), with great views and delicious country cooking.

Continue down on #1 toward Col Raiser. Before reaching Col Raiser, trail #1 splits off to the left to the Regensburgerhütte/Rifugio Firenze. After reaching the *hütte*, you can loop back on trail #4 to Col Raiser and the lift down to Plan da Tieja. Or, if you wish, at the fork to the Regensburgerhütte, continue to Col Raiser ahead, the shorter way. Exiting the lift station, walk down the hill on the road and turn right, following signs to S. Cristina, to catch one of the frequent buses to Selva.

Walk #9

A Walk Through the Vallunga/Langental—Selva to Selva
Walking Easy Time: 3 to 5 hours
Rating: Comfortable

This hike through the Vallunga Valley or Langental can be reserved for a cloudy or drizzly day as no lifts are involved. You'll walk into the Vallunga, the only unspoiled glacial valley in the Parco Naturale Puez. The trail ascends gently from 5355 to 6890 ft. (1632 to 2100 m.), and then climbs seriously into the rugged Dolomites to Rifugio Puez at 8121 ft. (2475 m.). But today, *Easy Walkers* will walk only as far as they feel comfortable, remembering that a two-hour walk ascending into the valley will be about a ninety minute return. The early part of the trail winds through open, grassy meadows filled with many picnic opportunities, which eventually works its way through a narrow pass with towering mountains on either side, climbing to high peaks at the distant end. The return to Selva is along the same path. *Note: There are no restaurants or facilities in the valley. Remember to pack a picnic lunch and plenty of water.*

Directions: You can either drive or walk to the start of today's hike. There is a small parking area at the beginning of the trail. Please follow the Selva village map to the large "P" (parking) just below and past Castle Wolkenstein at the entrance to the valley and the nature park. If you are walking, follow the signs to Vallunga/Langental and check the village map.

Start: Enter the park at the end of the parking area on trail #4-14. This is the only path that goes deeply into the valley. As you walk through the meadows, note the tiny, early eighteenth-century chapel, recently restored. Take a few minutes to enter and discover its old frescoes and lovely altar. The ascending trail proceeds through the valley—a popular, rocky path. Trail #4 splits off to the left, rising steeply into the Puez Alps, but continue ahead on #14 for as long as you feel comfortable. At 6890 ft. (2100 m.), the trail begins to ascend dramatically to Rifugio Puez. Most *Easy Walkers* will reverse direction here and return to Selva on the same path.

CORTINA D'AMPEZZO

Spectacular! There is no lens but that of the human eye that can catch and truly comprehend the stark grandeur of the Dolomites' Cortina d'Ampezzo, and even that fine instrument can sometimes be overwhelmed by the majesty of Cortina's compelling surroundings. In summer, dramatic sunsets silhouette the gigantic ruptures of earth and stone, the soft verdure of the Ampezzo Valley lying snugly within these finely etched mountains. Photographers must surely experience intense emotions as they try to capture this ever-shifting, almost primeval scene on film. The colors of the landscape change constantly as the sun moves across the sky, the azure lakes reflect the hard-edged peaks. The delicate green meadows ablaze with wild flowers versus the unforgiving, jagged rock formations make for an intriguing dichotomy. *Easy Walkers* are in for the time of their lives—day-hikes in the incomparable beauty of the Dolomites and casual evenings strolling the pedestrian streets in the elegant town of Cortina d'Ampezzo.

The first outsiders to visit the Ampezzo Valley were mountain climbers who heard about Cortina from Déodat de Dolomieu, the French minerologist who first described these soaring peaks and discovered their geological properties. Foreign tourists soon followed, spreading stories about the wondrous sights around Cortina, and the town became famous in winter for its incomparable skiing, in summer for its mountain climbing and hiking. Cortina attracted illustrious guests: kings, princes, movie stars, politicians, authors, and business leaders. It was, and still is, chic to see and be seen in Cortina, and visitors stroll up and down the Corso Italia (the main pedestrian thoroughfare) between 5:00 and 7:00 P.M., filling the stores, window shopping, or sipping a predinner aperitif on this fashionable street lined with hotels, art galleries, antiques shops, jewelers, boutiques, cafes, and restaurants. Grand hotels built in the 1920s and 30s lend an elegant touch to Cortina, and the hills above are dotted with the charming country chalets of important Italian families who come to Cortina for winter sports and August holiday.

Cortina is a different type of base village for *Easy Walkers*—its streets crowded with "beautiful people," rather than hikers and backpackers—yet Cortina's Dolomite trails are filled with walkers, hikers, backpackers, and mountain climbers. Cortina may be more expensive than other Italian base villages during the month of August, so *Easy Walkers* should consider the month of July for their Cortina d'Ampezzo walking holiday.

Trail in the Dolomites

Cortina, at 3970 ft. (1210 m.), is surrounded by many peaks over 10,500 ft. (3200 m.), and visitors arriving in Cortina for the first time are stunned by the magnificent sight of these surrounding Dolomites, the mountain groups of Tofane, Pomagagnòn, Cristallo, Sorapis, and Croda da Lago—and the Boite River running through town. The eastern slopes of the Pomagagnòn and Punta Fiames Mountains are spectacular at sunset; Cristallo sparkles in the afternoon sun; and Tofana gleams golden in the early morning sunrise. Cortina was the scene of the 1956 winter Olympic Games and has forty-five ski lifts spread over the varied slopes surrounding this beautiful valley. While these lifts service a network of over 62 miles (100 km) of ski runs and cross-country trails, many lifts also operate in summer, bringing hikers to the beginning of fascinating day-walks.

It's difficult to believe that Cortina is only a two-hour drive from the wonders of Venice, and *Easy Walkers* can experience a one-day walking itinerary in this magical city. (See Venice chapter.) Twisting, scenic mountain roads also take travelers from Cortina through the Dolomites, off-the-beaten-track south to Alleghe's beautiful lake. A drive west over the Passo Pordoi brings walkers to the Val di Fassa and Vigo di Fassa in another *Walking Easy* valley. Cortina is only forty minutes from the Austrian border, close enough to Lienz, Austria, for an interesting one-day excursion.

In August, Cortina is filled with happy Italian families who come for the healthy, dry climate and the hiking. The trails here are varied enough to meet the needs of all levels of walkers—supported by a multiple-lift system providing easy and exciting ways to visit the many *rifugi* in the surrounding mountains. Explore the dozens of places around Cortina that offer *Easy Walkers* a variety of paths and scenery—from the solitude of a walk through the forest to Rifugio Miétres to the pleasant company of dozens of hikers around Tre Cime, from the silent chairlift rising above peaceful Lake Misurina to the large, three-stage cable car called "The Arrow in the Sky," rising to 10,644 ft. (3244 m.) at Tofana di Mezzo. A summer *Walking Easy* trip to the Italian Alps should definitely include the "Queen of the Dolomites," Cortina d'Ampezzo.

Transportation

By Plane - The closest international airports are Munich, Milan, and Venice. Car rental agencies are available at all airports. We suggest the use of a car in this region.

By Train - Cortina's closest train station is at Dobbiaco/Toblach, 20 miles (32 km) to the north, on the Bolzano/Lienz line. Local bus service to Cortina and car rental agencies are available.

By Car - From the west and north, leave *autostrada* A22 at the Brixen-Pustertal exit and take 49 toward Dobbiaco/Toblach, from there driving south on 51 to Cortina. From the east and southeast, take 51 from near Pieve di Cadore to Cortina. From nearby areas in the Dolomites, use local roads over the Passo Pordoi and Passo Sella, or Passo Pordoi to Passo Falzarego, continuing on to Cortina d'Ampezzo.

The *Grand Strada delle Dolomiti*, the Great Dolomite Road from Ora/Auer east to Cortina d'Ampezzo (State Highway 48), was opened in 1909, a remarkable engineering feat linking some of the most dramatic parts of the Dolomites. The road passes through varied landscapes of unrivaled beauty and traverses high, stark passes and green, peaceful valleys. Leaving Ora, the first pass crossed is Passo San Lucano, at 3612 ft. (1101 m.), then the Val di Fiemme and the Val di Fassa, climbing to the highest point on the road at Passo Pordoi, 7346 ft. (2239 m.). The road descends in wide curves with fabulous views of the surrounding mountains—on the left passing by the Sella group and on the right by Padòn, behind which Marmolada and its glacier can be seen. At the foot of the pass is the summer and winter resort of Arabba, at 5256 ft. (1602 m.), with a network of cable cars and chairlifts, a fabulous view in front of the Marmolada glacier, and a seventeenth-century church, now a national monument. Further along the road, past Arabba, high on the mountainside at 4807 ft. (1465 m.), stands the little village of Livinallongo, with breathtaking views of Civetta, Pelmo, Marmolada, and Sella. At 4685 ft. (1428 m.) is the hamlet of Andraz, a cluster of old alpine houses, and the ruins of a tenth-century castle perched on a rocky spur that can be seen on the winding road to Falzarego. This pass is at 6907 ft. (2105 m.) and has a cable car rising to 9010 ft. (2746 m.) at Lagazuoi on the left and the much-photographed climbing rocks of Cinque Torri on the right. As the pass descends toward Cortina, you proceed through Pocol, at 5010 ft. (1527 m.), and when the car leaves the Crepa Tunnel, suddenly—in front of you—is a splendid view of the Valle d'Ampezzo and Cortina, your *Walking Easy* destination.

By Bus - There is local bus service in the Cortina area on the Autobus Cortina d'Ampezzo, and SAD buses make the Great Dolomite Road trip once a day.

Favorite *Walking Easy* Hotel

Hotel Aquila
Three-Star; Owner - Gaspari Family
Corso Italia 168, 32043 Cortina d'Ampezzo
Tel: 04 36 26 18 837 86, **Fax:** 04 36 86 73 15
E-mail: haquila@sunrise.it
Internet: www.sunrise.it/cortina/alberghi/aquila

A family owned and operated hotel, the Aquila is situated on Cortina's famous walking promenade. Casually decorated, the Aquila offers excellent regional cooking, and we highly recommend reservations with dinner included.

This moderately priced hotel has thirty-nine rooms with private facilities, indoor swimming pool, sauna, and Jacuzzi. The Gaspari family is always in attendance, ensuring a comfortable stay. Cortina is a busy hiking area in summer, so book early.

Lifts in and around Cortina d'Ampezzo

Tondi di Faloria - A two-stage cable car leaving every half-hour, this lift brings *Easy Walkers* to 7667 ft. (2343 m.) and dramatic views of Cortina, and the Tofane, Sorapis, and Cristallo Mountains. The base station is near the bus terminal. (See Walk #4.)

Tofana di Mezzo - This awesome, three-stage cable car rises to 10,673 ft. (3244 m.) every half-hour. Called "Arrow in the Sky," it was built in 1969 and renovated in 1997. Its base station is near Stadio del Ghiaccio or Olympic Ice Rink. The view from the third stage at the top offers panoramas extending into the Austrian mountains, the Central Alps, and the Po Plains. (See Walk #3.)

Lagazuoi - The Lagazuoi chairlift and cable car can be accessed from Passo Falzarego, west of Cortina. The view from the top is considered the best panorama of the Dolomites, and in the distance are Civetta, Pelmo, Marmolada, Gruppo Sella, and the Pale di San Martino Mountains. (See Walk #7.)

Cinque Torri - Located off route 48 to Passo Falzarego before reaching the Lagazuoi cable car, this chairlift to 7763 ft. (2366 m.) affords spectacular, close-up views of the surrounding mountains. The Cinque Torri are five towers of vertical rock, not particularly tall, but used by climbers to train for the high peaks because they range from easy to very difficult. The most popular rock tower is a fourth level climb named "Miriam"! (See Walk #6.)

Cristallo - This covered chairlift, located on the road to Misurina, can take you up to San Forca at 7333 ft. (2235 m.), where you transfer to a gondola rising to the jagged peaks of Cristallo at 9502 ft. (2896 m.), with stunning panoramic views. (See Walk #4.)

Miétres, Col Tondo - The double chairlift rises first to Col Tondo, then to the *rifugio* and Miétres, with its outstanding views of the Pomagagnon range. (See Walk #4.)

Excursions

Cortina's Tourist Office or *Azienda Promozione Turistica* is located on Piazetta San Francesco, 8.

Fax: 04 36 32 35
E-mail: infocortina@apt-dolomiti-cortina.it
Internet: www.apt-dolomiti-cortina.it

1. Cortina - Visit the lovely Baroque parish church built in 1775, with its

243-foot-high (74 m.) bell tower rising over the rooftops—the village landmark. It's located on Cortina's pedestrian street, in the heart of town.

The following museums are all situated in the same building, on the corner of Corso d'Italia, located off the pedestrian street near the church, and are supported by a group interested in preserving the ethnic inheritance of the Ampezzo Valley. The **Museum of Modern Art (Mario Rimoldi)** houses a remarkable collection, including paintings and sculptures from some of the twentieth century's major Italian artists. The **Paleontologic Museum (Rinaldo Zardini)** contains millions of years of earth's history, a remarkable collection of marine fossils from the region of the Dolomites surrounding Cortina. The **Ethnological Museum of Ampezzo**—actually a museum of tradition—exhibits crafts, costumes, and the daily work habits of people living long ago in the Ampezzo Valley.

2. Pocol - Pocol is a tiny suburb outside of Cortina, on the Falzarego Pass road. Follow signs and walk to the **Belvedere,** at 5049 ft. (1539 m.), where the panoramic view of the Ampezzo Valley and its surrounding peaks is best seen at sunset. Nearby is the **Sacrario,** containing the remains of 10,000 soldiers who died in World War I.

Directions: *By bus - Bus service is available from Cortina every hour. By car - Follow signs to Passo Falzarego.*

3. Pieve di Cadore - This pretty town, located southeast of Cortina, is one of the oldest holiday resorts in the Dolomites and has drawn walkers and mountain lovers since the mid-nineteenth century. It's the birthplace of the famous Renaissance painter Titian, born in 1478—his home may be visited in Pieve along with the **parish church** containing one of his paintings. Note also the **Magnifica Comunità del Cadore** building in the center of the village, with its beautiful rooms, and the **Cadore Museum's** Roman and Venetian archaeological exhibits.

Directions: *Take 51 south from Cortina (driving in the direction of Venice) into Pieve.*

4. Dobbiaco/Toblach - Lying north of Cortina in the Val Pusteria or Pustertal, this busy Tyrolean village is a good base for exploring the Sesto/Sexten region of northern Italy. Dobbiaco lies at the junction of several valleys and is on the road to the northern Dolomite areas. Note the town's characteristic old houses and stop in at the Rococo **parish**

church, dating from 1782, with its stucco work and magnificent ceiling frescoes. The Austrian composer Gustav Mahler frequently stayed in this area, where he composed his ninth and tenth symphonies. *Easy Walkers* might enjoy taking the **Mt. Radsberg Chairlift** to the 5,269-foot (1606-meter) summit for vistas of the Sesto/Sexten Dolomites and the Höhlenstein Valley.

Directions: By car - Drive on 51 north into Dobbiaco. By bus - A morning bus from Cortina arrives in Dobbiaco in 45 minutes.

5. **Sesto/Sexten Dolomites Natural Park (Parco Naturale Dolomiti di Sesto) -** This park is a mountain hiker's dream—its irregularly shaped peaks and quiet valleys make this rugged, remote area a place of exceptional beauty, and the surrounding valleys are home to tiny, gleaming Südtirolean villages. The park covers 28,750 acres (11,635 hectares) around Dobbiaco/Toblach, San Candido/Innichen, and Sesto/Sexten. Early astronomers used the park's densely packed peaks for orientation, and these summits were once referred to as "the world's most impressive sundial." During World War I, over 10,000 soldiers fought in these mountains as Austrian Tyroleans tried to defend themselves against invading Italians. Victims are buried in a military cemetery in the Höhlenstein Valley, and there is a Peace Trail (Via della Pace/Friedensweg) on Monte Piana and on Mt. Fanes—a memorial to the horrors of war.

Directions: Drive 30 miles northeast of Cortina toward Dobbiaco.

6. **Sesto/Sexten -** A quiet, charming Tyrolean village with a population of only 1800, Sesto has only a few hotels, but it is proud of its many flower-bedecked *pensioni.* Rudolf Stolz, a local painter (1874–1960), lived in Sesto, and his home is now a museum. The Monte Elmo lift in Sesto offers panoramas of the surrounding Sesto Mountains. Or, walk to Moso/Moos, a neighboring village, and take the cable car up to the Rotwand Meadow, at 6316 ft. (1925 m.). The scenery around and between Sesto and Moso is considered to be some of the most beautiful in the Dolomite valleys.

Directions: Take 51 north to Dobbiaco. Drive east on 49 to San Candido, then 52 south to Sesto and Moos.

7. **San Candido/Innichen -** Lying east of Dobbiaco/Toblach at the entrance to the Val di Sesto, set in larch and pine forests on the River Drava, the

small village of San Candido is home to a **cathedral,** considered to be the Südtirol's most important Romanesque structure. The **Innichen Monastery,** founded in 769, was replaced in 1170—with other parts of the church dating from the twelfth to the fourteenth centuries. Note the monumental wooden statues, carved in the early thirteenth century. The cathedral's treasures are displayed in an adjacent museum. the **Museo Mineralogico Dolomythos** houses a bizarre geological and mythical history of the Dolomites.

Directions: By car - *Take 51 north to Dobbiaco/Toblach, picking up 49 east into San Candido.*

8. Bressanone/Brixen - See the Selva/Gardena chapter, Excursion #4.

Directions: Take 51 north from Cortina to Dobbiaco, picking up 49 west and driving south to Bressanone/Brixen.

9. Chiusa/Klausen - See the Merano chapter, Excursion #8.

Directions: Take 51 north to 49 west, picking up 12 south near Bressanone/Brixen into Chiusa. To return, try a circle route. Take 12 south and pick up 242 east through Ortisei and Selva to 48 east. Drive over the Passo Sella, the Passo Pordoi, and the Passo di Falzarego into Cortina. This magnificent drive back along the Dolomite Road is much slower because of all the hairpin turns on the mountain passes.

10. Brunico/Bruneck - This main town in the Puster Valley was founded in 1251 by the bishop of Brixen. Fortification of the town was completed in the fourteenth century, and remnants of these walls are still visible today. The medieval quarter is just below the thirteenth-century **Bishop's Castle.** On Stadtgasse, the old main street, visit the **City Apothecary** with its vaulted rooms, frescoes, and coats of arms. Northwest of the St. Ursula Gate is the Baroque **Church of St. Ursula,** completed in the 1500s and renovated in Gothic style in the late 1800s. Just above where the Ahrn and Rienz Rivers meet is Brunico's Stegen District and the **Parish Church of St. Nicholas** with paintings from the 1400s. A folklore museum now occupies the quarters of the courtier Mayr and recreates a typical local village built around a 300-year-old mansion.

Directions: Drive on 51 north to 49 west and follow the signs for the local road into town.

11. Lienz, Austria - Lienz, the capital of the eastern Tyrol district of Austria, lies in the shadow of the Dolomites and was cut off from the main part of the Tyrolean province when the Puster Valley (in the Südtirol) was transfered to Italy in 1919. A half-mile west of town center, pay a visit to **Bruck Castle (Schloss Bruck) and the Museum of East Tyrol (Osttiroler Heimatmuseum).** The castle was a fortress and now houses this impressive museum with its collections of local antiquities, folklore, and handiwork of the region. The **Knights' Hall,** or **Rittersaal,** is a good example of how the castle appeared in the Middle Ages. The **Albin Egger-Lienz Gallery** offers paintings of a local artist (1868–1926) whose work was often inspired by the Tyrol and its inhabitants. Another section displays ancient Roman artifacts uncovered at Aguntum. **Church of St. Andrew (St. Andrä)** is noted for its Gothic nave, but during restoration in 1968, murals from the fourteenth to the seventeenth centuries were uncovered. Under the gallery are the sixteenth-century Salzburg marble tombs of local nobility.

Directions: Drive on 57 north to Dobbiaco and pick up 49 east over the Austrian border, becoming 100, into Lienz.

12. Belluno - See the Alleghe chapter, Excursion #6.

Directions: By car - Follow signs to Venice, then local signs to Belluno. By bus - An early morning bus from Cortina arrives in Belluno in two hours.

13. Lake Misurina - At 5761 ft. (1756 m.), Lake Misurina is one of the oldest known mountain resorts in the Dolomites. (See Walks #2 and #5.)

Directions: Follow signs in Cortina and drive over the Tre Croci Pass to Lake Misurina, about a twenty-minute drive.

14. Bus Tours - Various travel companies in Cortina organize bus excursions to **Monte Piana, Croda da Lago, Lienz, Krimml Waterfalls, Venice, Südtirol Castles, Salzburg,** and **Val d'Isarco.** Check the back of the Cortina bus schedule for information or inquire at the Tourist Office and the bus station.

Cortina d'Ampezzo Walks

Recommended Maps:

- ❖ Tabacco Carta Topografica #03–Cortina d'Ampezzo e Dolomiti Ampezzane
- ❖ Tabacco Carta Topografica #10—Dolomiti de Sesto/Sextener Dolomiten

Walk #1

Introductory Walk along the Passeggiata
Walking Easy Time: 2 to 4 hours
Rating: Gentle

This gentle walk can be taken on the afternoon of arrival and is a good introduction to the environs around Cortina. It's on a paved path, or *passeggiata*, numbered 208 on the Cortina d'Ampezzo #03 hiking map. This path, now reserved for walkers *and* bikers, runs north and south through Cortina and the Ampezzo Valley, past the hamlet of Zuel, with views of Tofana to the west, Sorapis to the east, and Cristallo to the north—three of the famous Dolomite mountains surrounding the Ampezzo Valley. *Easy Walkers* will be hiking on trails in and around these mountains and valleys during their Cortina vacation.

Start: Walking down from the top of the pedestrian street, Corso Italia (at the Hotel Aquila), turn left at the bust of Angelo Dibona at the bell tower next to the church. Walk up and around this street, past the Hotel Ampezzo, crossing the main auto road. Turn right and walk past the Faloria lift station. Continue on to the paved path reserved for walkers and bikers and walk south to Zuel. Cross the auto road before reaching Zuel and pick up the walking path again. Return on the same path, now walking north, with views of the dramatic Pomagagnon range and towering Cristallo. The round-trip from Cortina to Zuel is about ninety minutes. Returning to Cortina, if you have time, continue past the Faloria lift station, walking through the bus parking area for a short while, and pick up the paved *passeggiata* again to the north. After about an hour, you'll reach a group of signs directing hikers to Fiámes and Ospitale. *Easy Walkers* might then return to Cortina on the same path and visit the church, the museums, the shops, and the Tourist Office.

Walk #2

Rifugio Auronzo to Rifugio Lavaredo to Rifugio Tre Cime Locatelli/Drei Zinnen Hütte and Return

Walking Easy Time: 4 hours

Rating: Comfortable

Today's walk is a *must do*, and it is suggested that *Easy Walkers* make this their first extended hike in the Cortina area. Make sure to leave an entire day for this hike—you'll enjoy the full exposure to the grandeur of the Dolomites. The day begins with a bus or auto ride over the gentle Tre Croci Pass in the direction of Lake Misurina: a 21-mile (34-km) ride to Rifugio Auronzo. This popular hike proceeds along Tre Cime (Three Summits), one of the best-known, most dramatic formations in the Dolomites. You'll also visit Rifugio Lavaredo and climb comfortably to an incredible, scenic viewpoint.

After viewing this remarkable natural phenomenon, you'll proceed toward your next destination for rest and repast at the Rifugio Locatelli/Drei Zinnen Hütte. If you look carefully along the way, you'll see the scars of a World War I battleground, involving mountain troops of Italy and Austria. The *rifugio* will be filled with hikers who've come from around the world for the best views of these deeply crevassed "pale mountains." As the sun moves across the sky, the colors change, the shadows deepen—a kaleidoscope in slow motion. The walk ends with a return over the same trail, back to Rifugio Auronzo and your car or bus.

Directions: Leaving Cortina, drive over the Tre Croci Pass and follow signs toward Lake Misurina. After passing this tranquil lake, a sign, RIF. AURONZO, will direct you to the right. Pay a local toll and drive up to Rifugio Auronzo, where the walk begins. On busy summer days, parking attendants will direct you into an available spot. If you prefer to take the bus, there are two morning buses from Cortina, arriving at Rifugio Auronzo an hour later. For the return to Cortina, there are two afternoon buses. *Note: Check the bus schedule carefully before you leave Cortina.*

Start: Where you park will determine how you access the well-engineered path toward Rifugio Lavaredo. If you arrive early and are fortunate enough to park at a level close to Rifugio Auronzo, walk to the *rifugio* and pick up the wide path numbered 101-104. If the lower parking is filled, you'll be directed higher up and closer to dramatic Tre Cime. You may then enter the path below by descending on a narrow trail that meets the main path, which is probably one of the most widely used trails in the Dolomites. You'll have lots of company on today's hike.

As you walk toward Rifugio Lavaredo and its sun-terrace, hold some enthusiasm in reserve—this is only the beginning of one of the finest scenic hikes in the area. On the left is the famous Tre Cime, and when bathed in sunlight, its pastel colors are revealed, depending on the sun's position and time of day. Just before Rifugio Lavaredo, at 7691 ft. (2344 m.), the path forks, with #101 rising steeply up to the left. *Easy Walkers* should walk straight ahead on main path #101–#104, past the *rifugio*.

After a while, the wide path narrows. Follow the sign up to Rifugio Locatelli/Drei Zinnen. You'll reach the Paternsattel, at 8052 ft. (2454 m.), in another half-hour, offering additional spectacular views of the Dolomites. To the far right is Rifugio Locatelli/Drei Zinnen Hütte, your destination. Note however, two paths are visible in the direction of the *rifugio*. Take the lower, wider path in preference to the narrow, hillside trail above, for the one hour walk. As you get closer to the *rifugio*, there is a narrow trail ascending steeply up to the right, blazed red and white, but continue on the main path, eventually walking up and around to the right to the *rifugio*.

The hike from the parking lot to the *rifugio* takes about two hours. After lunching, resting, and taking in the outstanding scenery, return on the same path. On the drive back to Cortina, you might enjoy a stop at beautiful Lake Misurina, ringed by pine forests. (See Walk #5.)

Walk #3

Cortina Lift to Tofana di Mezzo, Walk Col Drusciè to Lago Ghedina to Cortina
Walking Easy Time: 2½ hours
Rating: Comfortable

A triple lift to Tofana, at 10,644 ft. (3244 m.), is the beginning of your excursion to one of the locations used in Sylvester Stallone's *Cliffhanger* movie. Remember that this excursion can be fully enjoyed only on a clear day. At the top station, walk on to a large sun-terrace for extensive views of the Dolomites. For those who wish, there is the opportunity to ascend several flights of steps to walking paths along the peak at Tofana. This is a rugged mountain, and you should visit the peak only if you don't mind the high altitude and narrow paths. The peak is a popular starting place for mountain climbers, and you might have the opportunity of watching them prepare to disappear over the cliff on hair-raising *ferrata*, or iron-assisted hikes, to other Tofane locations. Plan to spend at least an hour on Tofana to absorb the remarkable visual impact of this stark, mountain wilderness.

To begin the hike, you'll take two sections of the lift down to Col Drusciè, at 5837 ft. (1779 m.), where the walk to Cortina starts by way of Lago Ghedina.

Directions: The Tofana lift is a twenty-minute walk from the church in Cortina, past the ice rink. There is ample parking at the lift station, but it's much easier not to drive through busy Cortina.

Hint: Easy Walkers *who are not happy at great heights or who may be affected by the altitude should enjoy this part of the excursion from the sun-terrace and not attempt to ascend the narrow paths on Tofana.*

Walk *up* the pedestrian street past the Hotel Aquila and follow signs to the ice rink and the Tofana Lift. Purchase a round-trip ticket to the top station, Tofana, which involves three cable cars. The first stop is Col Drusciè, the next is Ra Vales, and the last one is at Tofana.

Start: At Tofana, walk on to the large terrace for views of the Ampezzo Valley, the major peaks of the Dolomites, and on a clear day, as far as the Hohe Tauern in Austria. Take the steps in back of the terrace up to engineered paths along the ridges of the Tofana peak. Guide ropes are provided as a precaution for walkers who want to enjoy the thrill of getting as close to the peak as possible.

When ready, return to the first lift station at Col Drusciè for the walk. At the rear of the Col Drusciè lift station, note a sign pointing right, LAGO GHEDINA #413. Walk to the right, descending easily on a grassy meadow, part of a ski run. The grassy path turns sharply right, but *Easy Walkers* will turn sharply *left* up a forest path for a short ascent. Turn right on the jeep road numbered #410 on your map. Continue, bearing right at the first intersection. Snake down the mountain to the auto road where you turn right again, following the sign RIST. GHEDINA.

This small, sheltered, trout-filled lake is bordered by a pleasant walking path. The restaurant overlooks the lake, but if you prefer, you can picnic under the trees across the lake.

As you leave the restaurant area, turn right

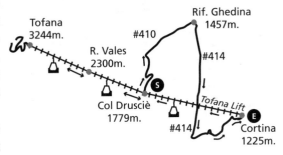

on the road (#414) for a pleasant walk through the forest to a three-way auto intersection. Turn left on the lower left paved road (still on #414) and descend to the main road. Turn left for a few meters and then turn right, past a bus stop, on a minor road that leads to Cortina, descending with the church tower as your guiding beacon.

Walk #4

Cortina Lift to Faloria, Walk to Ristorante Rio Gere to Rifugio Miétres to Rifugio Col Tondo to Cortina (Optional Excursion to Cristallo)
Walking Easy Time: 2½ to 5 hours
Rating: Comfortable

Today, you'll take the cable car from Cortina to the top station at Faloria. You can continue by walking up on a steep, wide trail to Rifugio Tondi or taking a private jeep at Faloria for the ride to the top and additional, spectacular views from Tondi. You'll then walk down from Rifugio Faloria to Ristorante Rio Gere, on a descending, wide jeep road, continuing through the forest to Rifugio Miétres and incredible views of the dramatic Pomagagnon range. (At Rio Gere, if the weather is clear, take the lifts to Cristallo for exceptional vistas of another area of the Dolomites where the *Cliffhanger* movie was filmed.) The walk continues through the forest down to Rifugio Col Tondo. There is an option at Rifugio Miétres to take chairlifts between Miétres and Col Tondo instead of walking the entire way to Cortina.

Directions: At the bust of famed guide Angelo Dibona in front of the bell tower at the church, turn and walk up and around to the main thoroughfare, passing the Hotel Ampezzo on your left, and crossing the main auto road to the Faloria lift station on the right. Purchase a one-way ticket to the top station, transferring to the waiting cable car at the mid-station.

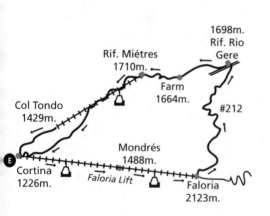

Start: The walk begins as you leave the cable car at Faloria, 6966 ft.

(2123 m.). *Easy Walkers* have two options here before today's itinerary begins:

1. Walk up the mountain to Rifugio Tondi, at 7635 ft. (2327 m.), along a rocky, wide jeep path for outstanding views of the Dolomites on the other side of Faloria, walking back to Faloria when ready.

2. If you don't wish to make the climb of almost 700 ft. (215 m.) but would like to visit Tondi, take the private jeep taxi that will take you to and from the peak for a fee.

If you take the excursion and return from Tondi or choose to hike immediately, the walk begins to the left, as you exit the lift station, on a signed wide, jeep road (#212 on the map), in the direction of Rio Gere. This is a one-hour descent, mostly on a ski run, to the Ristorante Rio Gere, located on the main auto road to Cortina next to the Cristallo chairlift. Watch for the sign #212 RIO GERE on the left and enter the forest trail. When you reach Rio Gere, if the weather is clear, take the enclosed "Sky Walker" chairlift to Son Forca, at 7267 ft. (2215 m.), at the base of Cristallo, transferring to the gondola for the breathtaking ride to Rifugio Lorenzi, at 9620 ft. (2932 m.)—the start of serious climbing expeditions over these jagged peaks and yet another *Cliffhanger* location. There are *no* hikes up there for *Easy Walkers*!

When ready, return to the base station next to the Rio Gere restaurant, where the hike continues. Walk down the auto road for a few hundred feet, and on the right, enter a path through the forest marked #211 MIÉTRES, blazed red and white. As you enter the path, walk through a turnstile, following the red-and-white blazes. After about twenty minutes, this path ends at a gravel road. Turn right and walk between the farmhouse and the barn at Malga de Larieto, at 5460 ft. (1664 m.), still following Miétres signs. The path ascends gently toward Miétres at 5611 ft. (1710 m.). At a sign to Miétres, turn sharply left on a narrow, mountain trail. This trail can be wet and muddy as it goes through the forest. Within a few minutes, you'll leave the forest and enter a meadow, heading for the sun-terrace of Rifugio Miétres, framed by the jagged peaks of the Pomagagnon group—one of the most dramatic sites in the Cortina area. *Easy Walkers* now have two options:

1. Take one or both of the chairlifts that descend from Miétres to Col Tondo, at 4689 ft. (1429 m.), with an easy walk back to Cortina.

2. Walk down to the jeep road, all the way to Col Tondo, and into

Cortina—ninety minutes of *Walking Easy*.

With either option, at the bottom, follow the descending, paved road back toward the church steeple in Cortina.

Walk #5

Lago di Misurina/Lake Misurina Lift to Col de Varda, Walk to Rifugio Città di Carpi and Return, Lake Misurina Circle Walk
Walking Easy Time: 3 to 4 hours
Rating: Comfortable

Today, *Easy Walkers* will drive to Lago di Misurina and the Col de Varda chairlift, taking this *seggiovia* to Col de Varda, at 6939 ft. (2115 m.). The ninety-minute walk to Rifugio Città di Carpi is on a nicely graded trail with outstanding views of Cristallo, Sorapis, Tre Cime, and the Cadini di Misurina above you. The path continues on a well-blazed, easy-to-follow mountain trail to Rifugio Città di Carpi.

This *rifugio* welcomes picnickers on its outside tables, and after lunch and mountain viewing, you'll return to the Col de Varda lift station along the same path. This walk, plus an hour's rest at the *rifugio*, will take about four hours round-trip. On your return to the base station, a gentle, one-hour ramble around Lake Misurina provides a different perspective of the surrounding mountains. On the way back, you might enjoy a stop at the restaurant at Lago Scin on the road above Cortina for *cappuccino* and dessert.

Directions: Leave Cortina by car for the thirty-minute drive over the gentle Passo Tre Croci, following signs to Lake Misurina. Just before the lake, turn right to Seggiovia Col di Varda parking area. If you prefer to take the bus to Misurina, there are two morning buses from Cortina, arriving at the lake in thirty-five minutes. *Note: Check the afternoon bus schedule carefully for your return.* Purchase a round-trip ticket on the chairlift.

Start: At the back of the top station, follow the sign CITTÀ DI CARPI, #120 on your hiking map, walking ahead on a wide path that turns down to the right and around the mountain, descending to 6375 ft. (1943 m.). The rugged Cristallo is in full view on your right, the massive Sorapis group across the valley ahead, and the jagged peaks of the Cadin are above.

The path splits—continue to walk ahead following the sign to Città di Carpi, ascending on a mountain trail through the forest, then hiking up to your left to 6923 ft. (2110 m.) and the welcoming Italian flag flying above the *rifugio*. The level of ascent steepens on the last part of the hike—take it slowly.

The small *rifugio* welcomes hikers to use their outside tables and benches for picnics, inside is a restaurant serving local specialties. When ready, return to Col de Varda along the same path, remembering that your initial descent at the chairlift is now an ascent. Take the chairlift down to Lago di Misurina for the pleasant, one-hour stroll around the lake before returning to your car and driving to Cortina or catching the late afternoon bus.

Walk #6

Cinque Torri Lift to Rifugio Scoiattoli, (Optional Walk to Rifugio Averau), Walk to Rifugio Cinque Torri to Rifugio Bái de Dónes (Base Station Cinque Torri Lift)

Walking Easy Time: 2 to 4 hours
Rating: Comfortable

Plan the better part of the day for this hike—you'll want to spend extra time watching climbers scale the famous Cinque Torri peaks. The Cinque Torri lift is on the Passo Falzarego road, a twenty-minute drive from Cortina. The chairlift ascends from 6198 ft. (1889 m.) at its base station on the pass to 7300 ft. (2225 m.) at Rifugio Scoiattoli. Here, you'll find new views of Tofana across the valley and the incredible five towers of Cinque Torri a few minutes walk from the restaurant's sun-terrace. You can walk up to the foot of the Cinque Torri and watch climbers scaling the vertical faces of these rugged peaks. This area is a favorite training ground for climbers, from beginner to expert.

An optional walk begins back at the *rifugio* at the top station of the chairlift and ascends to Rifugio Averau's restaurant and facilities at 7917 ft. (2413 m.) on a wide path that steepens closer to the *rifugio*. At this altitude, there are no trees or grass, only barren, rocky terrain, but the views from the terrace at Averau are worth the 600-foot (188-meter) climb. The walk continues back down to Rifugio Cinque Torri and then descends along the road and through the forest on a mountain trail to the Cinque Torri/Bái de Dónes chairlift base station and your car.

Directions: Driving from Cortina, follow signs to Passo Falzerago for the twenty-minute drive to the Cinque Torri Lift. Turn left into the large parking area at the sign 5 TORRI PARKING. Buy a one-way ticket to the top.

Start: The walk begins at Rif. Scoiattoli with its restaurant and sun-terrace. Before starting, observe the mountain climbers in action by walking to the left on one of the little trails going up to the base of the Cinque Torri peaks. Athletes of all ages and both sexes climb the sheer faces of Cinque Torri at various levels of proficiency, and it's remarkable to see how quickly and efficiently they scale the peaks. You'll probably spend about an hour taking in the action.

Return to Rifugio Scoiattoli and proceed on the optional hike up to Rifugio Averau, located on the mountain ridge in front of you. The wide path is rocky, devoid of any vegetation, and becomes steeper toward the *rifugio*. Take it slowly and reap the rewards of panoramic vistas at the top. Return on the same path toward Rifugio Scoiattoli, then turn right on the wide, descending path just before the *rifugio* to the trail (sometimes unsigned), leading to Rifugio Cinque Torri down on the right.

If you prefer *not* to take the climb up to Rifugio Averau, follow the sign to Rifugio Cinque Torri in back of Rifugio Scoiattoli and descend on a narrow path, leading to the wider trail below. This path offers additional views of the climbers on Cinque Torri, now on the left.

Walk past the *rifugio* on the rarely used auto road, following the sign RIFUGIO BÁI DE DÓNES, down and around the other side of Cinque Torri. After fifteen to twenty minutes on the road, look carefully to the left for the sign and trail into the forest to Rifugio Bái de Dónes/Seggiovia. This narrow forest trail descends for another thirty to forty minutes to the parking area at the Cinque Torri lift.

Walk #7

Lagazuoi Lift, Walk to Rifugio Scotoni to Cabin Alpina with Private Bus/Jeep to Lagazuoi Base Station
Walking Easy Time: 4 hours
Rating: More challenging

Note: This hike begins at a higher altitude than other hikes listed in the Cortina area. It was suggested by Giorgio Peretti of the Gruppo Guide Alpine Cortina. Due to time constraints, the authors did not have the opportunity to take this hike.

Directions: Leave Cortina on the Passo Falzarego road for the thirty-minute drive to the Lagazuoi Lift Station at Passo Falzarego, at 6890 ft. (2100 m.). Purchase a one-way cable car ticket to Rifugio Lagazuoi, at 9161 ft. (2792 m.), perched high on barren, rocky terrain.

Start: Coming off the lift, turn left and then sharply right and walk down trail #20 on your hiking map, descending steeply at first, to Rifugio Scotoni at 6513 ft. (1985 m.), a descent of 2651 ft. (808 m.). This trail goes along

Hint: Confirm the availability of the private bus/jeep service at Cabin Alpina with the Tourist Office before taking this hike. It's usually available in July and August.

the Alta Via Dolomiti #1 path and continues to Cabin Alpina, at 5663 ft. (1726 m.), where there is private van or jeep service to take hikers back to the Lagazuoi parking area at the base station.

MERANO/MERAN

An alpine Garden of Eden, its streets and parks lined with palm trees, Merano (not to be confused with Venice's Murano), lies in the South Tyrol (Südtirol/Alto Adige) of northeastern Italy, in a wide, fertile and sunny valley with a delightfully mild climate, protected by the snow-capped peaks of the Italian Alps. In summer, nearby alpine pastures are covered with a carpet of colorful flowers, and autumn brings an abundance of fruit in the many vineyards and apple orchards. Merano is a grand European resort, with elegant boutique shopping under medieval arcades, ancient churches and castles, notable museums and works of art, elegant, turn-of-the-century hotels, daily free concerts, a casino, and racetrack.

There are hundreds of kilometers of walking paths in and around Merano's environs, bringing *Easy Walkers* to neighboring villages and tiny rural inns specializing in the best of local, South Tyrolean cuisine. These trails will also lead you into the high mountains surrounding Merano, to grand castles and stark fortresses and to the *waalwege*, gentle paths following the irrigation channels along the contours of hillside orchards and vineyards.

The Passer/Passirio River cascades through town under gilded, elegant bridges and is lined by gentle, tree-shaded walks—on one side the Winter Promenade and on the other the more shaded Summer Promenade. One of the most famous *Walking Easy* paths in Merano is the Tappeiner Weg, named after the doctor who planned it, built it, and in 1892, donated it to the town. This path, with magnificent views over Merano and its valley, meanders gently along the sides and slopes of Mount St. Benedetto and is bordered by tropical and subtropical trees and flowers.

An internationally famous health center, Merano's spas offer treatments that rival the best in the world—the Spa Center on the banks of the Passer River is furnished with modern therapeutic equipment, including an indoor swimming pool filled with thermal water. It is believed that freshly pressed grape juice, the Meran Grape Cure, is beneficial for people with metabolic, heart, and circulation problems, as well as those with kidney trouble and hepatitis.

The city first made its appearance in recorded history in the year 857, gradually assuming greater political importance, as witnessed by the large number of area castles that you can visit. Its fame dates back to the fourteenth century when the Castle of the Counts of Tirol gave the country its name, and Merano became its first capital. Its narrow, arcaded streets; ancient churches; and castles still attest to Merano's importance as the medieval capital of the Tirol. By the fifteenth century, however, Innsbruck had become the capital, and Merano was no longer the home of princes—just a small country town surrounded by ancient walls.

This changed in the early 1800s when Merano first earned its reputation as a health resort, attracting members of European royal families, nobility, and the aristocracy. It's currently a city of 34,000 residents—a business center, a holiday resort, and a market town—the most popular resort in the Südtirol region of the Italian Alps. As mentioned previously, the Südtirol/Alto Adige/South Tyrol was formerly part of Austria and was ceded to Italy over seventy-five years ago. Today, the Südtirol is an autonomous province where all have the right to use and teach their native language, a model for the treatment of linguistic and ethnic minorities in Europe.

The ancient city of Bolzano/Bozen is easily accessible from Merano and offers visitors a fascinating day-excursion to its Old Town and the museum housing the famous Ötzal Man. Another day trip can take you south of Bolzano to the beautiful Kalterer See, where wine enthusiasts might enjoy visiting the Wine Museum in Ringberg Castle. One of the off-the-beaten-path valleys near Merano, the Ultental, with its high-alpine landscape and old farmhouses perched on steep mountainsides, is an unspoiled delight. The Passiertal, with its spectacular waterfalls, has also retained much of its alpine individuality, and its high mountain passes lead into the Wipptal with the Timmelsjoch and the Jaufenpass and the Ötzal of Austria. Many fascinating places, such as Innsbruck, Austria, and St. Moritz, Switzerland, are near enough to Merano to visit on day trips.

Merano is a place to indulge yourself—bask in the warmth of the sun, relax in the thermal baths, and enjoy the local cuisine—while *Walking Easy* in the Italian Alps. Your itinerary should definitely include Merano, one of the most beautiful towns in the Südtirol: charm, style, elegance—and walking trails everywhere!

Transportation

By Plane - There are international airports in Milan, Venice, and Munich, with train connections to Merano via Bolzano/Bozen.

By Train - Train connections are available from Milan, Venice, Innsbruck, and Munich via Bolzano, where trains run every hour for the forty-minute trip to Merano.

Hint: *The local bus system in and around Merano is terrific. Use it wherever possible to get to the beginning and at the end of hikes. Buy a bus pass for economy and convenience at your hotel desk, tobacco shops, or the main bus station ticket office in Merano. The complete bus schedule can be found in the booklet* A Guest in Merano, *available at your hotel.*

By Car - From Bolzano, drive northwest on the new Merano-Bolzano expressway, following signs into Merano. From Innsbruck, Austria, take the A13 *autobahn* (becoming the A22 *autostrada* in Italy) south through the Brenner Pass and exit at Bozen-Sud. Pick up the new Merano-Bolzano expressway to Merano.

A favorite route from western Austria is 315 south from Landeck, crossing the Italian border at the gentle Reschenpass, the road becoming route 40 in Italy, then picking up 38 into Merano.

From southern Italy, pick up A22 *autostrada* north, exiting at Bolzano-Sud exit, following signs into Merano.

By Bus - Buses leave frequently from Bolzano for Merano, depending on the time of day. The bus ride takes an hour.

Favorite *Walking Easy* Hotels

Easy Walkers are fortunate to have the following choices of hotels in Merano, depending on their personal preferences and budgets. We've stayed in each hotel, and enjoyed them all.

Hotel Bavaria, Four-Star: **Hotel Palma,** Three-Star; Sister hotels under the direction of Mr. H. Wunderer.

I-39012 Merano/Südtirol; **Tel:** 04 73 23 63 75, **Fax:** 04 73 23 63 71

E-mail: bavaria@dnet.it

Hotels Bavaria and Palma share the same parklike setting, in a quiet, residential section of Merano, only a ten-minute walk from the center of town. Both hotels offer comfortable facilities, with a century-old tradition of hospitality. The Bavaria has fifty rooms, and the Palma has twenty rooms—both hotels with modern, private facilities. Half-board reservations are strongly suggested, with excellent, five-course dinner service for all guests in the Bavaria dining room. You'll enjoy the indoor and outdoor pools, comfortable sitting areas, and peaceful gardens.

Hotel Castel Rundegg

Four-Star; Managing Director Peter Castelforte

I-39012 Merano/Südtirol; **Tel:** 04 73 23 41 00, **Fax:** 04 73 23 72 00

E-mail: info@rundegg.com, **Internet:** www.rundegg.com

The small, luxurious, seventeenth-century Castel Rundegg sits on a quiet hilltop, a fifteen-minute walk to the center of Merano. Of course, the Rundegg has been updated into a small, exclusive beauty farm and spa. *Easy Walkers* who prefer the ultimate in spa facilities, gourmet food, and service will be pampered under the personal direction of Peter and Adriana Castelforte, long-time Walking Easy enthusiasts. The cost is a bit more—but you're worth it! Ask for Mr. Castelforte and the special *Walking Easy* hiking package.

Excursions

The Merano Tourist Information Office is in the center of town at 35 Freiheitsstrasse/Corso Liberté, next to the Kursaal (casino).

> **Fax:** 04 73 23 55 24
> **E-mail:** info@meraninfo.it
> **Internet:** www.meraninfo.it

1. Merano

Castles - The fifteenth-century **Castle of the Counts (Landesfürstliche Castle)** is located behind City Hall and contains collections of furniture, weapons, paintings, and tiled stoves. The restored **Castle Tirol,** built between 1200 and 1300 near the town of Dorf Tyrol, offers visitors a magnificent panorama of the Merano area. It is now used for summer concerts. Visit its archaeological museum and note the chapel portals. The first Tyrolean eagle, dating from about 1280, adorns the door to the Great Hall. The poet Ezra Pound's grandson now runs the agricultural museum house at **Brunnenburg Castle,** rebuilt in 1904. **Rametz Castle,** built about 1200 and surrounded by gardens and vineyards, is now a wine cellar near Rametz Bridge. Visit the new botanical gardens at Trauttmansdorff Castle, easily accessible by city bus.

Shopping - The **Meran Arcades,** Merano's main shopping street, is lined with traditional buildings now housing modern shops and restaurants. A large, bustling **weekly market,** primarily food and clothing, is held every Friday morning near the railroad station.

Near Merano

Spas - On the banks of the Passer/Passirio River, the thermal spa center is furnished with modern equipment for treatment of illnesses and boasts an indoor swimming pool filled with thermal water, as well as doctors and technicians on hand to perform a vast selection of treatments. Merano is also famous for the autumn "grape cure" at harvest time. The freshly pressed grape juice is supposedly helpful to those with metabolic problems, improving the heart and circulatory systems, as well as helping patients with kidney and liver problems.

Horse Racing - Located outside of Merano, one of the most beautiful race tracks in the world is also the largest in the Alps. The Grand Premium Steeple-Chase is run the last Sunday in September in connection with a huge national lottery. It brings together famous jockeys, horses, and trainers from around the world. The course features high fences and arduous water jumps—a challenge to horses and jockeys.

Churches - The **Parish Church of St. Nicholas (Sankt Nikolaus),** a fourteenth-century Gothic church with an ornate bell tower, stands in the heart of the Old Town on Piazza del Duomo and is a landmark of Merano. Inside the church are paintings and sculptures, and in the tower entrance are ancient frescoes. Behind the church are many old gravestones—until 1848 this was Merano's official cemetery. The Gothic, octagonal **Church of St. Barbara (Cappella di Santa Bar-**

bara) is located behind St. Nicholas and boasts a lovely pietà and fifteenth-century frescoes. The **Chapel of St. Peter above Gratsch** features recently discovered and restored stuccos and frescoes from the eleventh century.

Museums - The **Civic Museum (Museum Civico)** is located on Via delle Corse. Exhibits include four huge, carved, prehistoric *stelae* called "menhir" found near Algund, Bronze Age artifacts, local arts and crafts, paintings, and Gothic sculptures.

Architecture - Gunpowder Tower, located on the Tappeiner Promenade, was mentioned in historical writings in 1377 and was used to store gunpowder after 1629. Three of the four original **city gates** are still standing: Bozen Gate on the south side of Merano, Passeirer Gate on the north side, and Vinschger Gate on the west side.

2. **Riffian -** With a monumental **church** that is an important place of pilgrimage, the village of Riffian is east of Dorf Tyrol. The church houses a famous sculpture from 1420, and the adjacent cemetery chapel was constructed about 1400.

   Directions: Take a public bus or drive north out of Merano toward Vipiteno/Sterzing.

3. **Schenna/Scena -** On a hill across from Riffian, visit **Castle Schenna**, built in 1350, open now as a museum; the **Church of St. Martin;** and the neo-Gothic **mausoleum** of the archdukes of Austria. Above Schenna is the small **Church of St. George,** a circular building built about 1200, with fifteenth-century Gothic frescoes.

   Directions: Take a public bus to Schenna or drive toward Riffian.

4. **Bolzano/Bozen -** The capital of the province of the Südtirol/Alto Adige/South Tyrol is a cultural city at the meeting of the Isarco and Talvera Rivers. In 1991, the sensational discovery of the "Ice Man," or **Ötzal Man,** who perished in an alpine storm over 5000 years ago, shed new light on ancient peoples living at the start of the Copper Age in northeastern Italy. The frozen mummy (now familiarly called Ötzi after the Ötzal area northwest of Merano on the border of Austria) is on display at the **Museo Archeologico dell'Alto Adige,** around the corner from the Piazza delle Erbe, in the city center. You might have to wait on line for an hour to see Ötzi—it will be well worth it—don't miss this re-

markable exhibition. His frozen mummy is lying in a special room repro-
ducing the cold and humidity of the glacier. All his clothing and gear are
miraculously intact and displayed. Audio guides in English are available
for a small fee.

The heart of Bolzano is the **Piazza Walther** walking street, named
after a twelfth-century, wandering German minstrel. At one corner of
the square is the Gothic **cathedral (duomo),** with its lovely green-and-
yellow roof. Take Via Posta from the other side of the square to Piazza
Domenicani and visit the **Dominican Church,** now a music conserva-
tory, with its paintings and frescoes. In adjoining **Cappelle di San Giovanni,** note the fourteenth-century frescoes, considered the best
medieval work in the Alto Adige.

Via Goethe leads to **Piazza delle Erbe** and its imposing **statue of
Neptune.** This piazza is home to a daily fruit and vegetable market and is
the beginning of Bolzano's main shopping street, **via dei Portici,** lined
with boutiques under Tyrolean arcades. The **Museo Civico** houses a collection of traditional costumes, wood carvings, and archaeological exhibits.

If time permits, you might enjoy an unusual excursion from
Bolzano—a visit to the **Earth Pyramids,** a strange geological forma-
tion—a veritable forest of tall, thin, needlelike spires, each with a
boulder on top, formed by erosion. These pyramids are on the
Renon/Ritten Plateau above Bolzano and can be reached by way of the
Soprabolzano cable car, leaving from Via Renon, left of the Bolzano
train station. At the end of this lift, a rack railway takes visitors to Col-
lalbo, where you follow a path to the pyramids.

*Directions: By car - Take the new Expressway, following the
Bolzano/Bozen signs. By bus - A morning bus from Theaterplatz in
Merano arrives in Bolzano in one hour. By train - Trains run every hour
to and from Merano and Bolzano, a forty-minute ride.*

5. **Trento -** The Trento Tourist Office is across the street from the train and
   bus stations on Via Alfieri. **Piazza Dante,** in front of the station, is a convenient place to park and begin exploring this capital of the Trentino region. Next to the station, visit the twelfth-century collegiate **Church of
   San Lorenzo.** Walk on via Pozzo and via Orfane to the elegant, pink Renaissance **Santa Maria Maggiore** church. Via Belenzani runs one block
   east of the church and is lined with palaces: **Palazzo Pone Geremia,
   Palazzo Tauen, Palazzo Quetta,** and **Palazzo Malfatti Ferrari.**

The street ends at **Piazza Duomo** and the eighteenth-century **Fountain of Neptune.** Trento's magnificent Romanesque **cathedral,** completed in 1515, is a treasure-trove of paintings, sculpture, and stained-glass windows. The **Palazzo Pretoria** is next door to the Duomo and houses the **Museo Diocesano Tridentino,** containing the Duomo's treasures. East of the cathedral is the Baroque **Palazzo Sardagna** and the **Museo Tridentino di Scienze Naturali.**

A **cable car** leaves from behind the bus station to Sardagna on Monte Bondone. Buses continue from there to the Vaneze and Vason ski resorts. From Vason, another cable car ascends to a summit at 6884 ft. (2098 m.). A bit further sits Viotte and its excellent **Botanical Garden,** on the banks of two artificial lakes, with over 2000 species of alpine flora from around the world.

Directions: By car - Take the Expressway to Bolzano, following signs to the A22 autostrada south into Trento. By Train - The train from Merano to Bolzano runs hourly. Transfer in Bolzano for the southbound train to Trento.

6. **Vipiteno/Sterzing -** Located 43 miles (69 km) north of Bolzano, Vipiteno is a picturesque town and a popular all-season resort. It's the first town of any size on the Italian side of the Brenner Pass from Austria. Walk down its main street, closed at one end by the **Torre delle Dodici,** erected in 1468, lined with fifteenth- and sixteenth-century Tyrolean houses, arcades, and wrought-iron signs. Stop at the **Museo Multscher** in the Piazza Città to admire works by the fifteenth-century painter Hans Multscher. The **Museo Provinciale delle Miniere Jöchisturn** celebrates the town's silver mining era. Note the ancient houses along **via Città Nuova,** and stop at the **Municipio** to see a third-century B.C. Mithraic altar.

Because of its strategic location near the Brenner Pass, Vipiteno's stores offer an extraordinarily wide selection of merchandise: leather, wine, and fashionable clothes from Italy; ham, sausage, bread, and sports equipment from Austria and Germany.

Directions: Drive 44 north from Merano, through the Passeiertal, winding through the mountains over the Jaufenpass into Vipiteno.

7. **Bressanone/Brixen -** See Selva/Wolkenstein chapter, Excursion #4.

Directions: Drive on the Expressway out of Merano to Bolzano and take the A22 autostrada north to the Brixen/Pustertal exit, following local signs to Bressanone/Brixen.

8. **Chiusa/Klausen -** South of Bressanone/Brixen, Chiusa has maintained its old Tyrolean character in houses and wrought-iron signs. The **parish church** was finished in 1498 on the ruins of a sixth-century church, and the **Capuchin Monastery,** constructed in 1697, now houses the **Museo Civico.** However, **St. Sebastian** is the oldest church in Chiusa, built about 1213. This round church can be found outside of town in an orchard. On the **Säben Cliff,** at 650 ft. (200 m.) above the town, an ancient settlement was built, and in the fourth century, a church and fortifications were constructed. A Benedictine monastery was built on the site in 1681, still standing today. The **Church of the Holy Cross** is part of the Säben Monastery, dating from the seventeenth century, but standing on the original sixth-century church foundations on the high point of the cliff.

   Directions: *Drive on the Expressway to Bolzano and pick up 12 north into Chiusa/Klausen.*

9. **Glorenza/Glurns -** North of Merano in the Lower Vinschgau Valley (Val Venosta), not far from the Swiss border, lies the smallest walled city in Europe. Glorenza/Glurns has retained a great deal of medieval charm and contains ancient high walls along with three gate towers and four round corner towers. In fact, the town and its buildings are now protected by a preservation order, and strict limitations are set on new building and remodeling. Ancient Glorenza was totally destroyed in 1499 after the German Emperor Maximilian lost a crucial battle to the Swiss. However, it was rebuilt in the sixteenth century. Take special note of the old arcades where craftsmen now work, and enjoy the many pedestrians-only streets.

   Directions: *Drive on 38 northwest out of Merano. At Schluderns, follow signs to Glorenza/Glurns.*

10. **Verona -** This "Venetian Arc" city on the banks of the Adige River ranks second only to Venice as a tourist attraction in this part of Italy. Verona has a picturesque, medieval Old Town center, immortalized by Shakespeare in *Romeo and Juliet.*

    A good place to begin walking is at the **Piazza delle Erbe (Square**

of Herbs), one location of the Tourist Information Office, where you can pick up a city map and brochures. Walk to the **Piazza Brà,** a large and spacious square at the center of the city, and visit the **Arena di Verona** (closed on Mondays). Built by the Romans in the first century, this was among the largest arenas in the Roman world, accommodating 25,000 spectators. It has perfect acoustics and now hosts musical performances.

Running off the Piazza delle Erbe is the **Piazza dei Seignori,** surrounded on all sides by stately old buildings, a **statue of Dante** in its center. Check out the twelfth-century **Palazzo della Ragione** and **Loggia del Consiglio.** At one end of the square is the **Palazzo del Governo,** where the della Scalas once ruled Verona. Off this end of the square are the **Tombs of the Scaligers (Archa Scaligere),** magnificent Gothic tombs of the ancient rulers of Verona. In the same area is the Gothic **Church of Sant'Anastasia** and the Romanesque **cathedral (duomo),** consecrated in 1187. Inside the Duomo, note the remarkable main doorway adorned with figures of the prophets, the classic red-marble pillars, and the Titian altarpiece on the first altar to the left as you enter.

Cross the Adige River at Ponte Nuovo, and walk in the **Giusti Gardens (Giardino Giusti),** the grounds of a palace dating from 1580, laid out in terraces and mazes. Walk up to the top on a shady path for a fine view of the surrounding countryside. Recross the Adige River on Ponte Pietra, pick up Corso Sant'Anastasia, which becomes Corso Pörta Borsari and Corso Cavour, leading to the **Old Castle** and **Bridge of the Scaligers (Castelvecchio).** This fourteenth-century castle with massive walls, towers, turrets, and a huge courtyard contains a **museum of art,** exhibiting paintings, sculptures, arms, and jewelry. From the castle, you can walk along Rigaste San Zeno and via Barbarani to **St. Zeno Major (Chiesa di San Zeno Maggiore),** one of the finest Romanesque churches in Northern Italy, set between two medieval bell towers.

Directions: By car - Take the Expressway to Bolzano, picking up the A22 autostrada south, then following local signs to Verona. There are parking areas near the train station, the arena, and Corso Porto Nuova, near your exit off route A4. By train - Take the hourly train to Bolzano and change for the train to Verona, a 1¾-hour trip. City buses #71 and #72 link the railway station to Piazza delle Erbe (or walk for fifteen minutes along Corso Porta Nuova).

11. Ortisei/St. Ulrich - See the Selva/Wolkenstein chapter, Excursion #2.

Directions: By car - Drive on the Expressway to Bolzano. Take 12 north to 242 east to Ortisei.

12. Bus Tours - If you prefer public transportation on excursions around Merano, contact the Tourist Office. There are bus trips to a variety of places, including **Venice, Lake Garda, Val Gardena/Alpe di Siusi, St. Moritz, Verona, Bolzano, Kaltersee/Lago di Caldero** and **local vineyards.**

Merano Walks

Recommended Map:
 ❖ Tabacco Wanderkarte #011—Merano

A hint about *waalweg* walks: When the snow melts in the mountains around Merano, the water is caught in a system of irrigation channels called *waale* in German. This water is used to irrigate the apple orchards and vineyards planted on the terraced hillsides and in the valleys. The trail alongside the *waal*, known as a *waalweg*, is usually reached by a path from the road and is level once it has been attained. Although this system of irrigation has been replaced in many places by modern technology, most of the *waale* are still kept working, and the paths are well-groomed, well signed, and very popular with walkers (with *weinstuben* and restaurants located along the paths). An interesting note about the *waale:* the man taking care of a *waal* (a *waaler*), listens for the water bell (*waalschelle*), which has been placed inside the *waal.* If the noise of the bell has stopped, he knows that something is obstructing the water, which makes the device turn and the bell ring, and he investigates immediately, thus preventing any flooding it might cause.

Walk #1

Introductory Walk—Algund to Merano Along the Algunder Waalweg and Tappeiner Weg
Walking Easy Time: 3 hours
Rating: Gentle

This walk is a good introduction to the marvelous walking around Merano, with views not only of this medieval town, but also of the acres of vineyards and apple orchards that fill the fertile valley. The walk can also be taken on an overcast day as an alternative to high-mountain hiking. The first part of the walk, on the Algunder Waalweg, is reached by a short bus ride from Merano to the outskirts of the little village of Algund. After a ninety-minute walk, the *waalweg* ends, and you'll descend to Merano on the popular Tappeiner Weg, strolling through the ancient shopping arcades back to your hotel.

Directions: Take the #13 bus, asking the bus driver to let you off *past* the village of Algund, where the Algunder Waalweg begins.

Start: After exiting the bus, walk ahead on the road and turn right into the parking area, following the large Algund sign. Once on the path alongside this miniature irrigation canal, you'll be walking through grape arbors and apple orchards with views of the Meran Valley on your right. Continue following the *waalweg* signs. After about ninety minutes, with the imposing Schloss Thurnstein high on your left, the *waalweg* ends at a paved auto road. Turn right, walk down the road, and in a few minutes the entrance of the famous Tappeiner Weg will appear. From here, it is a leisurely hour's stroll into Merano. Just after entering the Tappeiner Weg, you might wish to stop at Cafe Unterweger for lunch and/or snack, enjoying the superb views of Merano.

Walk #2

Ifinger Lift to Piffing/Merano 2000, Walk to Meraner Hütte to Falzeben to Hafling
Walking Easy Time: 3½ hours
Rating: Comfortable

One of Merano's frequent buses will take you to the base station of the Ifinger Lift, where you'll board the cable car to Merano 2000 and the Chalet Piffing, at 6250 ft. (1905 m.). The first part of the hike takes you up a wide jeep road. Eventually, you'll proceed up to the Meraner Hütte after passing Kirchsteiger Alm. There are several starting points for hikes to higher-altitude destinations that *Easy Walkers* may choose to take on another day. The regional specialties at the Meraner Hütte are worth stopping for. There are several chefs behind a cafeteria-style counter serving traditional Südtirolean dishes, such as *kaiserschmarren, knödelsuppe,* and *bratwurst.* After you indulge a little, the walk continues from the Meraner Hütte down to Hafling through Falzeben for the bus return to Merano.

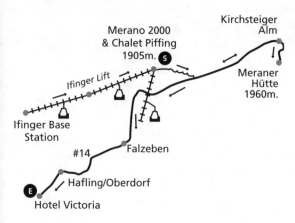

Note: Check local bus schedules before leaving on today's hike.

Directions: Take the bus to the Ifinger Lift Station and purchase a one-way ticket to the top station.

Start: After exiting the lift, follow the sign at the Piffing Restaurant to Meraner Hütte, walking straight ahead on the wide road. Shortly, turn off to the right on a narrow mountain trail marked MERANER HÜTTE, descending through the forest. After about twenty minutes, the path spills out on to wagon trail #14. You'll ascend from 5971 ft. (1820 m.) all the way up and around, passing Kirchsteiger Alm and its restaurant as you turn right up the wagon path to the Meraner Hütte, at 6431 ft. (1960 m.).

Return by the same trail until you reach the little path coming out of the forest that you walked on earlier today. Stay to the left on the road for a gentle descent, following signs FALZEBEN #14. It's also possible to return by bus to Merano from Falzeben, but if the weather is nice, you might continue walking down to Hafling, where there are numerous opportunities to return to Merano by bus. The #14 path from Falzeben leaves from behind the bus stop, just to the right of the road, and descends to 5414 ft. (1650 m.). It crosses the road several times as it continues to descend toward Hafling/Oberdorf. Eventually, you'll come to a sign for the Hotel Victoria, across from the bus stop, for the return bus to Merano.

Walk #3

Dorf Tirol Lift to Hochmut, Walk to Tiroler Kreuz to Dorf Tirol (Optional Excursion to Schloss Tirol and/or Schloss Brunnenburg)
Walking Easy Time: 3 to 4 hours
Rating: Comfortable

The bus system in Merano is very efficient and is used by many to reach locations throughout the valley. Today's hike leaves from Dorf Tirol, a short bus ride from Merano. A second bus takes you from Dorf Tirol to the base station of the Dorf Tirol-Hochmut cable car. The walk begins at Hochmut, at 4465 ft. (1361 m.), and descends through Talbauer. The path leads down through the forest on the Muter Weg to Tiroler Kreuz. You'll return to Dorf Tirol along the road and visit one or both castles—Schloss Tirol and Schloss Brunnenburg—before taking the bus back to Merano. For those who would like to extend today's hike, it is possible to descend from Schloss Brunnenburg on a trail down to Café Unterweger and return to Merano along the Tappeinerweg.

Directions: Take the local bus to Dorf Tirol, about a ten-minute ride. At Dorf Tirol, take a second bus for the quick ride to the Hochmut cable car and purchase a one-way ticket to the top.

Start: Exit and walk to your left, departing from the front of the little restaurant, following the sign DORF TIROL. This mountain trail is largely in the open as you wind around the valley, with views of Dorf Tirol below on the right. The trail descends on #24 to 3967 ft. (1209 m.) at the Talbauer Restaurant and, in another few minutes, descends further to your right at a fork in the trail. The left path (#24 Meraner Höhenweg) leads up to Longfallhof, another *Walking Easy* hike. The path to the right descends through the forest and is signed toward Dorf Tirol, #23 Muter Weg on your map, by way of Tiroler Kreuz, at 2645 ft. (806 m.). There is a cut-off toward the bottom of this trail marked FARMERKREUZ. Do *not* take that trail but continue on the main forest path to Tiroler Kreuz.

The path eventually comes out onto a road in front of the Tiroler Kreuz Restaurant, where it is possible to take a bus back to Dorf Tirol. But it's a short, pleasant walk on the road to Dorf Tirol, where you can visit one or both of the castles: Tirol and Brunnenburg. The nearest castle is Schloss Brunnenburg, easily accessible from the village center. It's also possible to walk down from the back of this castle to the Tappeinerweg for a pleasant, hour's stroll to Merano. Or, walk back up to Dorf Tirol and take the bus to Merano.

Walk #4

Forst to Lana along the Marlinger Waalweg
Walking Easy Time: 2½ hours
Rating: Gentle

Today's popular, low-level walk takes place on the Marlinger Waalweg, passing through apple orchards and grape arbors on the gentle slopes along the Merano Valley. You'll take a bus from Merano for the short ride to Forst, with its famous brewery, where the walk begins. It's necessary to ascend along a road for about twenty minutes before accessing the *waalweg* path. The Marlinger Waalweg is on a low balcony, overlooking all of Merano. There's a higher balcony walk above the **waalweg,** the Marlinger Höhenweg that *Easy Walkers* can take on another day. The entire length of the walk traverses orchards and vineyards, and along the way, winestubes and restaurants are strategically located for rest and relaxation. The path ends above Lana, where you'll take the bus back to Merano.

Directions: Take bus #11 at Theaterplatz/Piazza Teatro, in the heart of Merano, for the short ride to Forst. Exit the bus at the last stop in Forst.

Start: Cross the road and walk up the gently ascending auto road, following the sign to the *waalweg*. Once there, walk in the direction of Merano, following the *waalweg* signs past Marling, perhaps stopping at the little *winestube* for *traubensaft* (freshly harvested grape juice) and thick pretzels. The *waalweg* ends in the hills above Lana. Follow signs into town and the bus station and take the Lana bus back to Merano.

Walk #5

Dorf Tirol Lift to Hochmut, Walk to Longfallhof on the Meraner Höhenweg to
**   Tiroler Kreuz to Dorf Tirol**
Walking Easy Time: 4 hours
Rating: More challenging

Today's hike starts from Hochmut after taking the bus to Dorf Tirol from Merano. The beginning of the hike is similar to Walk #3, but after descending to Talbauer, you'll take the left fork on Meraner Höhenweg #24 instead of descending directly to Tiroler Kreuz. The Meraner Höhenweg climbs on to a more challenging but well-defined mountain trail, through the forest, up to 4758 ft. (1450 m.). It descends again, quite steeply at times, to the road below Longfallhof for the walk back to Dorf Tirol past Tiroler Kreuz. This walk can be shortened by taking the bus from Tiroler

Kreuz to Dorf Tirol.

Directions: Buses run to and from Dorf Tirol every half-hour. Get off at Dorf Tirol and change for the short ride on the *Gästebus* to the Dorf Tirol-Hochmut cable car station. Purchase a one-way ticket to the top at 4466 ft. (1361 m.).

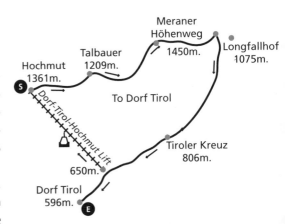

Start: After exiting, follow mountain path #24 in front of the restaurant in the direction of Talbauer and Dorf Tirol. The trail descends around the mountain to 3967 ft. (1209 m.) at the Talbauer Restaurant, but it soon turns *up* the mountain to the left (do *not* take the right path down to Dorf Tirol). Turning left, the trail climbs through the forest, ascending to 4758 ft. (1450 m.) before descending to the auto road just before the Restaurant Longfallhof, at 3527 ft. (1075 m.). At the road, turn right for the easy walk to Tiroler Kreuz, at 2645 ft. (806 m.). You have two options here:

1. Wait for a bus that comes every twenty minutes for the short ride into Dorf Tirol and another bus back to Merano.

2. Continue walking on the road into Dorf Tirol for the bus to Merano.

Note: Walks #6 and #7 were suggested by other Easy Walkers—they were not taken by the authors because of time constraints.

Walk #6

Dorf Tirol Lift to Hochmut, Walk on the Hans-Friedenweg to Leiter Alm to Vellau

Walking Easy Time: 4 to 5 hours

Rating: More challenging

This walk features some exposed areas with rocky ascents and steep descents, but it should present no problems for experienced walkers.

Directions: Take the bus to the Dorf Tirol cable car and buy a one-way ticket to Hochmut.

Start: Walk from Hochmut, at 4466 ft. (1361 m.), on the Hans-

Friedenweg, with its amazing views, to Leiter Alm, at 4994 ft. (1522 m.). From here you can either walk to Vellau or take the gondola down. From Vellau, take the bus for the return to Merano.

Walk #7

Merano to Schenna to Merano
Walking Easy Time: 3½ to 4 hours
Rating: Comfortable

Start: Walk up and along the Passer River on trail #5 on your hiking map, making a right turn across the bridge, just past Schenna, high up on the mountain. Walk up to Schenna for a visit to this lovely, hilltop town and its castle, Schloss Schenna. Return to Merano by bus or by walking along the Passer River on the Schenna side on trail #4.

ALLEGHE

In the geological age of the Dolomites, Lake Alleghe (Lago Alleghe) is "the new kid on the block," formed about 200 years ago when a giant landslide destroyed a dozen tiny hamlets, and formed this serene lake. The village of Alleghe, at 3196 ft. (974 m.), is off the beaten path and sits on the lake's shores in a peaceful corner of the Agordine. The surrounding scenery includes close-up views of the massive wall of the mountain of Civetta, towering above lake and village at 10,564 ft. (3220 m.), one of the most compelling images in the Dolomites. During early morning and late afternoon, this peaceful, trout-filled lake reflects rugged peaks and dark pine forests in dramatic contrast to high-altitude scenes of the sharply shadowed crevasses of the Dolomites. After-dinner walks along the lake add a pleasant dimension not available in most other alpine base villages.

Invigorating hikes and excursions are available throughout the Agordine. Malga Ciapela, a few dozen kilometers from Alleghe, is the site of a triple cable car lift and a not-to-be-missed, sensational visit to the Marmolada glacier, at 10,965 ft. (3342 m.). Still visible on the glacier are signs of the bitter fighting that took place between the mountain troops of Italy and Austria during the First World War. The Fedaia mountain pass drive to Lago di Fedaia, at 6896 ft. (2100 m.), invites *Easy Walkers* to a level walk along the reservoir with a ride in an unusual, two-person, open bucket standing lift that rises to the lower side of the Marmolada glacier. A short detour to Rocca Pietore while driving to Malga Ciapela and Lago di Fedaia brings *Easy Walkers* to one of the prettiest villages of the Agordine, and its notable parish church with an ancient, sixteenth-century triptych. Agordo, south of Alleghe, is the most important town in the valley and is surrounded by forests and famous Dolomite peaks. The town's central square is dominated by the parish church with its double towers and the seventeenth-century Palazzo Crotta. The Agordo Valley stretches south for a *Walking Easy* visit to the old village of Canale d'Agordo, birthplace of Pope John Paul I. Canale sits at the head of an unspoiled valley, closed in between two groups of high mountains, with a popular walk through the Val Garés forest to the tiny, remote village of Garés. Of the five *Walking Easy* base villages in the Italian Alps, Alleghe is closest to Venice—for a one-day excursion, it's a ninety-minute drive.

While Lago Alleghe is serene, many of the area hikes are challenging, with ascents to the mountain *rifugi* of Coldai and Venezia—and the unspoiled realms of eagles, marmots, and chamois even higher up in the mountains. Other hikes take *Easy Walkers* to picturesque valleys, rushing waterfalls, and through cool forests—with a comforting blaze on a rock or tree and directional signs nearby. Not many Americans have discovered this treasure of a village and its tiny lake, surrounded by the stark beauty of the mountains and valleys of the Dolomites—a scenic and unique *Walking Easy* village.

Transportation

By Plane - The closest international airports to Alleghe are in Milan, Venice, and Munich. Car rental agencies are available at all major airports.

By Train - The closest railroad station is in Belluno, 30 miles (48 km) from Alleghe. The station at Bolzano is 50 miles (80 km) from Alleghe.

By Car - From the south, exit the A22 *autostrade* at Ora/Auer. Pick up 48 east to Moena, then 346 east, to 203 north into Alleghe. From the north on A22, exit before Bolzano and pick up 241 to Vigo di Fassa. Drive south on 48 to Moena and take 346 east to Cencenighe. Then drive north on 203 to Alleghe.

Note: It is recommended that Easy Walkers *rent a car if using Alleghe as a base village. Most of the hikes and sightseeing excursions require auto transportation.*

Favorite *Walking Easy* Hotel

Sporthotel Europa
Four-Star; Owners - Case Family
32022 Alleghe (BL); **Tel:** 04 37 52 33 62, **Fax:** 04 37 72 39 06
E-mail: sporthoteleuropa@dolomiti.it, **Internet:** www.sporthoteleuropa.it
  The Sporthotel Europa is located on lovely Lake Alleghe, its front rooms overlooking the trout-filled lake, the side bedrooms facing the massive wall of Civetta. The hotel's bedrooms, all with modern, private facilities, have been renovated recently. The high incidence of repeat guests, both in summer and winter, attests to the quality of care and attention of the Case family. The comfortable public rooms are filled with an abundance of fresh flowers and are utilized in the evening by guests playing cards and games, reading, or just relaxing.
  Breakfast is a bountiful buffet, and dinner includes salad bar, appetizer, main course, and dessert. Each week in summer, a picnic is held at Piani di Pezzè, the mid-station of the Alleghe lift. Members of the

Case family are very much in evidence at the Sporthotel Europa, with its comfortable rooms, new fitness center, warm ambiance, and excellent cuisine.

Excursions

The Alleghe Tourist Office is in the center of town at Piazza Kennedy 17.

Fax: 04 37 72 38 81

E-mail: infoalleghe@apt-dolomiti-cortina.it

1. Alleghe - There are three lifts in and around Alleghe:

Alleghe Funivie - Take a ten-minute gondola ride to Piani di Pezzè, at 4823 ft. (1470 m.).

Chairlift Piani di Pezzè - This chairlift picks up where the Alleghe gondola leaves off, taking you on another ten-minute ride from Piani di Pezzè to Col dei Baldi. (See Walk #2.)

Marmolada Triple Lift - A visit to Marmolada on a triple cable car lift is a must for *Easy Walkers*. After a short drive from Alleghe to Malga Ciapela, you will board the first of three cable cars taking passengers to the Marmolada glacier, largest in the Dolomites. Although there are no *Easy Walker* hikes here, this excursion should have a high priority on your "things to do" list.

Directions: Drive north out of Alleghe to just past Caprile. Pick up the road west to Passo Fedaia. You'll reach the lift (before the pass) in about 11 miles (18 km).

2. Agordo - Agordo lies 12 miles (19 km) south of Alleghe and is the only sizeable town in the southeastern Dolomites. At 2,005 ft. (611 m.), its elevation is low compared with many other towns in Italy's alps, but its location is superlative—it lies in an open hollow with a mild and reliable climate, surrounded by pine forests and majestic Dolomite mountain groups. A wide piazza sits in the center of town, dominated by a large, Baroque church with a double bell tower. You might also visit the seventeenth-century Palazzo Crotto.

Directions: Drive south on 203 from Alleghe to Agordo.

3. Falcade - See the Vigo di Fassa chapter, Excursion #11.

Directions: Drive south of Alleghe on 203, turning right at

Alleghe

Cencenighe toward Canale d'Agordo and Passo San Pellegrino.

4. Selva di Cadore - At 4380 ft. (1335 m.) in the Val Fiorentina, on the south side of the Passo Giau, this village is in a sunny setting with dramatic views of Mt. Pelmo.

  Directions: *Drive north through Caprile, turning right at the sign to Selva di Cadore.*

5. Cortina d'Ampezzo - See the Cortina d'Ampezzo chapter.

  Directions: *Head north out of Alleghe through Caprile, following signs and driving over the Passo Falzarego to Cortina.*

6. Belluno - With the Dolomites to the north and the Belluno pre-Alps to the south, the city of Belluno developed on a rocky rise where the Piave and Ardo Rivers meet. Its foundations are on an ancient Roman settlement. The heart of the Old Town is made up of Renaissance streets, and when you walk in the Piazza del Duomo, the **Palazzo dei Rettori** stands out; it is currently the headquarters of the prefect. On its left is the old **Bishop's Palace.** The southern side of the square is dominated by the majestic **cathedral (duomo),** completed in the sixteenth century. Note the beautiful paintings and the crypt, illuminated by four large windows facing in the direction of the Valle del Piave. Next to the Duomo rises one of the most elegant Baroque **campinile (towers)** in Italy, created in

1743. The town center is closed at its southern end by the twelfth-century **Porta Ruga,** among streets and houses preserving the aura of medieval Belluno. Don't miss the cobblestone via S. Maria dei Battuti with its square, and the **Church of San Pietro,** rebuilt in the 1700s on the foundations of the existing medieval church. Inside are two large, wooden altarpieces considered to be important works of art. Between the small Piazzetta delle Erbe and Piazza del Duomo is the eighteenth-century **Palazzo dei Giuristi** and the headquarters of the **Museo Civico,** with exhibits of Venetian and Roman archaeological finds.

Directions: Drive on 203 south through Agordo. When 203 splits, take the left or east fork into Belluno.

7. Venice - See the Venice chapter for details.

Directions: Take 203 south through Agordo, and when it splits, go east to 50 east and pick up autostrada A27 into Venice. You'll go over a long causeway and arrive at a busy and confusing area, the Piazza Roma, a dead end for car traffic. On your right are a pair of large, eight-story garages where you can park your car. There can be a long line of cars trying to get into these garages if you don't arrive by 9:00 a.m. Walk from the garage across the top of Piazza Roma to the Grand Canal piers and take the large, inexpensive, public water-bus, or vaporetto, to San Marco.

Hint: *A tip of a few American dollars might facilitate your entry into a convenient parking area.*

8. Canazei - See Vigo di Fassa chapter, Excursion #2 and Walk #6.

Directions: Drive on 203 north to 48 west, over the Passo Pordoi into Canazei.

9. Pieve di Cadore - See Cortina d'Ampezzo chapter, Excursion #3.

Directions: Drive north on 203 out of Alleghe through Caprile to 48, turning east to 51 south into Pieve.

Alleghe Walks

Recommended Maps:

- ❖ Tabacco #015—Marmolada, Civetta
- ❖ Tabacco #025—Dolomiti di Zoldo and Agordine
- ❖ Cartina dei Sentiere, Estate Ciretta, Alleghe

Walk #1

Introductory Walk around Lago di Alleghe
Walking Easy Time: 1½ to 2 hours
Rating: Gentle

This brief walk can be taken on your day of arrival and provides views of the lake, the village of Alleghe, and the impressive wall of Civetta, towering over the village.

Start: From the Sporthotel Europa on the lake, walk to the right as you face the lake, with the lake on your left. Turn left at a path on the auto road and proceed until you arrive at a playground on the left. Walk through it to the canal and turn right, continuing until you reach the bridge. Turn left, cross the little suspension bridge, and then turn left on a narrow dirt path.

This short walk brings you to the other side of Lake Alleghe and a road. Walk along the path on the left side of the road, with the lake on your left, back to Alleghe. Note the gondola lift across the road on your right, which you'll take on another day. Walk up the hill, past the ice rink, to the center of town for a visit to the Tourist Office and the short walk back to your hotel.

Walk #2

Alleghe Lifts to Col dei Baldi, Walk Col dei Baldi to Rifugio Coldai to Col dei Baldi (Optional Walk Col dei Baldi to Piani de Pezzè)
Walking Easy Time: 4 to 5 hours
Rating: More challenging

If you can tear yourself away from tranquil Lake Alleghe for a walk in the mountains, you'll take the gondola from Alleghe to the mid-station at Piani di Pezzè, at 4823 ft. (1470 m.), and transfer to the chairlift to Col dei Baldi, at 6306 ft. (1922 m.). The walk proceeds gently downhill to 5844 ft. (1781 m.) at Malga Pioda and then rises to Rifugio Coldai, at 6995 ft. (2132 m.). For strong walkers, this hike can continue up to the ridge overlooking Lake Coldai, at 7031 ft. (2143 m.). As this open, rocky trail ascends the mountain, it gets steeper for the last fifteen minutes of the walk before reaching Rifugio Coldai. The views are dominated by Mt. Pelmo rising to 10,399 ft. (3168 m.) across the valley, the site of two other *Walking Easy* hikes.

This is a popular hike, and you'll share the trail with many other walkers. You'll also notice serious hikers (denoted by the size of their backpacks!), who will continue on this high, Dolomite trail all the way to Rifugio

Tissi, at 7382 ft. (2250 m.), for a night's stay. Return to Alleghe along the same trail to the top station, where you'll find the chairlift to continue the descent. There are restaurants at the lift stations and at the *rifugio*.

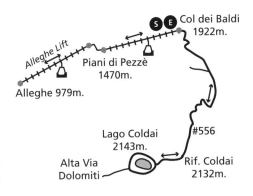

Directions: From the front door of the Hotel Europa turn left, walking along the lake to the ice rink. Cross the auto road to the lift station and purchase a round-trip ticket to the top station. Board the gondola for the ten-minute ride to Piani di Pezzè, at 4823 ft. (1470 m.). Walk through the large parking area, filled with cars of families who have come to this mid-station plateau for a day's outing. There are pony rides, restaurants, and families picnicking and sunbathing throughout the meadow. Continue to the chairlift station on the right for the ten-minute ride to Col dei Baldi, at 6306 ft. (1922 m.), where the walk begins.

Start: After leaving the chairlift, walk ahead in the direction of Pelmo, the impressive mountain in front of you. Follow red-and-white signs for RIF. COLDAI #561. Walk under the end of a ski lift on a wide path through a grassy meadow. Bear right on the wide wagon path and follow it down and around the meadow until you reach the farm in the valley below. It's possible to take some shortcuts down through the meadow directly to the farm, and that's okay, providing the trails are dry—if muddy they can be slippery. At Malga Pioda, bear to the right, following the sign RIF. COLDAI #556. This is a rocky trail that immediately begins to ascend the mountain. There are many little spin-offs, but we recommend staying on the well-defined main trail.

The last few minutes of the trail is steeper. The *rifugio* is a welcome sight and offers drinks, snacks, and facilities; it will be filled with hikers enjoying their

Hint: Easy Walkers *should make this ascent at their own comfortable pace, allowing other hikers to pass, which they most certainly will! Rest as needed. Your pace can be slow but steady. Be careful, this path is rocky—do your viewing standing still.*

holiday. If you wish, continue on the path up to the ridge for a view of the lake below, noting many hikers continuing on for a night's stay at Rifugio Tissi.

When ready, return by following the trail you came on to the top station of the lift for the descent to Alleghe. It's also possible to walk down to Piani di Pezzè by following the jeep road just past Malga Pioda—an hour's downhill walk to the gondola station for the ride to Alleghe.

Walk #3

Walk around Lago di Fedaia, Excursion to Marmolada Glacier

Walking Easy Time: 1 hour (Allow the better part of a day for today's walk and excursion.)

Rating: Gentle

Today, you'll have an opportunity to explore deep into the Dolomites for some fabulous views at the foot of the giant glacier on Marmolada. You'll also have the joy of driving on narrow, twisting Italian roads, rising from 3281 ft. (1000 m.) at Alleghe, through the Passo di Fedaia, to the Fedaia reservoir, at 6736 ft. (2053 m.). Restaurants are available at the *rifugi* and lift stations, but a picnic with views of Marmolada can be fun.

Directions: Drive north from Alleghe in the direction of Caprile. Outside Caprile, turn left following signs for ROCCA PIETORE and PASSO FEDAIA. Drive through the tiny communities of Bosco Verde and Malga Ciapela, the site of the start of a major triple lift to another vantage point of the glacier at Marmolada, an *Easy Walker* excursion for another day.

Start: At the top of the pass, park your car at the Rifugio Passo Fedaia, a restaurant and souvenir store just before the reservoir. Walk ahead on an unused road along the left side of the reservoir. It's a thirty-minute walk to the Marmolada bucket lift that will take you up to 8613 ft. (2626 m.) and

> **Hint:** It is suggested that you watch others get on the standing lift as it moves through the station. No more than two people are allowed, and the lift platform is numbered indicating where each passenger should stand just before the open car arrives. There are attendants to help you on and off, but you must be swift and hop on as the car passes. The gate will be closed behind you. Getting off at the top or bottom is also tricky—attendants will help—so move quickly.

the leading edge of the glacier. *Easy Walkers* have the option of joining many others for a rocky climb to 8859 ft. (2700 m.) to the *rifugio* at the glacier. There's a steep, rocky trail descent back to the bottom base station that is not recommended, but you'll enjoy meandering through the rocky fields (or the snowy fields, depending on the month) as you look up at the glacier. Part of the thrill, other than the sensational views from Marmolada, which

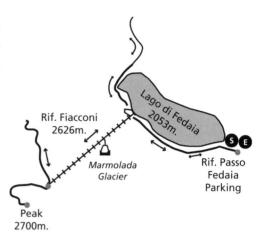

reached to the jagged Dolomites around Cortina, is the open, standing, two-person lift cage that will take you up and down the mountain.

When ready to leave the glacier, board the lift car for the breathtaking descent to the reservoir, observing hikers climbing up and down the rocky trails below. After getting off at the base station, walk across the top of the dam to the other side and note the trails that lead steeply up the mountain. Climb as far as you feel comfortable, but you can enjoy a grassy, meadow rest and/or picnic with views of the lake, the glacier, and Marmolada.

Recross the dam and return to your car on the same traffic-free road at the side of the reservoir that you walked on earlier. On the road back to Alleghe, consider stopping at the tiny, colorful village of Pian and visiting a few of the interesting metal workshops.

Walk #4

Walk to Rifugio Città di Fiume to Malga Prendera along the Alte Via Dolomiti and Return

Walking Easy Time: 3 to 4 hours

Rating: Comfortable

This sensational hike will give *Easy Walkers* unparalleled views of Mt. Pelmo and the impressive Roccetta range on a pleasant, ascending path through forest and meadows. The day begins with an auto ride on a mountain road from Alleghe, through Selva di Cadore, to Pescul and beyond. From the parking area, the trail rises gently from 5358 to 6293 ft. (1633 to 1918 m.) at the picturesque Rifugio Città di Fiume. The path you will use to the *rifugio* is a jeep road—now closed to traffic and well used by hikers. After an hour's walk to the *rifugio*, the trail continues up to 6890 ft. (2100 m.) on an easily ascending, wide meadow trail with spectacular views of the Agordino's jagged Dolomite peaks. This second part of the hike, on the Alta via Dolomiti Trail, will have walkers gasping at the beauty of la Roccetta. You'll return to the *rifugio* and your car by the same path.

Directions: We promise not to take you on any auto routes that are considered to be perilous. There may be a few moments when you hold your breath—just remember, let the passengers do the viewing while the driver concentrates on arriving at the destination safely. To drive to the start of today's walk, leave Alleghe to the north, driving through Caprile (*not* taking the cut-off mountain road to Selva di Cadore at the entrance to Caprile). Turn right at the *second* Selva sign and stay on the major auto road in the direction of Cortina, turning sharply right at Rucava and following the sign SELVA DI CADORE. Drive through Selva, and at about 2½ miles (4 km) past the end of Pescul, after a major hairpin turn, you'll see on your left a large yellow-and-black sign and a parking area for Malga Fiorentina and Rifugio Città di Fiume. This drive takes thirty to thirty-five minutes.

Start: The walk begins on the wide, unused road, blazed occasionally in red and white and marked #467 on your hiking map. The road winds through the forest and rises steadily but comfortably for an hour to the *rifugio*. This popular *rifugio* provides picnic tables for visitors and a grassy meadow for sunning, along with spectacular views of Mt. Pelmo.

To continue ahead, walk back down the road for a few meters. Turn left at the first intersecting path in the road. Walk over a muddy path to a sign that directs you *left* on #467 (*not* on #480 to the right). Follow the trail around and up the mountain, ascending easily. The path becomes fairly level, with outstanding views of the Dolomites. As you walk and the sun changes position, the colors and shadows change also—a dramatic and unusual sight. After about forty-five minutes, the path veers to the left at an open, grassy meadow, but walk out onto the plain for magnificent views of la Rocchetta in front of you. It may be hard to tear yourself away—the photographic opportunities are endless!

When ready, continue back to the path, walking along this Alta via Dolomiti Trail, which eventually leads to the Rifugio Croda da Lago Palmieri.

This walk to the lake is too far for *Easy Walkers* today—when you think it's appropriate, return on Dolomiti Trail, leaving enough time to get back to your car. On your return drive, you may want to stop and investigate some of the tiny, picturesque villages along the way.

Note: Returning to Selva di Cadore, you'll see a sign directing you down to the left to Caprile and Alleghe. This is the little mountain road you did not take earlier. It's a shortcut and will save you some time, but it starts off on a very narrow road, and you might feel more comfortable returning on the same road you came up on. However, after the first five minutes, the road is excellent, and it does cut out ten to fifteen minutes of driving time.

Walk #5

Rifugio Staulanza to Rifugio Venezia to Rifugio Staulanza
Walking Easy Time: 6 to 7 hours
Rating: More challenging

Mt. Pelmo is the center of attention on today's hike, which extends halfway around the base of this imposing mountain. After a drive from Alleghe to Passo Staulanza, at 5794 ft. (1766 m.), you'll hike along the Anello Zoldano Trail from the western side of the mountain, around the south to the Rifugio Venezia on the east. If you visited Città di Fiume on another *Walking Easy* hike that offered views of Pelmo from the north, you will have viewed Pelmo from all directions.

This walk is a long one for *Easy Walkers*, and it will take at least three and one-half hours of hiking to reach Rifugio Venezia. With an hour's rest at the *rifugio* and a two-and-one-half to three-hour walk back, you'll need a minimum of seven hours for today's hike. This does not include the one-hour round-trip drive from Alleghe or time spent for rest and photography. Still, if you are out of your hotel before 9:00 A.M., you should be back by 5:00 P.M.

The early part of the hike rises steadily on a forested mountain trail from 5794 to 6234 ft. (1766 to 1900 m.). It then rolls on with little change in altitude until you start to walk around to the east side of the mountain, where there are ascents and descents before you reach Rifugio Venezia at 6385 ft. (1946 m.). Experts who plan on climbing Pelmo often spend the night at this *rifugio* so they can get an early start in the morning for the challenging peak climb. Walkers are always on the trail for this popular hike, which crosses all types of terrain—meadows, mountains, plateaus, and forests. Much of the early part of the walk is in the shaded forest, and it can be extremely muddy in spots, so this walk should not be taken after a rainy period. *Note: This hike is rated more challenging, not because of its difficulty, but because of its length.*

Directions: Leave Alleghe by car in the direction of Caprile, taking the second right turn on the major auto road to Selva di Cadore. (Watch for this sharp right turn to Selva di Cadore.) Drive through Pescul for almost 3½ miles (5½ km), parking along the road in front of Rifugio Staulanza.

Start: The walk begins across the road from the *rifugio* on the route signed #472 RIF. VENEZIA. The path is signed and blazed all the way, and just after beginning the walk up the hill, a branch of #472 splits to the left to Città di Fiume. However, follow the markings to Rifugio Venezia. Except for occasional variations, the path ascends on a narrow, rocky, dirt trail until you reach a plateau, where the trail stays level for several kilometers. Your map shows this trail as #472 Anello Zoldano. In about an hour, note a signed trail up to the left marked *dinosauri*, leading to an imprint made by a dinosaur millions of years ago. Continue on #472 to the *rifugio*. After leaving the forest, the views to the left are of the southern face of Pelmo, eventually changing to views of its rugged east wall. Views to the right are of ski trails across the valley and the little town of Zoppe in the valley below. At an intersection, cut sharply left, going up to the *rifugio* for rest, scenery viewing, and lunch break. When ready, your trip back is along the same trail.

Walk #6

Alleghe to Masarè to Sala to Forchiade to Masarè to Alleghe
Walking Easy Time: 3½ to 4 hours
Rating: Comfortable

This low-level walk can be reserved for a cloudy day. *Easy Walkers* will proceed from Alleghe, along the road to Masarè, up to the hillside overlooking the gorge and river. The altitude change is about 263 ft. (80 m.), gently ascending through le Foppe and bringing walkers down to Sala on a mountain trail through a cool pine forest. The return is on a path in the gorge, entered at the hamlet of Forchiade, turning back to the road just before Masarè for the final walk into Alleghe.

Start: Turn left as you leave the Sporthotel Europa. Walk along the lake, past the ice rink, turning right on the path along the auto road, with Lake Alleghe on your right. Walk through Masarè and turn left into a parking area, just before the bridge over the river. Walk through the parking area to a paved road and turn right, and right again, onto a wagon path. This logging road rises gently from 3281 to 3491 ft. (1000 to 1064 m.), bringing you to a sign directing you ahead to Sala. There are signed options that send strong walkers up to Casamatta, at 4147 ft. (1264 m.), and on to Rifugio Tissi, at 7382 ft. (2250 m.), not a recommended destination for *Easy Walkers* today.

Pine needles cover this trail through the forest to Sala as you descend several hundred meters into the old village. After passing some interesting old barns and houses, make a right turn onto the main auto road. Cross the bridge over the river and walk down to the right on the first paved road into the gorge in the direction of Masarè and Alleghe. At the split in the road, just past a few houses (Palle), stay to the left, not descending to the right down into the gorge. This paved path eventually rejoins the main auto road several hundred meters before Masarè. Walk on the path next to the auto road and continue on to Alleghe.

Walk #7

Excursion to Canale d'Agordo, Walk through the Val di Garès
Walking Easy Time: 3 to 4 hours
Rating: Comfortable

Canale d'Agordo is an unspoiled treasure of a village, deep in the Agordo Valley. It's located off a road that traverses the mountains between the Agordine and the Fassa Valleys, at the entry point of the San Pelligrino Pass. Canale d'Agordo has managed to maintain its rich heritage and has restored barns and homes from past centuries. Note the Casa delle Regole in the center of town, dating from 1640. A walk through the tiny streets of the village will reveal the reverence that local people feel for their community. Religion plays an important part in the lives of the townspeople. This is the birthplace of Pope John Paul I—the ancient church boasts a carved, wooden altar dedicated to him—and the village was also the recipient of an historic visit by Pope John Paul II.

After you drive to a parking area on the outskirts of the village, Canale d'Agordo is the start of a walk through the Val di Garès. The walk begins on a wagon path through tall, pine forests at 3609 ft. (1100 m.). It proceeds along the picturesque Liera River and ascends gently through the Val di Garès to tiny Lago di Garès, at 4265 ft. (1300 m.).

Directions: Drive south through Masarè to Cencenighe and make a right turn to Canale d'Agordo. Turn left into the village and park near the church. After a visit, continue driving through the village for a few kilometers until you reach a parking area on the left and the entrance to picnic grounds. Park your car.

Start: Walk through the picnic grounds on the left, onto a pedestrian-only path, and into the cool, shaded forest. This trail continues through the pine trees, with the running stream on your right, all the way through the Val di Garès, crossing the stream before reaching the little lake where *Easy Walkers* have the following options:

1. Turn left around the lake and walk up to the waterfalls at Comelle. Then, continue around and down a narrow hillside path to the tiny hamlet of Garès.

2. Turn right at the intersection before the lake and walk directly up to Garès.

With either option, it's possible to walk back on rarely used, paved road, or return to your car on the same path you came on. However, it might be cooler and more scenic returning through the forest.

Walk #8

Walk Malga Ciapela to Rifugio Falier (Optional Excursion by Triple Lift to Marmolada)

Note: The following walk was not taken by the authors due to time constraints, but was described to them by other Alleghe hikers:

Directions: Drive north out of Alleghe to just past Caprile. Pick up the road west toward Passo Fedaia. You'll reach Malga Ciapela after about 11 miles (18 km). Make a left, turn past the campgrounds, and park at the end of the road.

Start: Walk up the trail (#610)—a short, steep climb—and go left on an unused auto road on #689. Turn right picking up mountain trail #610 again as it ascends along the Valle Ombretta, passing through Malga Ombretta, at 6247 ft. (1904 m.). Continue all the way to the Rifugio Falier, at 6805 ft. (2074 m.). Return to your car on the same path. If time permits, drive back to Malga Ciapela and the Marmolada triple lift for a sensational cable car ride to the glacier at Marmolada.

VIGO DI FASSA

The Val di Fassa (Fassa Valley), rising from the villages of Moena, at 3885 ft. (1184 m.), to Canazei, at 4807 ft. (1465 m.), is one of the Dolomite valleys where the Ladin culture and language are still preserved, as well as some elements of the Austrian character of the nearby Südtirol/Alto Adige/South Tyrol. The small country villages of the Fassa Valley are dwarfed and dominated by the high peaks of the Dolomite mountain ranges of Catinaccio and Latemar. These friendly villages attract winter sports enthusiasts enamored with the excellent cross-country skiing and summer hikers who take advantage of the large network of cable cars, gondolas, and chairlifts that crisscross the mountains, meadows, and valleys. Charming *ristoranti* and comfortable *rifugi* situated along a myriad of trails provide sun-terraces with extraordinary views and mouthwatering, local menu specialties, adding extra incentives and additional dimensions to the days' activities.

The village of Vigo di Fassa offers modern facilities existing in harmony with its traditional history. Located between Canazei and Moena, Vigo was chosen as a *Walking Easy* base village because of its easy access to the area's hikes, and because it is on an open, quiet, green hillside, away from the main auto road bisecting the valley. A major cable car in the center of Vigo rises to Ciampedie, at 6555 ft. (1998 m.), the start of several *Walking Easy* hikes. Campitello, a few kilometers to the north, boasts one of the largest cable cars in the Italian Alps, having the capacity to bring 130 passengers to Col Rodella, at 7874 ft. (2400 m.), for additional hikes with unforgettable panoramas. Canazei is the main base for exploring the magnificent peaks of Marmolada, Sella, and Sassolungo. A twenty-minute drive through the Karer Pass/Passo Costalungo to the Rosengarten Chairlift near Lago di Carezza/Karersee takes walkers to more challenging hikes and close-up views of the Catinaccio/Rosengarten range.

Local legend tells the story of dwarf-magician King Laurin who owned a magnificent rose garden. One day his enemies overwhelmed him, and his empire disintegrated. He begrudged his enemies the splendor of his rose garden, and he laid a curse on it: The roses were not to shine any more— neither by day nor by night. However, Laurin forgot the twilight, which is why the Catinaccio/Rosengarten glows a magnificent rose color shortly before the sun sets.

In the Val di Fassa, *Easy Walkers* have the opportunity to take low-altitude walks through the valley on *passeggiate* or taste *compagne cucina* (country cooking) at high-altitude *rifugi*. Store extra rolls of film in your backpack to capture the remarkable views and subtle colors of the Dolomites, especially at sunrise and sunset.

From Vigo di Fassa, travelers must pass through Canazei at the northern end of the Fassa Valley to enter the Passo Pordoi. From here, a twisting, mountain road heads to Arabba, Cortina d'Ampezzo, and south into the Agordine to such scenic base villages as the lake town of Alleghe. Another sensational mountain auto road north of Canazei climbs over the Sella Pass, with the majestic Sella mountain group on the right and impressive Sassolungo on the left, snaking down to the tranquil Val Gardena and Selva, another base village for *Easy Walkers*. The Fassa Valley continues south from Canazei through the villages of Campitello, Pera di Sopra, Pozza di Fassa, Vigo di Fassa, and the ancient town of Moena—the commercial anchor of the valley and an important entrance to the San Pellegrino Pass, providing easy access to Falcade and on to the Agordine. The inhabitants of the Val di Fassa hold a deep respect for their origins, honoring their Ladin identity, while working to meet the needs of the ever-growing numbers of tourists and hikers who come to this area each year. Unlike Cortina d'Ampezzo with its sophisticated shops and clientele, the Val di Fassa attracts casual Italian families for country vacations offering regional menu specialties, inexpensive wines, and comfortable, family-owned three-star hotels.

There are many hikes and *rifugi* in the Dolomites, and Vigo di Fassa and the Fassa Valley offer *Easy Walkers* a wide menu from which to choose a variety of day-walks and excursions.

Transportation

By Plane - The closest major international airports to Vigo di Fassa are in Munich, Venice, and Milan (car rental is preferable).

By Train - There are trains into Trento and Bolzano where buses then connect to Vigo di Fassa.

By Car - If you fly into Munich, drive south to Innsbruck, Austria. Cut south through the Brenner Pass into Italy where the road becomes *autostrada* A22. Exit before Bolzano and take 241 east into Vigo. From Trento, Verona, and the southern regions, leave the Brenner *autostrada* A22 at the Ora/Auer exit and take the S.S.48 delle Dolomiti road through Cavelese, Predazzo, and north to Moena. About 3 miles (5 km) past Moena, watch for the left turn to Vigo di Fassa.

From the east and Cortina d'Ampezzo areas, drive west on 48 through the Passo di Falzarego and the Passo Pordoi, through Canazei, picking up the right turn to Vigo di Fassa just past Pozza di Fassa.

By Bus - Local bus service connects from Bolzano, Merano, Cortina d'Ampezzo, Trento, and other cities, towns, and villages in the Dolomites and South Tyrol regions. Buses run frequently in the Fassa Valley, with excellent service between Canazei and Moena and all the small villages in between.

Favorite *Walking Easy* Hotel

Hotel Cima Dodici

Three-Star; Owners - Pierino and Mario Casari

38039 Vigo di Fassa; **Tel:** 04 62 76 41 75, **Fax:** 04 62 76 35 40

E-mail: hotelcimadodici@tin.it, **Internet:** www.fassa.com

Since 1963, the chalet-style Cima Dodici has been owned by the Casari family. The original hotel was built in 1956 and renovated a few times since. Its thirty-five hotel rooms, located in a quiet section of Vigo, are quite comfortable, with ample closet space, balconies, and private facilities. The public rooms in the bar area are well used, especially after dinner, when families congregate for their evening *cappuccino*, games, cards, and good conversation.

The kitchen, under the supervision of chef Mario, features excellent local cuisine, with a first course of soup or pasta; second course of veal, fish, etc.; a salad bar; and a choice of dessert. The menu is posted every morning, and the chef is quite accommodating if the main course is not to your liking. Breakfast is basically "continental," with juice, rolls, butter, jam, plain cake, and a hot beverage. Pierino's wife, Maria, and three daughters, Daniela, Roberta, and Barbara, also work in the hotel. With an Italian-English dictionary, many smiles and gestures, and a lot of per favores and grazies, you'll get along just fine.

Excursions

The Tourist Office in Vigo di Fassa is on the main street at via Roma, 18 in the center of town:

Fax: 04 62 76 48 77

E-mail: infovigo@fassa.com

Internet: www.fassa.com

1. **Vigo di Fassa -** Seven *comuni* in the Fassa Valley preserve their Ladin culture and language, especially Vigo, site of the **Majon di Fashegn** or **Ladin Cultural Institute,** and several traditional wooden cabins called *tablà*. The **Funivia Catinaccio** is a large cable car, rising to the top station at Ciampedie, with a fabulous view of the Catinaccio/Rosengarten. (See Walks #3 and #5.)

2. **Towns of the Val di Fassa -** The Fassa Valley is 12½ miles (20 km) long, with about 8500 inhabitants living in its villages, at an average altitude of 4429 ft. (1350 m.). The seven villages of Vigo di Fassa, Pozza di Fassa, Soraga, Mazza, Moena, Campitello, and Canazei make up the Val di Fassa in the heart of the Trentino Dolomites, at the center of Italy's most famous mountain ranges: the Catinaccio/Rosengarten, Latemar, Marmolada, Monzini, Sassolungo, and the Sella.

   Pozza di Fassa - Less than 2 miles (3 km) from Vigo, Pozza di Fassa is at the widest part of the valley and carries on the mountaineering tradition of this Dolomite region. One of the greatest climbers of all time, Tita Perez, "Devil of the Dolomites," was born outside of Pozza. The village is dominated by peaks of the magnificent Cima Undici and Cima Dodici. Nearby are areas of geological and mineralogical significance, including the ancient Monzoni range of mountains, dating back tens of millions of years.

   Soraga - 2½ miles (4 km) south of Vigo is Soraga, a tiny, tranquil village in magnificent surroundings. Near the village, on the right side of the Aviso River, the most ancient rocks of the Fassa Valley appear. The Soraga church was built in 1514 on the site of an even older church. When the river flooded in 1885, it destroyed its ancient bell tower.

   Mazzin - This peaceful village, 4½ miles (7¼ km) north of Vigo, surrounded by spacious green fields, is the heart of the valley and an area where many high-altitude walks begin. The nearby Doss dei Pigui is an area of great archaeological significance—major discoveries of prehistoric remains continue to be found there. These relics can be seen in the local museum.

   Moena - Four and one-quarter miles (7 km) south of Vigo di Fassa lies Moena, the largest town in the Val di Fassa with 2600 inhabitants. Moena also treasures its Ladin culture and language, and in local legend, this village is the kingdom of mythical King Laurin and is called "Fairy of the Dolomites." At sunset, the surrounding mountains take on the fiery red hue made famous in photographs of the area. Enjoy the spectacular views of the Catinaccio and Sassolungo Mountains. Note the Roda di Vael stones silhouetted against the sky: Use your imagination here to see a profile of legendary King Laurin. Moena has two churches of note, the twelfth-century **Sa Vigilio** and the small **San Wolfgango,** richly decorated with fifteenth-century frescoes.

Campitello - Situated 6 miles (10 km) north of Vigo, Campitello is dominated by the Col Rodella, forming a natural balcony onto the Dolomites. This upper Fassa Valley village is the home of the Ciamorces, famous alpine guides who proudly boast of their mountaineering feats and countless daring rescue missions. Campitello is also the site of one of the largest cable cars in the Italian Alps, the **Col Rodella,** rising to panoramic views of the Val di Fassa, Gruppo Sella, and Sassolungo. (See Walk #2.)

Canazei - Located 8 miles (13 km) north of Vigo, Canazei lies on the main Dolomite Road to the famous Sella, Pordoi, and Fedaia Passes. It's close to the Marmolada range, and you can drive east of the village for a superb view of this area, framed by the Catinaccio, the Torri del Vaiolet, the Sella massif, and Marmolada. Explore Canazei with an interesting piazza, inviting shops, and intriguing architecture. (See Walk #6.)

San Giovanni di Fassa - This tiny hamlet is located right below Vigo di Fassa and depends on Vigo for all its services. Its name derives from the Pieve di S. Giovanni, the largest religious and artistic monument in the Fassa Valley. Its Gothic **Church of Santa Giuliana a Vigo** was built in late 1400 on the site of an earlier church built about 1000. Each time the bell rings in this church, a legend is perpetuated. Supposedly in 1549, while the bell was being cast, a woman threw a bronze vessel full of precious metals that her husband had stolen from the Turks into a large melting pot. Soldà was going to kill his wife because of the lost treasure, and because he felt the bell would be damaged. However, when the bell was cast, the sound was perfect, and since then, the villagers attribute its beautiful sound to the precious metal stolen from the Turks in the sixteenth century! Visit the **Museo Ladino di Fassa,** with exhibits of archaeology and ethnography.

3. Bolzano/Bozen - See the Merano chapter, Excursion #4.

Directions: By car - Take route 241 over the Passo di Costalunga/Karer Pass, through the Valle D'Ega/Eggental, following signs into Bolzano/

Bozen. By bus - A morning bus from Vigodi Fassa arrives in Bolzano/Bozen in eighty minutes.

4. Trento - See the Merano chapter, Excursion #5.

   Directions: *Drive through Moena on 48, staying east on the road at Predazzo until you reach Ora/Auer, where you pick up 12 or the A22 autostrada south into Trento.*

5. Cortina d'Ampezzo - See the Cortina d'Ampezzo chapter.

   Directions: *Drive north on 48 through Canazei, then over Passo Pordoi, and Passo Falzarego to Cortina.*

6. Merano/Meran - See the Merano/Meran chapter.

   Directions: *Follow directions to Bolzano/Bozen and pick up 12 south. After a short drive, take the new expressway into Merano.*

7. Rovereto - Second only to Trento in population and political importance, and called the "Athens of the Trentino," Rovereto is a medieval town with the fourteenth-century **Castello di Sabbionara** looming over its houses. The town's Venetian connections are still visible in the **Palazzo Municipale** and the **Church of San Marco.** The third oldest museum in Italy, the **Museo Civico,** houses collections of archaeology, natural sciences, the old silk industry, and a new planetarium.

   During World War I, thousands of Italian and Austrian troops were killed in this area, and one of the largest bells in the world, the **Bell of the Fallen (Campana dei Caduti)** on nearby Miravelle hill, tolls one hundred times each sunset to eulogize war victims around the world.

   Southeast of Rovereto, at Lavini di Marco, follow the **Path of the Dinosaurs,** marked by footprints left 200 million years ago but only discovered in 1991.

   Directions: *Take 48 west toward Bolzano, then drive south on 12 into Rovereto.*

8. Egna/Neumarkt - Egna is an ancient town south of Bolzano/Bozen, established in 1189 as a trading post. For centuries its craftsmen and merchants enjoyed trade between Germany and Italy. When the railroad was introduced into the area in the mid-1800s and bypassed the town, Egna/Neumarkt became a sleepy, rural backwater. However, its ancient arcades and narrow streets have been restored, and the **Museum for Common Culture** is an introduction to typical nineteenth-century lifestyles of the area along the Brenner Pass.

Directions: By car - Drive on 241 west to Bolzano/Bozen, not entering the A22 autostrada but picking up 12 south to Egna/Neumarkt. By bus - A morning bus from Vigo arrives in Egna in ninety minutes.

9. Ortisei/St. Ulrich - See the Selva/Wolkenstein chapter, Excursion #2.

Directions: Drive north past Canazei and pick up 242 north through the Passo Sella/Sellajoch. Drive past Selva, continuing on to Ortisei.

10. Bressanone/Brixen - See the Selva/Wolkenstein chapter, Excursion #4.

Directions: Take 241 west to 12 north or the A22 autostrada into Bressanone/Brixen.

11. Falcade - The tiny village of Falcade, between the Pale di San Martino, Civetta, and Marmolada, is in a wonderful position for both winter and summer sports activities. Visit the **Church of San Sebastiano** with its pointed steeple and fine interior paintings. The village is internationally known in the world of modern art because of wood sculptors Dante Moro and Augusto Murer. Their studios are also art galleries that are open to the public.

Directions: Drive to south Moena. Turn southeast for 6 miles (10 km) on 346 and drive over the San Pellegrino Pass into Falcade.

12. Bus Tours - Excursions are available from Vigo di Fassa by local Atesina bus—current prices and timetables are available at the Tourist Office. Destinations include **Innsbruck, Salzburg, Munich, Cortina d'Ampezzo, Lake Misurina, Corvara, Livigno, Brunico, Merano, Lago di Carezza,** and **Ortisei.**

Vigo di Fassa Walks

Recommended Maps:
- ❖ Tabacco Carta Topografica #06—Val di Fassa e Dolomiti Fassane
- ❖ Additional maps are available free of charge from any local Val di Fassa Tourist Office.

Walk #1

Introductory Walk—Vigo di Fassa to Larzonei to Vallonga to Vigo di Fassa
Walking Easy Time: 2 hours
Rating: Comfortable

This walk can be clearly followed on the local map of Vigo di Fassa/Pozza di Fassa, available at the Tourist Office, and you might want to pick up this map before you begin. This short walk serves as an introduction to the lovely meadow and forest area south of Vigo di Fassa and might be an activity for your arrival afternoon. The walk begins at Vigo's village center and winds down through the meadows on a *passeggiata,* almost all the way to Tamion. It then turns up through the forest to Vallonga and back to Vigo.

Start: Walk west through the village center along the road, crossing it just past the Spar market, and entering on to the small street signed VIA VALLE. Walk ahead on this picturesque, cobblestone street and, at the second shrine on via Belvedere, take the small, unpaved, middle path between two old, wooden barns. This path leads down the meadows to an unmarked *passeggiata,* where you bear right to the road into Larzonei. Follow the road around and pick up the signed path toward Tamion. The path descends through the forest, crossing over the river on a narrow wooden bridge. Follow the sign to the right, VALLONGA, as the path ascends for a rise of about 427 ft. (130 m.). This trail crosses the stream again, bringing you out to the main auto road. Cross the road and immediately take the ascending path to the lovely old church dedicated in 1700 to S. Giovanni Nepomuceno, located in the center of Vallonga. Make a right turn at the church and a left almost immediately, onto the walking path in the direction of Vigo di Fassa.

This gentle path descends to Vigo parallel to the auto road down on your right. Continue ahead in the signed direction of Vigo. Do *not* turn up to the left on another *passeggiata* in the direction of Vael. When the path ends, turn left on the main street for a walk through Vigo di Fassa to your hotel.

Walk #2

Campitello Lift to Col Rodella, Walk to Rifugio Friedrich August to Rifugio Sandro Pertini to Malga del Sasso Piatto to Rifugio Micheluzzi/Duron to Campitello

Walking Easy Time: 4 hours

Rating: More challenging

Reserve the better part of a clear day for this sensational hike. At Campitello, you'll take one of the largest cable cars in the Italian Alps, holding 130 people, for the ascent to Col Rodella and spectacular views of the Sella group, Sassolungo, Sassopiatto, and Catinaccio.

The walk begins with a descent to the Rifugio August and continues along the base of Sassolungo/Sassopiatto on the Friedrich Augustweg. This narrow, mountainside trail running between 7546 and 7874 ft. (2300 and 2400 m.) is mostly comfortable, but there are enough rocky scrambles to rate it "more challenging." The views of the Dolomites are dazzling, and it's possible to cross over into the next valley, the Val Gardena, through Alpe di Siusi. Today, though, *Easy Walkers* will descend at Malga del Sasso Piatto (dairy farm) through the valley to the Rifugio Micheluzzi, at 6103 ft. (1860 m.), for a view of one of the prettiest pastoral scenes in the Italian Alps. The hike ends with a walk down a traffic-free gravel road, all the way to Campitello and your car.

Directions: Drive to Campitello and park in the large parking area at the base station of the *Funivia* Col Rodella. Buy a one-way ticket to the top station and take the large, modern cable car for the seven-minute ride to Col Rodella at 7832 ft. (2387 m.).

Start: Upon exiting, follow the sign SASSO PIATO #594. Walk ahead past the Rifugio des Alpes, noting the sign to Rifugio Col Rodella located on the peak to the left. But *Easy Walkers* will walk straight ahead, down to an intersection visible below, just before Rifugio F. August. This is the starting point of

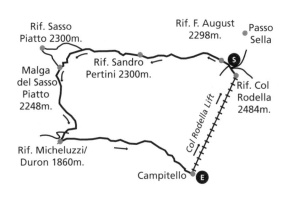

several walks, and it is well signed. Walk left and ahead, following directions to Rifugio F. August, at 7540 ft. (2298 m.), and then to Rifugio Sandro Pertini, at 7546 ft. (2300 m.). The trail to Rifugio S. Pertini is pleasant, fairly level, and well traveled—a forty-five-minute walk with astounding views of the surrounding Dolomites.

On leaving Rifugio Pertini, path #594 becomes a typical mountain *bergweg,* more challenging as it narrows because of rocky scrambles before descending to the small farm, Malga del Sasso Piatto, at 7376 ft. (2248 m.). The farm is reached by taking the *unsigned* mountain trail down to the left and splitting off the main trail *before* reaching Rifugio Sasso Piatto, visible up on the hillside. Toward the bottom of this descent, look for blue blazing and blue arrows on a huge boulder before the farm, directing you to the left on trail #533 to Rifugio Duron (called Micheluzzi on many maps).

This well-beaten, blazed trail descends in the meadows through the valley and near a mountain stream, eventually turning and crossing it. The trail continues down, steeply at times, into the forest and to a country road. Cross the road, picking up the path again, and within a few minutes, you'll be at the Rifugio Micheluzzi/Duron, at 6103 ft. (1860 m.). It's okay to picnic here at the *rifugio,* providing you purchase your beverages inside.

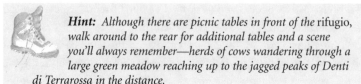

Hint: *Although there are picnic tables in front of the* rifugio, *walk around to the rear for additional tables and a scene you'll always remember—herds of cows wandering through a large green meadow reaching up to the jagged peaks of Denti di Terrarossa in the distance.*

When you're ready to leave, walk up to the road and turn right for the descent into Campitello. Walk down through Campitello on via Rodella with the river on the right and cross the auto road to the parking area at the cable car base station.

Walk #3
Vigo Catinaccio Lift to Rifugio Ciampedie, Walk to Rifugio Gardeccia to Pera di Sopra to Vigo di Fassa (Optional, More Challenging Hike to Rifugio Vajolet and Return)
Walking Easy Time: 4 to 6½ hours
Rating: Comfortable

Try to take this high-level walk on a clear day, as the views of the jagged peaks of Catinaccio/Rosengarten are breathtaking. You'll take the large cable car from Vigo di Fassa to Rifugio Ciampedie, at 6552 ft. (1997 m.), where the walk begins. The path to Rifugio Gardeccia, at 6398 ft. (1950 m.), is a popular, comfortable forest trail.

At Gardeccia, you have the option of a "more challenging" hike up to Rifugio Vajolet, at 7359 ft. (2243 m.), and hiking even further into the Vajolet Valley, ascending all the way to 8531 ft. (2600 m.). For those who don't wish to ascend the additional 961 ft. (293 m.) to Vajolet, the walk continues down along the side of a cobblestone road with fabulous views of the Catinaccio/Rosengarten above and the Sella group ahead. The road leads to the village of Pera di Sopra, where you can take a bus back to Vigo or walk through Maeda and Pozza to Vigo di Fassa.

Directions: In Vigo, take the cable car at the Funivia/Seilbahn Catinaccio and buy a one-way ticket for the short ride to the top at Rif. Ciampedie.

Start: At Rifugio Ciampedie, follow the sign ahead GARDECCIA NACH VAJOLET. After a few minutes, walk past Rifugio Negritella, where the path splits—#545 going down to Vigo by way of Rifugio Roda di Vael. Today, however, walk straight ahead on #540, eventually under a ski lift, emerging from the forest at Rifugio Catinaccio. Walk around the *rifugio* to the open, grassy plateau and the Rifugios Gardeccia and Stella Alpina. Trail #546 continues up and past Rifugio Vajolet, which sits high on the mountain for those *Easy Walkers* who would like more of a challenge on today's itinerary. The wooden benches in the meadow can be a great place for a picnic. *Note: For those who wish to shorten this hike for any reason, including weather, you can return comfortably on the same pleasant trail to the top lift station at Ciampedie and take the cable car down.*

To return to Vigo from Gardeccia, walk down to the left of the *rifugio* to the *unmarked*, stone jeep road (marked #546 only on your map), with the river on the right and the soaring peaks of Catinaccio up on the left. You might find it more comfortable walking on the small grassy strip alongside the cobblestone road. After about forty minutes, the road becomes paved, as you continue descending gently toward Pera, with impressive scenery in all directions. You might stop at Restaurant La Regolina on the right if a *cappuccino* break on the pretty sun-terrace seems indicated. Continue walking on the road until you come to a sign for the Regolina restaurant. Depart here from the auto road, descending to the right on a "chapel path" that winds down into Pera. Walk through Pera on via Tita Piaz to the main auto road, past some old barns, the church, and cemetery.

To walk back to Vigo, turn right on the main road in the direction of Vigo. Just past the auto dealer cross the road and walk to the Hotel Christina. Walk past the hotel, crossing the meadow in back of the hotel gently to the right (in the two o'clock direction), and walk over the bridge on the path up and through the meadow to the little village of Meida. Enter via Laurino, making a right on via Cavour. Cross the bridge and turn right immediately onto the *passieggiata*. In Pozza, cross another bridge to the right, then turn left and walk along the main road for a short time to Col da Prà, where you ascend to the main street in Vigo.

If you prefer to take the bus from Pera to Vigo, when you come off the chapel path, instead of turning right onto via Tita Piaz, turn left on to via Catanaccio and walk to the main road and the bus stop. (Check the bus schedules before taking today's walk.)

Walk #4

Rosengarten Chairlift to Rifugio Paolina, Walk to Monument Christomannos and Return, Walk to Base Station Rosengarten Lift (Optional Excursion to Lago di Carezza)

Walking Easy Time: 3 hours

Rating: More challenging

Today's walk begins at the Rosengarten/Catinaccio chairlift, a twenty-minute drive from Vigo over the Karerpass/Passo Costalunga, with a pleasant, double chairlift glide over a golf course and green meadows to Rifugio Paolina, at 6972 ft. (2125 m.). There are several walks from this point, but *Easy Walkers* will walk up 735 ft. (224 m.) on a twisting mountain trail to Monument Christomannos. Here, you'll find stunning panoramic views of the dramatic Latemar mountain group across the valley, the Catinaccio/Rosengarten group above you, and the soft green meadows and darker green forests below.

After returning to the lift station, you'll walk down the mountain on a zigzagging, well-defined trail that can be steep at times. This walk is rated "more challenging" because there is *no* level walking, only a steep ascent and a long descent. However, you have the option of returning to the base station by the same chairlift you came up on instead of walking down.

Directions: Leave from Vigo di Fassa on the main auto road through Vallonga and the Karerpass/Passo Costalunga, driving to the Rosengarten chairlift, located on the right side of the road. There's ample parking at the base station. Purchase a one-way ticket and board the chairlift for the fifteen-minute ride to the top.

Start: At the top station, walk to the right of Rifugio Paolina and follow one of several signs to MON. CHRISTOMANNOS. This highly visible, popular mountain path climbs to your destination under the peak of Roda di Vael. *Easy Walkers* may find the ascent steep, but the trail is usually filled with families—hikers from the ages of two to eighty. Take the ascent slowly and enjoy the view at the monument, a large bronze eagle dedicated to Dr. Cristommanos of Merano, who understood the importance of tourism in the area and proposed the now-famous Dolomite Road.

Return to Rifugio Paolina, the top station of the chairlift on the same trail, and after a picnic or lunch at the *rifugio*, walk down to the bottom of the chairlift and the parking area on the path marked SESSELIFT TAL STATION. This trail zigzags down the mountain to ease the level of descent, starting next to and under the chairlift, steeply at first, but easing off nicely onto the meadow and through the golf course to a road that winds down to the parking area at the lift station. This part of the walk should take about seventy-five minutes.

If time permits, drive five minutes further west for an excursion and short walk around Lago di Carezza, parking in a large area on the right for a small fee. Cross the road and walk around the pretty little lake, *Lago di Carezza*, through the Latemar forest. If you wish, you can walk on several small trails off to the right of the main split-fence trail. These reach further up into the forest, where locals search for wild mushrooms, a favorite pastime in this area. We've seen hikers come out of the forest with baskets filled, some mushrooms being as large as a foot across. There are, however, strict regulations concerning the picking of mushrooms, that is, con-

Hint: *Caution! Check with experienced "mushroomers" before eating any mushrooms you pick!*

cerning weight, size, amount, etc., and a permit is necessary—check with the Tourist Office. The walk around the lake takes about thirty minutes on a pretty forest path and can be a pleasant break in the day before returning to Vigo.

Walk #5

Vigo Catanaccio Lift to Ciampedie, Walk to Rifugio Negritella to Vigo di Fassa on the Alta Via di Fassa

Walking Easy Time: 2½ hours

Rating: Comfortable

This hike begins at Rifugio Ciampedie, at 6552 ft. (1997 m.), after you've ascended to this point on the cable car from Vigo di Fassa. The path goes through the southern forest of Ciampedie in the direction of the Rifugio Roda di Vael, and *Easy Walkers* can descend to Vigo on route #547 without having to ascend to the Rifugio Vael, a climb of 886 ft. (270 m.).

Directions: Purchase a one-way ticket at the Catinaccio lift station in Vigo for the quick cable car ride to Ciampedie.

Start: Walk to Rifugio Negritella by following the sign #545 RIFUGIO RODA DI VAEL. Watch for the ascending mountain trail on your right signed #545. This path is called the *Alta via di Fassa/Fassaner Höhenweg* and ascends and descends as it winds around the mountain to Rifugio Roda di Vael. After about seventy-five minutes, and before the *rifugio*, you'll meet another path. A hike to the right brings you up to Rifugio Vael, but a left turn takes walkers down to Vigo di Fassa on #547. This path meets a jeep road taking you into Vigo.

Walk #6

Canazei Lifts to Pecol and Belvedere, Walk to Lago di Fedaia via the Bindelweg/Viel del Pan (Optional Excursion to Marmolada), Return to Belvedere

Walking Easy Time: 3½ to 4 hours

Rating: More challenging

This sensational walk, using lifts in Canazei, offers new views of Marmolada across the valley and above Lago di Fedaia. It will also be possible to take the standing, bucket chairlift at the reservoir for a visit to the glacier at Marmolada if you haven't taken Walk #3 from Alleghe. *Note: The following options are important.*

   1. If you take the hike in its entirety to Fedaia, it is essential to take the bus from the Passo di Fedaia side of the reservoir back to Canazei. This bus usually operates during the months of June, July, August, and the first ten days of September.

   2. Check with the Vigo Tourist Office to make sure the bus is operating

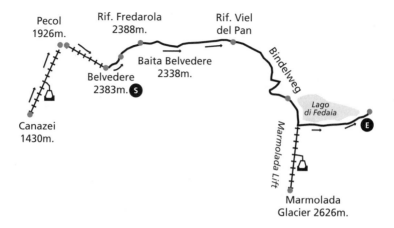

on the day you plan to take this hike. Ask for the afternoon bus schedule and plan the day's activities accordingly.

3. The path down to Lago di Fedaia from the *Bindelweg* (the last fifteen minutes of the hike) is on a steep, grassy slope and can be slippery. Take the descent slowly.

4. It's possible to shorten today's walk by *not* descending to Lago di Fedaia. Return along the same trail to Belvedere for the lift descent to Canazei.

Directions: Drive to Canazei, parking across from the lift station. Purchase a one-way ticket to Belvedere/Col dei Rossi, at 7819 ft. (2383 m.), via the Pecol mid-station.

Hint: *The two-person standing bucket lift requires some special attention when getting on and off. There are attendants who will help you. Move quickly and firmly and follow directions.*

Start: At Belvedere, follow signs #601 VIEL DEL PAN (the Ladin name for the *Bindelweg*). Walk down to the Baita Belvedere, at 7671 ft. (2338 m.), then up to Rifugio Fredarola, at 7835 ft. (2388 m.). Proceed past Fredarola to pick up the #601 Bindelweg to Rifugio Viel del Pan, at 7979 ft. (2432 m.). The views from this *rifugio* are breathtaking.

At this point, *Easy Walkers* have a few options:

1. Return along the same trail back to Belvedere for the double lift descent to Canazei.

2. Continue further on #601, finally winding down to the reservoir, Lago di Fedaia, on a steep trail. This walk, with views of Marmolada

and its glacier, should take about three hours.

3. If time permits, before catching the bus back to Canazei, walk across the road to the reservoir and up to the lift station for the standing, bucket lift ride to the leading edge of the glacier, the view you saw across the valley while walking on the Bindelweg. This is a spectacular trip—try not to miss it. You must check bus schedules carefully if taking this option. Also, please note the bus stops for your return to Canazei and your car.

Walk #7

Passo San Pellegrino to Albergo Miralago to Rifugio Fociade and Return
Walking Easy Time: 3 hours
Rating: Comfortable

Directions: The walk to Rifugio Fociade begins at the high point on the Passo San Pellegrino, at 6296 ft. (1919 m.), reached by driving to Moena and into the Valle di Pellegrino toward Falcade. Albergo Miralago is just off the main auto road that winds through the pass.

Start: The walk starts at the little lake next to the Hotel Miralago. The unused jeep road, #607 on your hiking map, rises gently from 6299 ft. (1920 m.) to Rifugio Fociade, at 6503 ft. (1982 m.). It passes through the tiny hamlets of Gherghele and Sprinz in the shadow of the high mountains of the Costa Bella, Sasso Valfredda, and Sasso Vernale groups. The walk back is along the same trail, with new views of the Dolomites across the Pellegrino Valley.

Walk #8

Walks through the Val di Fassa—Moena to Canazei

Although the Val di Fassa is usually bathed in bright sunshine, you might wish to take a low-level walk due to inclement weather or just "tired legs." There are *passeggiate* along the valley, never far from the auto road, many on easy, paved paths, some of which rise gently through the low foothills on either side of the valley. Follow the Val di Fassa local maps—Vigo, Moena, and Canazei—available free of charge at the village Tourist Offices.

VENICE

The proximity of romantic Venice to walking areas in the Italian Alps is a super bonus for *Easy Walkers*. For example, it's only a two-hour automobile ride on good roads from Cortina d'Ampezzo to the parking garages outside Venice. For those who prefer to avoid the hassle of Venice parking, bus tours are available from many base villages, leaving for Venice in early morning and returning the same evening. Check with your local Tourist Office for current details.

This chapter is intended to provide *Easy Walkers* with an informative and casual *one-day* walking tour of Venice. You should pick up a well-detailed street map, available at the *Azienda di Promozione Turistica* or Tourist Office, conveniently located under the arcade in the far left corner of Piazza San Marco, as you face the square from the basilica. Chances are you'll get lost—make the most of it and enjoy!

> **Hint:** *All streets lead to and from the Piazza San Marco. Look overhead for directional signs back to the piazza.*

Transportation to Venice

By Train - The Stazione Santa Lucia links Venice by train with Italy and the rest of Europe. Boats wait in front of the station to take you across to the island of Venice. Line #2 is an express connecting the train station to the Rialto Bridge, the Lido, and San Marco. Line 1 is the Grand Canal local.

By Car - Venice is linked to the rest of Italy by *autostrada*. From the Cortina d'Ampezzo area, take 51 south toward Belluno, following signs to *autostrada* A27 into Mestre and Venice. After driving over a causeway, you'll arrive at a busy and confusing area, the **Piazza Roma,** a dead end for car traffic. On the right are a pair of large parking garages for visitors' use. There can be long lines trying to get into these garages after 9:00 A.M., but a tip to the garage attendant may help convince him to let you pass into the garage where parking is usually very tight. There are attendants inside the garage who will help you find a spot. Parking costs depend upon the size of the car and can be $15 to $30 a day.

> **Hint:** *Put all belongings inside your locked car trunk for safekeeping and write down the location of the parking space and the floor.*

Walk from the garage across Piazza Roma to the Grand Canal piers (follow the crowds) and take the large, inexpensive, public water bus, *vaporetto*, for an exciting canal ride. Get off at the San Marco stop.

> **Hint:** *Take Vaporetto #1 (the Grand Canal local) and try to sit in an outside seat for your first views of incredible Venice. It's possible to take more expensive, alternative water transportation, but although the vaporetto takes a little longer, it serves as a fine introduction to the sights and sounds of Venice.*

Transportation in Venice

By Boat

Vaporetti circle the city and run the length of the Grand Canal, with twenty different lines or routes. Line 5 circles Venice and stops at the islands of Murano and Guidecca. Line 2 is an express connecting the train station to the Rialto Bridge, the Lido, and San Marco. Line 1 is the Grand Canal local. Timetables and ticket booths are at each stop. The cost is inexpensive, and you can buy discount passes, such as the **24-Hour Tourist Ticket (*Biglietto Turistico*).** This pass allows one-day travel on any route of the city's *vaporetti* and can be bought at most *tabacchi* and at some boat landings. *Vaporetti* schedules are listed in *Un Ospite di Venizia*, a free monthly guide you can pick up at the tourist office.

Motoscafi are sleek motorboats or water taxis and are expensive. *Always* agree on a set fare before beginning the trip—and remember that the minimum price doesn't take you very far.

Traghetti are a well-kept Venetian secret, used by many locals. They are two-person gondolas that ferry people across the Grand Canal at different points between its three bridges—the cheapest and shortest gondola ride. Look for their signs along the Grand Canal.

Gondola rides are a romantic, if expensive, way to see Venice's canals. Official prices are set, but tell the gondolier where you want to go and for how long.

Easy Walkers' "Must See" Venice

1. The Grand Canal Tour - *Vaporetto* Line 1 at the San Marco landing can take *Easy Walkers* on a leisurely cruise of Venice's main waterway, looping 2 miles through the city—red-and-white striped gondola boat moorings along the way. A seat in the prow will give a clear view of the sights: three bridges and almost 200 palaces built from the fourteenth to the eighteenth centuries. Leaving San Marco, at your left is the large, white, domed seventeenth-century Baroque church of **Santa Maria della Salute,** next to the **Palazzo Venier dei Leoni,** housing the **Peggy Guggenheim Collection of Twentieth Century Painting and Sculpture.** The **Gritti Palace Hotel** is across the canal on the right bank along with the Renaissance palace **Ca' Grande.** Just before the **Accademia Bridge** is **Palazzo Barbaro,** where author Henry James lived and wrote. This wooden bridge dates back only to 1934 and leads to the fabulous **Accademia Gallery.**

On the left bank, a few minutes past the bridge, note the Baroque mansion **Ca' Rezzonico,** poet Robert Browning's last residence. Further along on the left is the **Museum of Eighteenth Century Venice (Museo del Settencento Veneziano),** with fine Venetian paintings by Guardi, Longhi, Tiepolo, and others. On the left bank, the boat passes two identical fifteenth-century Gothic palaces, one the home of Richard Wagner where he wrote *Tristan und Isolde.*

Rounding a bend in the canal, note **Palazzi Mocenigo** on the right bank, four buildings with lion's heads (where Byron lived while writing *Don Juan*), then look for the Renaissance palaces **Palazzo Corner-Spinelli** and **Palazzo Grimani,** also on the right bank. Approaching the **Rialto Bridge,** the canal narrows, and just beyond it on the right is the Gothic **Ca' d'Oro,** housing the **Franchetti Gallery,** with its collection of tapestries, sculptures, and paintings.

A little farther down on the left bank are two museums, the **Galleria d'Arte Moderna** and **Museo Orientale,** housed in the Baroque palace of **Ca' Pesaro.** Also on the left is the white church **San Stae,** and if you exit the boat here, you'll walk through local neighborhoods filled with the trappings of day-to-day Venetian life. Be aware that street names change and numbers often don't follow in any order. Back on the boat, on the right bank is the Renaissance **Palazzo Vendramin-Calergi,** where Wagner died in 1883, now housing the **casino** in winter.

2. **Piazza di San Marco Area -** Exit the *vaporetto* at **San Marco** and walk straight ahead through the **Piazzetta** (the entrance to St. Mark's Square). Two columns face the waterfront here—one topped by a winged lion and the other with St. Theodore and his dragon.

The **Doge's Palace (Palazzo Ducale)** rises in pink-and-white marble splendor above the Piazzetta. The palace was not only the Doge's residence, but it also served as parliament, law courts, and the prison. Enter the palace through the ornate, fifteenth-century **Gate of the Paper (Porta della Carta)** into a large courtyard. Ahead you can see the **Stairway of the Giants (Scala dei Giganti),** flanked by immense statues of Neptune and Mars. To reach the rooms open to the public, walk along the arcade to a

Venice

central staircase leading to the **Anticollegio,** with paintings by Tintoretto and Veronese. The world's largest oil painting, *Paradise* by Tintoretto, hangs in the **Great Council Hall.** Guided tours, in Italian only however, are available to the palace's secret rooms. The **Bridge of Sighs (Ponte dei Sospiri)** is located outside the east wing of the palace. Leading to the prison, the bridge was given its name because of the sighs of prisoners being taken to jail.

Continue into **St. Mark's Square,** passing the **St. Mark's Bell Tower (Campanile di San Marco)** on your left. The bell in the tower, the Marangona, peals at sunrise, noon, and sunset. There is usually a long line of visitors waiting at the elevator that rises to the top of the tower, with its panoramic views of Venice. You might wish to spend your limited time elsewhere unless you can get in quickly.

Directly in front of you on a building facade is the animated clock **Torre dell'Orologia,** built in 1496, with Moorish figures that strike on the hour. The clock tells the time while matching the signs of the zodiac to the position of the sun.

To the right of the clock tower is **Saint Mark's Basilica (Basilica di San Marco).** The church was built from 1063 to 1073 and remodeled in a variety of styles. It is the piazza's treasure, considered one of Europe's most beautiful churches, and is laid out in a Greek cross topped by five domes—a mix of Byzantine and Romanesque styles. Visit the **atrium,** with its six mosaic cupolas depicting scenes from the Old Testament; the **basilica,** with a stunning composition of marble, alabaster, and mosaics; the **Baptistry,** with its preeminent baptismal font; the **Treasury;** and the **Presbytery,** with the Byzantine **Pala d'Oro** of gold and gemstones from Constantinople, considered the most valuable treasure of the church.

The atrium stairs outside the basilica lead to the **Marciano Museum (Museo Marciano)** with *Quadriga,* four horses yoked together, cast in the fourth century, and brought to Venice from Constantinople by crusaders in the early thirteenth century.

The **Museo Correr** at the far end of the piazza houses a priceless collection of paintings, sculpture, ancient documents, clothing, and currency.

Walk outside in **St. Mark's Square** for fabulous views of the basilica and the palace. Thousands of people compete for space with the pigeons, while colorful cafés provide live orchestras, *cappuccino*, and a comfortable (although expensive) place to view the passing parade. The streets around the square are lined with typical tourist stores, *trattorias* and fine restaurants, and elegant boutiques.

3. **Accademia Gallery (Galleria dell'Accademia) -** Leave the far end of St. Mark's Square near the Tourist Office and walk toward Campo San Stefano. Turn left to cross the canal on the Accademia Bridge to reach the Accademia Gallery. This art museum houses an impressive collection of Venetian paintings including works by Canaletto, Bellini, Tintoretto, Mantegna, Carpaccio, Giorgione, and Titian.

4. The **Peggy Guggenheim Collection,** housed at the eighteenth-century **Palazzo Venier dei Leoni,** is a museum of twentieth-century painting and sculpture. The gallery can be reached by following signs over the Accademia Bridge, one of only three bridges over the Grand Canal, or by taking a *traghetto* to cross the canal.

5. **Rialto Bridge (Ponte di Rialto),** built in the late sixteenth century, this bridge was constructed with arches high over the canal to allow ancient,

high-masted galleys to pass under it. The bridge is lined with windows of the stores inside. Vegetable, fish, and fruit markets are on one bank of the bridge, and chic boutiques are on the other. Leave St. Mark's Square adjacent to the animated clock, bearing diagonally to your right, following the overhead signs through the maze of streets to the Rialto Bridge.

6. **The Ghetto - Ghetto** is derived from the Venetian *getto*, meaning casting in metals. There was an iron foundry in the area to which all Jews were ordered in 1516. The Ghetto is an island, surrounded by a canal. You can visit the **Scuola Grande Tedesca,** the oldest of Venice's five synagogues, in the same building as the **Museo Comunità Israelitica/Ebraica.** The Ghetto is in the untouristy Cannargio area—check with the Tourist Office for directions.

FRANCE

The French Alps stretch from Lake Geneva to the Mediterranean Sea. Here are hundreds of miles of mountain scenery embracing three national parks—Mercantour, Ecrins, and Vanoise—and two regional parks—Vercors and Queyras—all created to protect the splendid natural habitat of this tranquil region. And the walking trails in the French Alps match the natural beauty and quality of those in its neighboring alpine countries. The trail system is supported by helpful local tourist offices and villagers anxious to share the wonders of their paths with day-walkers from around the world. *Walking Easy in the Italian and French Alps,* like its companion book covering Switzerland and Austria, is a how-to book devoted to each area's most scenic walks—that can be completed in one day by recreational walkers.

Any seasoned traveler can cite compelling reasons to visit France for a romantic summer holiday. These inducements might include Paris's sensual, late-night entertainment and dining at famous French restaurants, breathtaking vistas from the Eiffel Tower, tours of the extraordinary medieval ramparts of Carcassonne, a slow stroll through the flower fields of Provençe, or a ride as the fearless captain of a rented barge on one of France's scenic canals. Americans visit France for many reasons, but usually bypass what we consider to be one of the most romantic sojourns of them all: the French Alps. Take a moment and imagine the cool, crisp, clean alpine air, filled with the enticing fragrance of wildflowers; lush green meadows framed by graceful, snow-capped peaks; the tantalizing aroma of country cooking wafting from the weathered brick chimneys of mountainside restaurants and *refuges.*

It's recommended that *Easy Walkers* try to spend at least five days in each location—Chamonix, Megève, and Morzine in the Haute-Savoie; Méribel and Les Arcs/Bourg-Saint-Maurice in the Savoie; and Embrun in the Hautes-Alpes, establishing a base village from which the walks can be reached. We use Paris as the gate of entry and departure in spite of the proximity of the French Alps to Geneva because we feel that a trip to France is not complete without a visit to Paris, one of the major cultural capitals of Europe. To that end, this guide also includes a section detailing a short walking tour of Paris, written specially for *Easy Walkers.*

FRANCE

SWITZERLAND

Morzine ❖

Chamonix ❖
Megève ❖

Les Arcs/Bourg-Saint-Maurice ❖

Méribel ❖

ITALY

Embrun ❖

You can do it—just tuck a copy of *Walking Easy in the Italian and French Alps* in your backpack, and you're on your way!

Timing Is Everything

The French Alps are located south of Lake Geneva (Lac Léman)—from the Haute-Savoie south to the Savoie and the Hautes-Alpes, and south again to the Alpes de Haute Provence and the Alpes Maritimes, bordering on the Mediterranean regions. However, the famous winter ski towns of France—and their summer walking trails—are concentrated in the northern alpine regions, the high mountains of the Haute-Savoie, the Savoie, and the Hautes-Alpes.

The hiking season in the French Alps is a short one, usually beginning the first of July and lasting through the first week in September. If you have a choice of selecting the timing of your walking vacation, there are fewer tourists and cooler temperatures in the beginning of July and in early September. These are ideal months for walking, with cloudless blue skies the norm. Mid-July and August are warmer and much busier. Although cities are crowded with European summer vacationers, remember that the serenity of shaded forests and high alpine trails is hardly ever shattered by too many walkers.

> **Hint:** *Lifts are an integral part of* Walking Easy *itineraries, and they usually operate in the French Alps in July, August, and the first week of September. When planning your walking holiday, make sure you confirm lift operating schedules with the local tourist office.*

Arriving in France by Airplane

If you are flying to France for a walking vacation, many airlines offer non-stop flights to Paris, with a change of plane to other cities closer to the Alps, such as Geneva, Nice, or Lyon. If you haven't visited Paris, this might be a good time to extend your alpine walking vacation, as Air France offers direct flights to Paris. Geneva, Switzerland, is the closest large international airport to the French Alps. Milan, Italy, is a possible alternative, especially if your first stop is Chamonix, easily accessible from Italy by car via the Mont Blanc Tunnel. From your point of arrival, options are available to villages in the Alps by rental car, train, or bus. However, the fastest and most convenient means of transportation *between* the French alpine base villages is by automobile.

France by Train

The French National Railways (*Société Nationale des Chemins de Fer* or SNCF) is owned and operated by the French government. Included in this system are the TGV or high-speed *Train á Grande Vitesse*, EC (Eurocity), IC (Intercity), *rapides* or expresses, and car-carrying trains or TAC (*Trains Autos-Couchettes*). Only a few local railways are not part of this system. Reservations are required for certain trains; selected Eurocity, Intercity, and all TGV. In the United States, reservations can be made through Rail Europe, (800) 438–7245. In France, you can make your reservations at train stations and SNCF offices. Visit Rail Europe on line at www.raileurope.com or check schedule and fare information at www.sncf.fr.

Hint: *Train cars are marked with a large "1" or "2" to denote class. For daytime travel, save by booking second class; it's almost as comfortable and clean as first class.*

Discount Train Travel in France

France Railpass: The France Railpass includes the following:
1. Any three days unlimited train travel in a one month period
2. Choice of first- or second-class train travel
3. Special travel bonuses, including discount fares for Eurostar and Artesia trains, 50 percent discount on the private rail line from Nice to Digne, 30 percent discount on the SNCM ferry to Corsica, 50 percent discount on the Corsica Railways, additional discounts on many tourist attractions
4. The option of purchasing up to six extra days of train travel

France Saver Pass: Two or more people traveling together can receive a special rate.

France Rail 'n Drive Pass: This pass includes the following:
1. Any three days unlimited train travel in first or second class with one

month to complete the travel.

2. Two days Avis car rental with unlimited mileage and local tax included.

3. Choice of four car categories: three manual and one automatic transmission.

4. Free drop-off at any of the 520 Avis rental locations in France.

5. Options to purchase up to six extra days of train travel, extra days of car rental, and third and fourth person sharing the car need only buy France Railpass.

Senior Discount Pass: Senior discounts for train travel are available for men and women sixty years and older. You can buy an **A La Carte Senior Pass** at any French train station with proof of age and a photo. It costs about $40 in euros and allows seniors unlimited train travel for one year at a 50 percent discount, international train travel at a 30 percent discount. However, this pass *cannot* be used from noon on Friday to noon on Saturday and between 3:00 P.M. Sunday and noon Monday. It also provides reduced prices on some regional bus lines.

Hint: Buy all passes (except the senior discount pass) from your travel agent or Rail Europe (800–4–EURAIL) before leaving the United States.

France by Car

If you are going to be in France for a walking vacation in the Alps, it might be more convenient to have an automobile at your disposal for travel between base villages and for sightseeing. A car also gives *Easy Walkers* the opportunity of driving to the Alps from Paris or the Riviera on good roads through the lovely French countryside. United States citizens need a U.S. driver's license to rent a car in France. If you are going to leave France for another country in your rental car, inform the car rental agency staff in advance so proof of liability insurance can be checked. If you buy and use a car in France, you must have an International Insurance Certificate—called a "green card."

Hint: In addition to helping you rent and drive in Europe, an International Driver's Permit is also useful for additional, easily understood identification. It can be obtained in the United States through AAA for a nominal fee. It requires two passport-size photos.

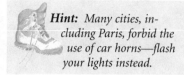

Hint: *Many cities, including Paris, forbid the use of car horns—flash your lights instead.*

Gasoline, called *essence*, is expensive and most cars require *essence super*. Unleaded gas is *sans plomb*, leaded is *avec plomb*.

In France, driving is on the right side of the road, the same as in the United States. Remember that a car coming from the right always has the right of way. Distances are measured in kilometers (1 kilometer = .62 miles). Speed is measured in kilometers per hour (km/h): 130 km/h (81 mph) is the speed limit on toll highways and expressways, 100 km/h (62 mph) on major highways, 90 km/h (56 mph) on country roads, and 60 km/h (37 mph) through towns and villages. Large fines can be imposed for exceeding the speed limits. French law requires seat belts to be worn in both the front and back seats.

Major highways (designated "A" on driving maps) are *autoroutes à péage* or toll roads. *Routes nationales* (N) are free roads, and *routes départementales* (D) are secondary roads. Michelin driving map #989 of France

Hint: *The French government has authorized confiscation of your driver's license if you are found driving more than 25 mph (40 km/h) above the speed limit. This applies to foreigners as well as the French, although the confiscated foreign license will be returned when you leave France.*

is a good choice for the entire country, but regional maps are also published for different areas, and you may want to purchase one for the alpine regions.

If you are going to be in Europe for more than three weeks, it might be more economical to use a "Purchase and Buy Back" program. This involves the actual purchase of a new automobile, with a guaranteed buy-back at

Hint: *Une panne means "car breakdown," but if you dial 17, the police will give you the telephone number of a nearby garage with towing facilities. On an expressway, use the emergency phone box for a direct connection to a facility that can help you.*

the end of a specified period of time. You'll pay a set charge, and this includes insurance in order to get the green card needed to drive in most European countries.

The *Routes des Grandes Alpes* in France is one of Europe's great drives. This north-south route makes use of mountain roads and steep, narrow passes (*cols*) between 5778 and 9187 ft. (1500 and 2800 m.). The highest passes are only open from mid-June through mid-October.

A journey from Menton on the Mediterranean Sea above Nice to Thonon on Lake Geneva (or the reverse) is a trip into the history of the French Alps on a legendary itinerary—through three national parks and two regional nature parks—the road winding past ancient fortifications, through tiny valley villages, over the high passes at Turini, la Cayolle, de Vars, d'Izoard, du Galibier, des Aravasis, de la Columbière, and the 9088-foot (2770-meter) Col de l'Iseran, made famous by cyclists on the Tour de France. The base villages of Chamonix, Megève, and Morzine lie along its 460-mile (742-km) route, as do the sightseeing villages of Val d'Isère and St-Veran. You'll visit the Alpes Maritimes, Alpe de Haute Provence, the Haute-Savoie, and the Rhône-Alpes and discover their architecture, works of art, flora, and geology. It might be fun to fly into Nice instead of Paris or Geneva and spend a few days driving north on the exhilarating and exciting *Route des Grandes Alpes*.

Hint: If you're planning a trip to Europe for seventeen days or longer and prefer to travel by car, there is an interesting cost-saving "Vacation Plan" offered by Auto France. A new Peugeot is delivered to your airport or city of choice, and insurance is included. There is no VAT (value added tax) and no maximum age restrictions. Check the Auto France Web site at: www.auto-france.com, and for further details call Auto France at (800) 572–9655.

Hint: Use IGN map: *Routes des Grandes Alpes.*

France by Bus

Regional bus companies are sometimes the only means, other than by car, of getting to out-of-the-way places, especially in the mountainous regions of the French Alps, because the gradients become too steep for train travel. Bus information is available from the local tourist offices.

France Up and Down

The following are important adjuncts to transportation in the French Alps:

Cable cars (*téléphériques*) - These are large, enclosed cars holding up to 180 people, running on a fixed schedule. Example: the giant cable car from la Saulire peak above Méribel down to Courchevel.

Gondolas (télécabines) - Gondolas usually hold four to eight people, are enclosed, and run continuously. Example: the Transarc gondola from Arc 1800 above Bourg-Saint-Maurice.

Chairlifts (télésièges) - Sit-down lifts that move continuously and are usually open to the weather. They can be single-, double-, or triple-chair systems. Example: the chairlift rising to the peak at Réallon, near Embrun.

Funiculars (funiculaires) - Mountain railways pulled up and down a steep incline by a cable. Example: the train linking Bourg-Saint-Maurice to Arc 1600.

Cogwheel railways or **rack-and-pinion railways** - These trains move by a toothed wheel connecting into the matching teeth of the rail. Example: the *Mer de Glace* mountain railway in Chamonix, winding its way up to one of Europe's largest glaciers.

Comfortable Inns and Hotels

Winter is more expensive than summer in alpine ski resorts. Hotel and apartment accommodations handle winter sports enthusiasts, and because they are not always filled in spring, summer, and autumn, rates can be lower— although advance reservations are always advisable. Accommodations in France range from world-class, deluxe, five-star hotels to comfortable rooms in rural farmhouses. The quality of a hotel (and its prices) can be judged by the number of stars it is awarded. In France, **** L is equivalent to five-star deluxe in other European countries; **** is equivalent to first class; *** indicates a superior, good quality tourist hotel; ** is a standard budget hotel; and * is a hotel meeting minimum standards. Many bedrooms in one- or two-star hotels do not have private bathrooms, but contain hot and cold water and a bidet, while others may have only a sink.

We usually recommend three-star hotels with *demi-pension* (half-board: breakfast and dinner) for comfort, quality of food, and overall value. If you prefer to dine at different restaurants each evening—more expensive but not necessarily better than dinner at your hotel on the half-board plan, try a hotel *garni*, a hotel that serves breakfast only, and which is rated on the same star system as full-service hotels.

Furnished chalets and rental apartments are a viable alternative to hotels, but they are usually rented for a one-week period. The tourist office in each French village can provide lists of places to rent. Write to the Tourist Office (*Office du Tourisme*) and then contact the home or apartment owner directly.

Hint: *When making hotel reservations, specify a room for two with twin beds, private bathroom facilities* (en suite), *and demi-pension (including dinner).*

Fédération Nationale des Logis et Auberges de France, or *Logis de France,* is an association of over 4,000 primarily one- and two-star, family-run, country inns and hotels, combining economy with comfort and cleanliness, located throughout France. In the Logis de France guide, hotels are graded by one, two, or three fireplaces, based on 150 different criteria, ranging from the quality of food and service to the standard of the room

Hint: *Many smaller hotels in rural or mountain areas do not accept credit cards. Check with your hotel, and if this is the case, make sure you have access to money or bring traveler's checks, as they do not accept personal checks drawn on United States banks.*

and general facilities. If you are interested in a bed-and-breakfast (*gîtes-chambres d'hôte*) in France, over 6,000 accommodations are listed with La Maison des Gites de France et du Tourisme Vert, 59 rue St-Lazare, 75009 Paris, France.

Many small hotels do not require a deposit. If you write, E-mail, or fax them, they will confirm the cost of your room and food arrangements, dates of arrival and departure. Remember, a complete listing and information about hotels in each town and village can be obtained by writing directly to the tourist information office in every city, town, and village.

Hint: *Prices listed for hotels include taxes, tips, and breakfast, unless otherwise noted.*

Regional Food Specialties

Cheese: The cheeses of alpine Savoie are varied in shape, color, and taste. Semihard Reblochon, produced more than any other area cheese, is made from the whole, unpasteurized milk of local cows, maturing in a cold cellar in only three to four weeks. Beaufort is called "the prince of Gruyère," a creamy cheese made in the traditional manner. Emmental, with its holes, smooth, shiny surface, and fruity taste, is made in the foothills of the Savoie and Haute-Savoie and needs about ten weeks to reach maturity. Tomme de Savoie is the oldest of the Savoie and Haute-Savoie cheeses. Tomme des Bauges is made with unpasteurized milk, only in the Massif des Bauges region in the heart of the Savoie Alps—it has a fruity taste with a coarse rind after maturing for forty days in humid cellars. Made in the mountains of the Haute-Savoie, the Chevrotin des Aravis is a farmhouse cheese produced from goat's milk. Made since the fourteenth century, Abondance comes from the milk of local cows in mountain chalets in summer and in dairies in winter. Tamié is made with whole, unpasteurized cow's milk, produced exclusively in the mountains by Trappist monks from the Abbey of Tamié near Albertville—look for its unique packaging, a white Maltese cross on a blue background.

Wine: Taste the wines of the Savoie Alps; the ancient vineyards from Lake Geneva south to below Chambéry overlook rivers and lakes on alpine slopes and flourish in the pure mountain air. The white wines are fruity and dry, best served cool with local fish, fondue, or raclette (a Swiss specialty featuring heated, shaved cheese). The red and rosé wines of the Savoie, light and fragrant, complement regional dishes and local cheeses. Try the Montmélian, similar to beaujolais. The sparkling wines, such as Seyssel, have an excellent reputation.

Hint: Drinking unlabeled house wine in bottles or carafes—vin de la maison—is less expensive.

Liqueur: After-dinner liqueurs such as Marc or Armagnac, called *digestifs*, are supposed to aid in the digestive processes. Brandy distilled from fruits or herbs such as Eau-de-Vie, or "Water of Life," has a very high alcohol content and is also drunk at the end of the meal. Marc and Brulôt Savoyard are traditional brandies.

Mineral Water: Bottled mineral water, with (*avec gas*) or without gas (*sans gas*), is available everywhere.

Where to Eat and Drink

Hotels: Three-star French alpine hotels usually offer a continental breakfast consisting of orange juice, hot beverage, a basket of rolls/bread and croissants, butter, and preserves. If you reserve a room with *demi-pension* (half-board), dinner can be a soup and/or appetizer, a main course of meat/fish/chicken with potatoes and vegetables, cheese and/or dessert. (Fresh fruit can usually be substituted for the dessert.) Coffee, tea, or hot chocolate are included with breakfast but always cost extra at dinner. Hotel food in France is uniformly excellent, and *Easy Walkers* can take advantage of lower costs by booking with *demi-pension.*

> *Hint:* An apéritif *before dinner supposedly awakens the appetite. It is also less expensive than scotch, vodka, or other such liquors.*

Restaurants: If you decide to eat in a restaurant outside your hotel, notify the hotel desk twenty-four hours in advance so the day's demi-pension charge can be deducted from your bill. In a restaurant, *plat du jour* means the daily special, while offering no choice of specific dishes that compose it. Less expensive restaurants may include a beverage in the menu price, called *boisson compris.* A 15 percent service charge (tip) is *always* included in your bill, but a few coins should be left on the table if you are pleased with the service.

> *Hint: Most diners prefer to take their after-dinner coffee later in the evening at an outdoor cafe or hotel sitting room.*

Picnicking: When planning a day of walking, we recommend taking a picnic lunch in your backpack. Fresh bread or rolls can be bought at the local *boulangerie* (bakery). Select a local cheese and/or sliced cooked meat in the *charcuterie* (delicatessen) or *boucherie* (butcher shop). Fresh fruit completes a healthy and inexpensive meal. Mustard can be bought in reusable squeeze tubes. Mineral water, juice, and soda are available in plastic bottles or cans at the *épicerie* (grocery store).

Few Americans have discovered the treasures of the French Alps so—brush up on your high school French, prepare your taste buds for the thrill of French country cuisine, and *marche facile en l'Alpes Française.*

> *Hint: It's polite to refer to your waiter as* monsieur, *NOT* garçon.

CHAMONIX

Chamonix's population of 10,000 residents includes the neighboring hamlets of Argentière, Montroc, le Tour, le Lavancher, les Praz, les Tines, les Moussoux, les Pélèrins, and les Bossons. This superb alpine area supports almost every summer sports activity imaginable: hiking, golf, summer bobsledding and skiing, fishing, swimming, paragliding, rafting, cycling, rock climbing, and tennis. The Chamonix Valley is lined with lifts, originally built to service winter skiers. Today, these lifts also bring thousands of summer hikers to trails traversing the north and south *balcons* (balconies) on the heights along the Arve River, which runs swiftly through the valley. There are 217 miles (350 km) of marked paths in the Chamonix area, many to be utilized by *Easy Walkers*. Several hikes are combined with excursions to high, panoramic lookouts, while others use mountain railroads or begin with breathtaking cable car rides over glaciers and high, craggy, rock formations. Many of the itineraries lead to remote *refuges* (mountain restaurants) for refreshment and relaxation before the return to Chamonix.

Site of the first winter Olympics in 1924 and surrounded by many of Europe's highest peaks, the Haute-Savoie's Chamonix, at 3402 ft. (1037 m.), is nestled under the 15,772-foot (4807-meter) Mont Blanc, the highest mountain in western Europe—intertwined with dozens of dramatic glaciers—in *Pays du Mont Blanc*, or Mont Blanc Country. The Tunnel du Mont Blanc wends its way beneath the Mont Blanc massif across the border to Italy and serves as an express route to the Aosta Valley, Milan, and other popular Italian destinations. Chamonix is easily accessible by car and train, less than two hours driving time from Geneva, with day-trips easily arranged to Lausanne and Montreux in Switzerland, Gran Paradiso National Park and Aosta in Italy, and beautiful Lake Annecy.

A "must do" *Walking Easy* hike is to the Swiss border, using gondola and chairlift from le Tour to Col de Balme, encompassing magnificent views of the Chamonix Valley and Mont Blanc from the east. Large cable cars carrying sightseers, climbers, and hikers operate during the summer to the Aiguille du Midi, at 12,599 ft. (3840 m.), Chamonix's most popular destination, with the option of a breathtaking gondola ride to Helbronner, and even further on to Italy on the opposite side of the Mont Blanc massif. Other excursions and walks utilize the Tramway du Mont Blanc, a little yellow-and-blue mountain train climbing at a 25-degree angle, rising all the way to the glacier at Nid d'Aigle, at 7875 ft. (2400 m.). Another hike includes a trip to the Mer de Glace and a return on the Tram du Montenvers, a mountain rack railway that winds its way down from 6280 ft. (1914 m.).

The Chamonix Valley has something for everyone: walking, sightseeing excursions, shopping, country cooking, and the hospitality of the French Haute-Savoie. Chamonix is the "granddaddy" of walking in the French Alps and is a *must* base village on any *Walking Easy* itinerary.

Bureau des Guides, Chamonix

Transportation

By Plane - The closest international airport to Chamonix is 51 miles (85 km) west at Geneva, with regular train and bus connections into Chamonix and car rental agencies at the airport. Flying into Paris is another option, with fast trains leaving regularly for Geneva.

By Train - TGV (high-speed trains) are regularly scheduled to and from Paris, and most require a change of train in St-Gervais, 12 miles (20 km) from Chamonix, with local trains into Chamonix. When traveling to Chamonix from Switzerland, there is always a change of train in Martigny, Switzerland.

By Car - From Geneva airport to Chamonix: Take superhighway A40 southeast, following CHAMONIX signs, about a ninety-minute drive.

From Charles de Gaulle Airport to Chamonix: From the car rental area in the airport, follow the *sentier* (exit) signs toward Paris. Once out of the airport, immediately follow signs toward MARNE LA VALLEÉ, then LYON on A104 all the way to A6, still in the direction of Lyon. Although it's possible to drive the 381 miles (614 km) to Chamonix in a full day, we don't recommend driving for more than three hours after a tiring international flight. Once on A6, consider stopping in Auxerre, with its incredible Romanesque church; the medieval town of Vézelay, or the old, fortified town of Avallon. After a good night's rest in any of these villages, continue driving on A6 south toward Lyon, leaving the highway at Macon and picking up A40 in the direction of Bourg-En-Bresse. Continue on A40, a major highway, toward Geneva. However, before Geneva, remain on A40 and follow the CHAMONIX/MONT BLANC signs.

By Bus - From the Geneva airport, two to six buses a day run to Chamonix, depending on the season, and daily bus service is available from Annecy, Grenoble, and the main resorts in the Mont Blanc area.

Local Public Bus Transportation in Chamonix - The convenient yellow-and-blue municipal bus line (navettes) operates regular shuttle service throughout the Chamonix Valley. Pick up a bus schedule and bus stop map at the Tourist Office.

Favorite *Walking Easy* Hotel

Hotel La Sapinière

Three-Star; Owners - Familie Cachat

102 rue Mummery, B.P. 85, 74402 Chamonix-Mont Blanc

Tel: 4 50 53 07 63, **Fax:** 4 50 53 10 14

E-mail: hotelsapiniere@chamonix.com

Internet: www.lasapiniere.com

This well-run hotel is in a quiet location, a five-minute walk from the center of Chamonix. An inviting terrace and shaded gardens surround the hotel; inside is a bar and lounge for after-dinner drinks and conversation. Most hotel rooms face south for views of the glacier, and the Cachat family had the foresight to donate the meadow in front of the hotel to the town as a greenbelt, thus ensuring that nothing can be built to destroy the view! Jeannie and Patrick Cachat take great pride in their establishment, originally built in the 1920s. The Cachats were one of Chamonix's founding families, arriving as farmers in 1650, with Patrick Cachat a third-generation hotelier.

The kitchen is excellent, and a full buffet breakfast is served. Dinners include soup, choice of appetizer, main course, and an array of delectable desserts. The accommodating staff will cater to special needs if notified in advance.

La Sapinière is a favorite hotel because of the quality of the food and service, the location, the view, and the friendly and helpful atmosphere created by American-born Jeannie and Chamonix-born Patrick.

Lifts in and around Chamonix

Mer de Glace (Sea of Ice) - Take a mountain cog railway from Chamonix's Gare du Montenvers to France's largest glacier, 4 miles (7 km) long. Visit the glacier by taking the small cable car down. Pay a visit to La Grotte de Glace (Ice Grotto), at a depth of 200 ft. (80 m.) into the glacier. Four months of work each spring create new scuptures in an eerie, subglacial atmosphere. At Montenvers, you can also see the Crystal Gallery and the Museum of Alpine Wildlife. (See Walk #1.)

Directions: Take the Montenvers cog railway, located to the left when facing the Chamonix railroad station (Gare SNCF). It runs every half hour.

Aiguille du Midi - This is an exciting, two-stage cable car: The first stage rises to 7602 ft. (2317 m.), with the second stage a nearly vertical ascent to the summit of the Aiguille, at 12,600 ft. (3840 m.). (See Walk #4.)

Directions: Walk west through town on the main street, rue Joseph Vallot, past the main post office, following the sign to Aiguille du Midi.

Le Tour - A ride to the top station at Col de Balme, at 7153 ft. (2180 m.), is interrupted only by a quick change at the mid-station from a gondola to an open chairlift. (See Walk #7.)

Directions: Take the Chamonix bus to the last stop at le Tour and buy a round-trip ticket to the top station.

Les Bossons/Les Planards - This chairlift rises to 4626 ft. (1410 m.) and takes you along the side of the magnificent Bossons Glacier, the largest ice cascade in Europe, a focal point of the scenery around Chamonix. (See Walk #6.)

Directions: At the main Chamonix bus stop, take the bus toward les Houches, asking to be let off at les Bossons chairlift.

La Flégère - Starting from 6158 ft. (1877 m.), this cable car rises to l'Index, at 8258 ft. (2525 m.), and descends to les Praz, at 3478 ft. (1060 m.). (See Walk #2.)

Directions: Take the Chamonix bus in the direction of le Tour and exit at la Flégère.

Le Brévent - This two-stage gondola and cable car ascends first to Planpraz, at 6562 ft. (2000 m.), then to le Brévent, at 8285 ft. (2525 m.). (See Walk #2.)

Directions: Walk into town, past the Tourist Office and the church, straight up the hill, following signs to le Brévent.

Tramway du Mont Blanc - (See Walk #6.)

Directions: At the central Chamonix bus station, take the bus to les

Houches. Exit at the last stop in les Houches and take the gondola up to le Prarion. Follow the directions in Walk #6. Check with the Tourist Office for other stops on the tram.

Excursions

The Chamonix/Mont Blanc Tourist Bureau (Office du Tourisme) is located on Place du Triangle de l'Amitié.

Fax: 4 50 53 58 90

E-mail: info@chamonix.com

Internet: www.chamonix.com

1. **Chamonix** - The **Alpine Museum** is located at la Résidence in the walking area of Chamonix and contains collections on the history of the area. The **casino** is situated in the town center, with roulette and black-jack. The **Merlet Alpine Animal Park** is located at Merlet toward les Houches. Visit alpine animals in natural, open surroundings. (See Walk #3.) The **Aguilles Rouges Nature Reserve** is located at Col des Mon-tets (Montets Pass) and contains many acres of flora and fauna, including a nature trail. Located at 67 Lacets du Belvédère, the **Mont Blanc Ob-servatory** is open weekday afternoons in July and August.

2. **Evian-les-Bains -** Situated on the shores of Lac Léman (Lake Geneva), Evian is 65 miles (104 km) north of Chamonix. World-famous "Evian" water was discovered here in the nineteenth century; the discovery turned a small, heavily fortified town into a Belle Epoque spa with mag-nificent hotels and sculptured gardens. From Evian, many boat trips are available, and while a cruise of the entire lake takes ten hours, it is only a thirty-five-minute boat ride to Lausanne/Ouchy on the Swiss side of the lake. Also, check out the "Garden of Waters," representing the different mineral waters from around the world.

   Directions: By car - Take N205 west out of Chamonix into Cluses. Turn right on D902 into Thonons-les-Bains. Drive east on N5 into Evian. For a return circle route, drive east out of Evian on N5, crossing the Swiss border at St-Gingolph (N5 becomes N21). Drive south toward Martigny, where you will pick up N115 in Switzerland and N506 in France—into Chamonix. By bus - Excursions to Lake Geneva, Evian, Thonon, le Chablais, and Morzine may be available with Chamonix Bus Excursions company, located next to the Tourist Office.

3. Les Gorges du Pont du Diable - La Vernaz, Le Jotty - Located 50 miles (80 km) northwest of Chamonix, the Devil's Bridge Gorges typify the power of erosion, with subterranean rock face, varied stone coloring, and an exceptional forest environment.

Directions: *Take N205 toward Geneva, staying off the main highway, and at Cluses, 25 miles (40 km) west of Chamonix, turn north on D902 and drive 27 miles (42 km) to the gorges.*

Overlooking Chamonix

4. Yvoire - A medieval village on the shores of Lake Geneva, Yvoire is a member of the Association of the Most Beautiful Villages of France and still boasts fourteenth-century fortifications and chateaux.

Directions: *Follow the directions as in Excursion #3, to the gorges, but continue further to Thonen. Turn west along the lake on N5 to Sciez, where you pick up D25 to Yvoire, a 75-mile (113-km) drive from Chamonix.*

5. Megève - Located about 22 miles (35 km) southwest of Chamonix, Megève is a cosmopolitan French ski resort and another *Walking Easy* base village, overflowing with trendy boutiques and outdoor cafes, with its downtown area bisected by an alpine stream. Plan to visit Megève on a Friday when mountain farmers sell local produce at an outdoor market next to the sports center. (See the Megève chapter.)

Directions: *Take N205 west, following signs to St-Gervais, from there following signs to Albertville and Megève on N212.*

6. Annecy - See Megève chapter, Excursion #4.

Directions: *Take N205 west out of Chamonix to St-Gervais, picking up D909 and then N212 through Megève. Take N508 toward Ugine and drive through Faverges. Continue around the left side of the lake to An-necy. You can return to Chamonix on a circle route. Pick up the A41 ex-pressway out of Annecy to superhighway A40 east. Follow signs to Chamonix/Mont Blanc.*

7. **Montreux, Switzerland -** Sometimes called "The Vaud Riviera," this popular resort on Lake Geneva is noted for its mild weather, producing a Mediterranean feeling in summer. Enjoy the path that runs for miles along the lake shore, planted with semitropical plants and flowers—a wonderful contrast to the snowy scenery and wintery pine forests around Chamonix.

The **Castle of Chillon,** made famous by the poet Byron, is only 1½ miles (2½ km) from Montreux. Check at the Montreux train station for a bus schedule to the castle if you prefer not to drive. From the Montreux railroad station, you can also take an excursion by mountain railroad to **Rochers de Naye,** at 7002 ft. (2134 m.), for a spectacular view of the lake, ringed by the French and Swiss Alps. From there, numerous pleasant walking paths wind through the countryside. Allow an hour each way for the train trip to Rochers de Naye.

Directions: By car - Follow N506 northeast from Chamonix over the Swiss border and through the Col de la Forclaz to Martigny. Take highway N9 north into Montreux by first following signs to Lausanne. By bus - A Chamonix Excursion Bus leaves about 1:00 P.M., goes to Mon-treux and Chillon, and returns to Chamonix in time for dinner.

8. **Lausanne, Switzerland -** Lausanne's **cathedral** is reputedly the most beautiful Gothic building in Switzerland—its picturesque towers and sculptured doors date from 1175 to 1275. Lausanne is home to the first museum in French-speaking Switzerland devoted solely to modern art. The **FAE Museum of Contemporary Art** is on the shore of Lake Geneva in Pully, about ten minutes from the city center. Ouchy, a bustling port on Lake Geneva, is now the lakefront for Lausanne, originally built up and away from the lake. Ouchy's shady piers provide delightful views over the port, the lake, and the mountains. Check out the **Olympic Mu-seum,** with an impressive view of the lake and surrounding Alps.

Directions: By car - Take N506 northeast out of Chamonix, over the Swiss border, and through the Col de la Forclaz to Martigny. Follow signs to Lausanne and pick up highway N9, past Montreux and Vevey, driving around Lake Geneva into Lausanne. By train - Take the train in Chamonix to Martigny and change for the train to Lausanne.

9. **Martigny, Switzerland -** Visit the Pierre Gianadda Foundation, with its exhibits of well-known artists, along with a Gaulish-Roman Museum, the Museum of the Automobile, and a sculpture park.

    Directions: By car - Take N506 through Argentière and over the border into Martigny. By train - Take the train east to Martigny.

10. **Evionnaz, Switzerland -** The largest maze in the world is comprised of more than 15,000 thuyas trees. We dare you to find your way out!

    Directions: Follow the directions in Excursion #9 to Martigny. Pick up local road 9-21, and drive 7 miles (11 km) north to Evionnaz.

11. **Courmayeur, Italy -** This well-known summer and winter resort at the foot of the Mont Blanc massif sits at an altitude of 4029 ft. (1228 m.). You can take the cable car from Courmayeur to Plan Chécrouit, rise to Altiporto, then to Cresta di Youla, where another cable car climbs to Cresta d'Arp, at 9065 ft. (2763 m.). Enjoy a splendid panorama of alpine peaks, including Mont Blanc to the north and the Matterhorn and Monte Rosa to the northeast. Allow at least two hours round-trip for lift travel time.

    About 2 miles (3 km) north of Courmayeur is **la Palud,** where you can ride the cable car up to Mont Blanc, crossing into France. The viewing platform at Helbronner is over 11,000 ft. (3353 m.) and is also the border with France. The next stage brings you over immense glacial snow fields and a viewing station above Chamonix. If you change cable cars, you can ride down to Chamonix! (See Walk #4.)

    Directions: By car - Drive through the Tunnel du Mont Blanc, continuing ahead on S26 into Courmayeur. By bus - A morning bus from Chamonix arrives in Courmayeur in forty minutes.

12. **Gran Paradiso National Park, Italy -** Created in 1922 and covering 1,390 square miles (60,000 hectares), this park originated as a hunting preserve of the Italian royal family and is now one of Europe's treasured wilderness areas. Its wildlife and flowers are protected by law so that many threatened species are thriving in the park. The park's alpine garden is at

Valmontey and contains over 2,000 species of flowers, as well as rocks, moors, marshland, lakes, and streams. The Gran Paradiso extends to the west; in France, it becomes the Parc National de la Vanoise.

Directions: By car - Drive through the Mont Blanc Tunnel, continuing ahead on S26 through Courmayeur and into the Aosta Valley toward Aosta. Turn south at Aymavilles, about four miles (6 km) west of Aosta, climbing into the Val di Cogne. The village of Cogne, at 5033 ft. (1534 m.), is 12 miles (20 km) up into the Valley, a good place to stop and enjoy the beauty and solitude of the park. By bus - The Chamonix Excursion Bus can take you to Parc National du Gran Paradis and Valley de Cogne et ses Dentellieres.

13. **Aosta, Italy -** This small city is the capital of the Aosta Valley, and its Roman ruins make it a popular tourist destination. The most important of these ancient relics are the **Pretoria Gateway,** three arches built of huge blocks of stone in 1 B.C.; the **Arch of Augustus** built in 25 B.C. when Rome defeated the Celtic Salassi tribe; and the **Roman bridge**. From the Pretoria Gateway you can reach the remains of the **Roman theater** and a recently discovered **Roman road**. The **Collegiate Church of St. Orso** boasts an eleventh-century crypt and a twelfth-century Roman bell tower. A rich treasure of sacred art and paintings is kept in the sacristy. Nearby is a small Romanesque **cloister,** dating back to the twelfth century. The **cathedral** is ornamented with sixteenth-century sculptures on its nineteenth-century facade; however, the rest of the church dates from the twelfth to the fifteenth centuries. Opposite the cathedral stands the ruins of a **Roman forum.**

Directions: By car - Take the Mont Blanc Tunnel, drive though Courmayeur on S26, continuing east into Aosta. By bus - The Chamonix Excursion Bus departs for Aosta at 1:00 P.M. and is back in Chamonix at 7:00 P.M.

14. **Geneva, Switzerland -** Geneva's Tourist Office is near the downtown railroad station on Place Cornavin and can provide *Easy Walkers* with information about the city, along with that indispensable city map. Geneva is divided by Lake Geneva and the Rhône River into two sections, the right bank and the left bank. The Old Town of Geneva is on the left bank—with Gothic, Renaissance, and eighteenth-century buildings, narrow alleyways, and cascading fountains. Geneva's top attractions are

the famous water fountain that has become the city's symbol, the **Jet d'Eau**; the **flower clock** in the Jardin Anglais; the **Old Town;** and its **museums**.

The **Musée d'Art et d'Histoire (Museum of Art and History),** at 2, rue Charles-Galland, displays prehistoric relics, Greek vases, medieval stained glass, Swiss watches and clocks, paintings, etc. (Take bus #3 or #33.) **Musée International de la Croix-Rouge et du Croissant-Rouge,** on 17, av. de la Paix, presents the history of the Red Cross. (Take bus 8 or F.) **Palais des Nations** in the Parc de l'Ariana is the second-largest complex of buildings in Europe after Versailles. It is United Nations headquarters in Europe and also contains a **Philatelic Museum** and the **League of Nations Museum.** (Take bus #8 or F.) The **Musée de l'Horlogerie (Watch Museum),** is at 15, route de Malagnou and displays everything relating to clocks and watches—from sundials to modern exhibitions. (Take bus #6.) Take tram #12 for a five-minute ride to the Carouge area and visit the **Carouge Museum,** with examples of the yellow Carouge creamware ceramics produced from 1803 to 1933.

You can begin your exploration of the old city on the **place du Bourg-de-Four,** on the site of an old Roman forum. In the **Old Town,** the dominating feature is the elegant **Cathédrale de Saint-Pierre,** built in the twelfth and thirteenth centuries and renovated over the years. Climb forty-five stairs to the top of the north tower for a great view of the city, the lake, and the distant Alps. Pay a visit also to the **Russian orthodox church,** with its glistening Byzantine domes.

Geneva has a wonderful public transportation system, beginning at place Cornavin in front of the main railroad station. No tickets are sold on buses or trams—you must buy them at the coin-operated vending machines at each stop. All tickets must be validated at the vending machine before entering the bus or tram.

Directions: By car - Take the A40-E205 expressway west of Chamonix, following signs to the city center. By bus - A morning bus from Chamonix arrives in Geneva in two hours. Or, you can take the 9:00 A.M. Chamonix Excursion Bus, arriving back in Chamonix in time for dinner.

15. Great Saint Bernard Pass and Hospice, Switzerland - The hospice stands at 8100 ft. (2469 m.), the highest point on the Great Saint Bernard Pass and Road, now bypassed by a tunnel. On the edge of a lake frozen 265 days a year, the hospice is the home of the grand, gentle dogs noted for carrying brandy to travelers stranded in the mountain snows. You should visit the **chapel,** with its pulpits and stalls dating from the seventeenth century, and the **museum's** pictures and memorabilia. The famous **Saint Bernard dogs** who accompanied the monks on their rescue missions are in kennels behind the hotel. Today, because helicopters have taken their place, the dogs sleep most of the day!

There is an enjoyable walking trail overlooking the small lake and ending at the customs station in Italy. As you leave the museum, pick up the path above the road on the right side. After a few minutes, you'll see a sign indicating Italy! Continue maneuvering on the narrow, rocky, descending trail, allowing entrance into Italy and bypassing the customs station. Within a few minutes you'll be at the souvenir stands on the Italian side of the border. To return to the hospice, walk back up the road through the customs stations.

Directions: By car - Take the Mont Blanc Tunnel and pick up S26 through Courmayeur, driving west to Aosta. Drive north on S27 but do not drive through the Saint Bernard Tunnel—take the old, winding road over the Col du Grand St. Bernard to the hospice, just across the Swiss border. For a circle route to return, continue north on 21 into Martigny and take N115, becoming N506 southwest across the border into Chamonix. By bus - The Chamonix Excursion Bus leaves Chamonix early in the morning for Col de la Forclaz, Bourg Saint-Pierre, Grand Saint Bernard, and Aosta and is back in Chamonix in time to make dinner.

16. Zermatt, Switzerland - A tourist and hiking mecca, Zermatt's surrounding mountains and glaciers encompass superb scenery, including the famous Matterhorn. An abundance of railroads and cable cars reaching the tops of Zermatt's high, snow-capped mountains makes this town a wonderful place for a long day-trip from Chamonix. You can pass the time in a trendy mix of souvenir shops and cosmopolitan boutiques, restaurants, and small cafes or choose any of the following exciting sightseeing options: **Gornergrat Cog Railway -** The entrance is across the street from the Zermatt Railroad Station. A 45-minute trip on the highest rack railway in Europe brings *Easy Walkers* to Gornergrat, at 10,272 ft. (3131 m.), with a fabulous view of the Matterhorn and the spectacular sight of the Monte Rosa and its glaciers at 15,203 ft. (4634 m.), the highest mountain in Switzerland. At the Gornergrat stop, with its Kulm

Hotel and restaurant, the large outdoor sun-terrace is filled with skiers, hikers, climbers, and sun-worshippers. From here, you can continue up to the **Stockhorn** peak, at 11,588 ft. (3532 m.), by way of a twenty-two-minute cable car ride, for an awe-inspiring, glacial panorama.

Klein Matterhorn Cable Car - Turn right on leaving the Zermatt railroad station, walk up the tourist-filled main street through town to the church, turn left, and you will arrive at the famous Zermatt cemetery. This well-tended cemetery serves as a testimonial to those climbers who lost their lives trying to scale the heights of the region's mountains. The tombstones spell out the history and courage of men of all ages and countries who tried to conquer the Matterhorn and failed. Passing the cemetery, cross the river, and turn right, where a short walk brings you to the lift station.

Easy Walkers will take connecting cable cars to reach the top of the Klein Matterhorn, at 12,684 ft. (3866 m.), the highest-altitude cable car station in Europe. The view of the Alps from France to Austria is breathtaking. Descending, the foot of the famed Matterhorn is your destination—its peak reflected in the still waters of Schwarzsee, a tiny mountain lake at an elevation of 8500 ft. (2591 m.).

Sunnegga Underground Railway - After arriving in Zermatt, walk straight ahead and follow signs to the Sunnegga Express Station. Sunnegga sits on a high, alpine plateau at 7500 ft. (2286 m.), with a southwest view of the Matterhorn and panoramic vistas of mountains, glaciers, valleys, and lakes. This underground railway takes twenty minutes to reach the Sunnegga station. From Sunnegga, a cable car continues up to **Blauherd,** at 8620 ft. (2627 m.), where a second cable car takes riders to the rocky summit of the 10,180-foot (3103-meter) **Unter Rothorn,** with exceptional views of the Findel Glacier, the Matterhorn, and Zermatt.

Directions: By car *(leave very early in the morning!) - Follow N506 northeast out of Chamonix, crossing the Swiss border to Martigny. Take 9 toward Brig, past Sion and Sierre, to Visp. Drive on 215 south to Täsch, parking in the giant parking area. Take the short train ride to traffic-free Zermatt. By bus - A bus-and-train excursion to Zermatt is available by Chamonix Bus Excursions, and it might be an easier way to travel.*

17. Bus Excursions - Mont Blanc and SAT (*Société Alpine Transporte*) buses run trips to **Lake Annecy, Evian, Yvoire, Thonon, Aosta, Zermatt,**

Geneva, etc. Leave the driving to the experts; check out times and costs at the bus depot.

Chamonix Walks

Recommended Maps:

❖ Carte des Sentiers de Montagne en Été - Vallée de Chamonix
❖ IGN Chamonix, 3630 OT

Walk #1

Lift to Plan de L'Aiguille, Walk to Mer de Glace on the Grand Balcon Nord (Excursion to Mer de Glace), Optional Walk to Chamonix
Walking Easy Time: 3 to 5 hours
Rating: Comfortable

Today's hike is one of the more sensational walks in the Chamonix area. The trail goes along the Gran Balcon Nord, overlooking Chamonix, the Valley, its neighboring villages, and the mountains on the opposite side of the Valley. This is a full day's excursion and utilizes the first section of the Aiguille du Midi cable lift, exiting at its mid-station. *Note: For those who are not planning to do Walk #4, this might be a good opportunity to take the second section of the cable car to Aiguille du Midi, returning to mid-station Plan de l'Aiguille for the beginning of today's walk.*

At Plan de l'Aiguille, at 7579 ft. (2310 m.), overlooking the dramatic Bossons Glacier, you'll walk along the Gran Balcon Nord to the Mer de Glace, one of Europe's largest glaciers, where it's possible to visit the glacier by descending in a small lift. The return to Chamonix is by the quaint Montenvers mountain railroad, or by a pleasant, two-hour descent through the forest to the valley.

Directions: Walk west through town on the main street, rue Joseph Vallot, past the main post office, following the AIGUILLE DU MIDI sign. Purchase a ticket to the mid-station Plan de l'Aiguille—unless you wish to visit the Aiguille du Midi today. Due to the popularity of this lift and the optional excursions, an early start is suggested. On busy days, your ticket will indicate the time and number of the cable car you've been assigned to. Take the lift to mid-station Plan de l'Aiguille and exit the car for the start of today's walk.

Start: Walk through the exit and turn left, following the MONTENVERS sign, on the steep trail down the mountain to the little refuge Plan de l'Aiguille—a ten-minute descent. *Note: This is the steepest part of today's hike, but it only takes a short time.* Follow signs at the side of the restaurant to Montenvers. This often rocky path takes you across the mountain to another glacier, on a well-trafficked, open trail, with views of the towering, jagged formations of the Aiguille on the right and Chamonix and the valley

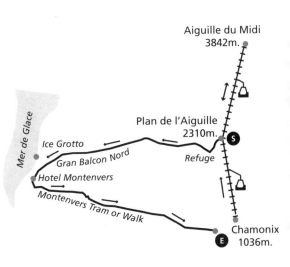

down on your left. There are some side trails descending steeply down to Chamonix—do *not* take them. Late in the walk, at a split in the trail, take the right ascending trail marked MONTENVERS SIGNAL. The walk rambles in and around 6562 ft. (2000 m.), and it then descends to 6156 ft. (1908 m.) at the Hotel Montenvers. Bear to the right at the hotel, and within minutes you'll arrive at the awesome sight of one of Europe's largest glaciers, the Mer de Glace, literally, the "Sea of Ice." The glacier, almost 9 miles (14 km) long, is the second-largest glacier in the Alps, and like all glaciers, it moves. It's possible to take a small cable car down for a visit to the glacier and the Ice Grotto. Ice artists work months in the spring preparing ice sculptures that look magical in the eerie blue light of the subglacial atmosphere. Spend some time at the Crystal Gallery and the Museum of Alpine Wildlife. To return to Chamonix, you have two options:

1. Board the Montenvers train for the twenty-minute return ride down. The last stop of the Montenvers train is adjacent to the Chamonix railroad station.

2. A walk down to Chamonix on the wide mule-path trail through the forest is also a nice way to end this exciting day. Judge your time and scheduling carefully, and if you decide on this two-hour hiking option, follow signs at Mer de Glace to Chamonix.

Walk #2

Lifts to Planpraz and Brévent, Walk Planpraz to la Flégère, Lift Down to les Praz, Walk to Chamonix

Walking Easy Time: 3½ hours

Rating: Comfortable

Today's walk and excursion will take most of the day so you should be on the road by 9:30 A.M. You'll walk from Chamonix to the Brévent cable car, where the second section of the lift takes you to the Brévent peak. After viewing the magnificent panorama of the Mont Blanc massif, you'll return by the same cable car down to the Planpraz Mid-Station, where the walk begins. The three-hour hike takes you to the cable car station at la Flégère, at 6158 ft. (1877 m.), on a typical, rocky, mountain path filled with ascents and descents.

The views across the valley over Chamonix are of the famous Mont Blanc massif, with the Glacier des Bossons to the right, as you walk in the direction of Mer de Glace across the valley. You'll view the 15,772-foot (4807-meter) Mont Blanc, and the 12,606-foot (3842-meter) Aiguille du Midi, towering over the Bossons Glacier as it appears to flow into the Chamonix Valley. As you hike toward la Flégère, you'll also see the Montenvers Railroad climbing the mountain across the Valley toward Mer de Glace, one of the largest glaciers in Europe. You'll descend to les Praz, at 3478 ft. (1060 m.), by lift and walk to Chamonix along a gentle river path.

Directions: Starting from the Chamonix Tourist Office, walk past the church and up the hill for about ten minutes, following signs to the Brévent cable car. Buy a ticket to Brévent, with a return to Planpraz. Take the gondola to the mid-station and change for the cable car and the ride to Brévent, at 8285 ft. (2525 m.). After viewing the fabulous Mont Blanc panorama across the valley, catch the next cable car down to the Planpraz Mid-Station, at 6559 ft. (1999 m.), where your hike begins.

Start: After leaving the Planpraz station, walk to the restaurant and turn left *up* the wide dirt path to signs pointing in the direction of LA FLÉGÈRE. Take this start of your hike slowly, reaching the ski lift and another sign pointing toward la Flégère. Walking on a wide, rocky path, stay to the left as you descend. Directional signs continue to confirm the trail toward la Flégère. After about an hour, you'll reach the Charlanon meadows, at 5945 ft. (1812 m.). The trail continues upward for a while and then levels off. You'll soon see your destination cable station ahead, across the valley from the Mer de Glace, and reach a series of steep, rocky steps with iron railings to aid your ascent, which lasts only a few minutes, bringing you to the level trail to the cable station. If it's early, you might wish to take the cable car up to l'Index, at 7825 ft. (2385 m.), for a superb view of Mer de Glace and the Chamonix Valley. If not, take the lift down to les Praz—cable cars leave on the hour and half hour.

On exiting the cable station at les Praz, you have two options:

1. Turn left to the river, and left again on the signed CHAMONIX path along the river, the gentle walk taking about thirty minutes, bringing you past the sports center into the main streets of Chamonix.

2. An alternative to walking the 1¼ miles (2 km) back to Chamonix is the Chamonix bus, with a stop outside the parking area on the street. Check the posted schedule.

Walk #3

Chamonix to Merlet to Chamonix—on the Petit Balcon Sud
Walking Easy Time: 2 to 4 hours
Rating: More challenging

This medium-level walk brings *Easy Walkers* to unparalleled views of the Bossons Glacier, directly across the valley from today's trail. The walk begins past the Brévent Lift Station and proceeds to Merlet along the lower entry to the *Petit Balcon Sud*, the site of a wild animal park. The trail ascends about 328 ft. (100 m.) during the first forty-five minutes on a wide, shaded, but rocky path through a cool pine forest, with views of the Bosson Glacier on the left. The path is well marked and signed, and *Easy Walkers* can return to Chamonix on the same path if they feel the last ascent to Merlet is too demanding There is an option at Merlet for the more energetic walker to continue the hike down to les Houches, at 3314 ft. (1010 m.), to catch the bus back to Chamonix.

Start: From the Chamonix Tourist Office, take the ascending auto road, following signs to the Brévent cable car. Walk left, past the lift station and stores, and continue on the auto road signed LES MOUSSOUX toward Merlet. This is the easiest and shortest route to the Petit Balcon Sud: the route des Moussoux. Views of the Bossons Glacier will be ahead on the left as you walk on the road through a residential area. After a few minutes, you'll see the sign PETIT BALCON SUD, and in about ten minutes, the road ends to enter the forest on a well-defined trail. A sign indicates MERLET - 1 HR., 45 MIN., but some walkers will take longer. Take the ascents slowly. Remember: They'll be descents on the way back!

After walking about thirty-five minutes, do *not* take the descending white-and-red blazed trail on your left. Continue ahead, ascending on the main trail, where signs continue to point ahead to Merlet. When the path forks again, continue on your left to Merlet, *not* taking the trail to the right up to Plan Lachat. Pass an entry to a descending trail on the left marked LES GAILLANDS that descends rather rapidly to the lakes on the valley floor. *Easy Walkers* will continue on the main trail to Merlet. When the path takes a sharp right turn, visit the lookout at this point for some remarkable views of the glacier, then continue on the main trail, which buttonhooks back to its original direction toward Merlet. After passing a steep, descending trail to les Bosson on your left, the rate of ascent increases dramatically until you reach your destination at Merlet. When the ascent increases, *Easy Walkers* can exercise two options:

1. Return to Chamonix along the same path, descending most of the way on the return.

2. For those who wish to continue, the ascending path remains well marked all the way to the animal park at Merlet, where additional decisions can be made.

    a. Continue the one-hour walk down to les Houches to return to Chamonix by bus. Walking on the forest road to les Houches will take longer than the path to the Christ-Roi statue, then to les Eaux Rousses, and further into the village and the bus.

    b. Return to Chamonix on the same path you walked up on.

Walk #4

Excursion to Aiguille du Midi and Helbronner, Walk to Lac Bleu and Return at the Mid-Station

Walking Easy Time: Plan a full day for today's excursion and short walk.

Rating: Comfortable

This excursion to the Aiguille du Midi is placed in the Walks section because the authors want to make sure that you don't miss this trip! However, it should be taken on the first clear day of your holiday in Chamonix! There's a short walk to Lac Bleu and back at the mid-station, but the real purpose of today's outing is a visit to the Aiguille du Midi and the ride over the Glacier du

Hint: Even on a hot, summer day, this station is usually well below freezing. Stow your insulated jacket in your backpack along with sunglasses and sunscreen.

Géant to Helbronner and Italy. *Note: There's some planning and preparation necessary for this full day's excursion, as the Aiguille du Midi is the most popular attraction in Chamonix.*

Start: The trip to the Aiguille du Midi leaves from the lift station on the outskirts of Chamonix, easily found after a short walk from the center of town. Follow signs and walk directly to the cashier's window indicating "reservations," if you made them earlier. If not, stand on the adjacent line and purchase a round-trip ticket from Chamonix to Helbronner, at 11,359 ft. (3462 m.), only if the weather is clear and that's your goal. Or, you can shorten today's outing by just visiting the Aiguille du Midi, at 12,606 ft. (3842 m.).

Take the giant cable car up to the mid-station at 7579 ft. (2310 m.) and continue by lift up to the Aiguille du Midi. After exiting at the Aiguille, cross the footbridge, walking to your right,

Pte. Helbronner 3462m.

To Courmayeur

Vallée Blanche

Aiguille du Midi 3842m.

Lac Bleu 2299m.

Plan de l'Aiguille 2310m. **S** **E**

Chamonix 1036m.

to visit the Mont Blanc Terrace. After fabulous views of Mont Blanc, you might wish to take the elevator to the Galerie du Mont Blanc at the summit. When ready, return to the footbridge, following the signs to Galerie de la Vallée Blanche, leading you to the Helbronner Gondola and the Ice Tunnel. Make sure you walk into the Ice Tunnel and on to the little ledge. If you're lucky, you'll see climbers coming out of the clouds after traversing the mountain below.

Follow the signs to Helbronner, for the forty-minute ride over the glacier in a small gondola. A round-trip and visit to the Aiguille can be as long as six hours, with a twenty-minute ride down from the Aiguille peak to return to Chamonix.

Hint: In summer, cable cars operate as early as 7:00 A.M. It might be a good idea to book your visit by telephone when you arrive.

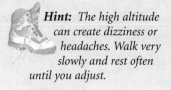

Hint: *The high altitude can create dizziness or headaches. Walk very slowly and rest often until you adjust.*

When ready to return from the Aiguille, follow the green CHAMONIX signs to the cable car departure area. On very busy days, boarding passes are distributed for the descent on your arrival at the information desk at the footbridge. Specify the time you'd like to return.

Return to the mid-station at Plan de l'Aiguille for a thirty-minute walk on an open, rocky trail to Lac Bleu, a little lake nestled in a hollow, surrounded by huge boulders. You should leave about an hour for the round-trip walk. When ready, descend to Chamonix by cable car from Plan de l'Aiguille.

Walk #5

Chamonix (on Petit Balcon Sud) to les Tines to les Praz to Chamonix
Walking Easy Time: 3 hours
Rating: Comfortable

This walk on the Petit Balcon Sud proceeds in an easterly direction through the forest, at about 3937 ft. (1200 m.). It's an enjoyable walk on a cloudy day because the trail is never very far from the valley floor in case of inclement weather. The most challenging part of today's walk takes place in the first forty-five minutes, when *Easy Walkers* will ascend from 3379 to 3953 ft. (1030 to 1205 m.), a rise of 574 ft. (175 m.). The trail is wide and rocky and climbs to reach the Petit Balcon Sud trail above les Nantes, overlooking the Chamonix golf course, where it then descends gradually to 3583 ft. (1092 m.). The return to Chamonix is on a level path along the Arve River, adjacent to the golf course, walking to les Praz and then into Chamonix.

Start: From the Hotel Sapinière, turn right exiting the hotel, and walk to the end of the street. Turn left. After a few minutes, note the marked path on the right, ascending to Petit Balcon Sud. This path is easily followed but rises steadily for about forty-five minutes—set a comfortable pace and rest as needed.

Once on the Petit Balcon Sud trail, proceed to your lower right, in the direction of Chalet de la Floria, still mostly through the forest. After another fifteen minutes, the road forks again. This time walk to the right, not following the ascending path to the left to the Chalet de la Floria, but contin-

uing ahead on the Petit Balcon Sud. As you walk, look down on the Chamonix golf course and the path for your return to Chamonix. The trail, bordered with wild blueberries and strawberries, continues to descend from
3937 to 3557 ft. (1200 to 1084 m.). Continue in the direction of les Tines
and Pont de la Forge. This path ends within a few minutes at the bridge over
the Arve River, where a gentle trail runs in both directions along the river.
Turn right, in the direction of le Paradis, for the return to Chamonix. This is
a level walking path through the forest, with several nice picnic areas on
your right and flowing streams from the Arve River on your left.

After about 1000 ft. (300 m.), you'll come to a small pathside restaurant with cabins and the recreation area of le Paradis des Praz. Walk
through. Within a few minutes, you'll reach the closed gates of the Chamonix golf course. Follow the path around to your left and over the river,
turning right again on this flat walking path. On your left is the entry to the
driving range. Because you won't have your golf clubs with you today, continue to walk through the golf course parking area to the auto road, passing
the Labrador Hotel. Turn right on the road for a few minutes, following
signs to la Flégère cable station. Make a right turn into the parking area,
walk past the station, and turn left in the direction of the sign pointing to
Chamonix. This level path takes you into Chamonix in thirty minutes. The
bus stop is outside the lift station parking area, if you prefer to ride back to
Chamonix.

Walk #6

**Les Houches Lift to Prarion, Walk to Col de Voza, Tram to Nid d'Aigle with Re-
    turn to Bellevue Lift to les Houches, Bus to les Bossons Glacier, Walk
    Glacier to Chamonix**
Walking Easy Time: 2½ to 3½ hours
Rating: Gentle

Easy Walkers will use many kinds of transportation to accomplish today's exciting walks and double-glacier excursions: Allow a full day for this outing.
You'll depart from Chamonix by bus to les Houches, with a gondola ride up
to Prarion. A short, gentle, downhill walk leads you to Col de Voza, where
you'll board the Mont Blanc Tramway for an exciting mountain train ride up
to Nid d'Aigle, at 7783 ft. (2372 m.), with views over the Glacier de Bion-
nassay. Here, you'll meet climbers in full mountain regalia coming and going
to the many high, mountain *refuges* in the area.

The Tramway du Mont Blanc has a long history of development, with work finished to the terminus at Nid d'Aigle in 1913. The engineers' original intention was to bring this tramway to the summit of Mont Blanc, but their goal was interrupted by World War I, and the railroad was never finished.

> **Hint:** *For best views, sit on the right side of the tram going to the glacier.*

After a visit, you'll return by tram to its first stop at Bellevue, where you'll take the Bellevue/St. Gervais cable car down to les Houches. Your next visit, after a short bus ride, will be to the imposing Bossons Glacier for a chairlift ride up to its leading edge. A walk back to Chamonix along the valley floor completes a very full and gratifying day.

Directions: Walk to the central Chamonix bus station next to the Tourist Office. Purchase a round-trip bus ticket to les Houches. Take a bus at about 9:00 A.M. for the twenty-minute ride. Exit the bus at the last stop in les Houches/les Chavants. Buy a one-way lift ticket to the top and take the short gondola ride up to le Prarion, at 6080 ft. (1853 m.).

> **Hint:** *You should make reservations for the return trip immediately on arriving at the glacier in order to make sure of your return time, because of the popularity of this scenic spot. The 12:30 P.M. return tram to Bellevue arrives at 12:50 P.M.*

Start: Walk up the hill past le Prarion Hotel and Cafe, following signed directions to COL DE VOZA. Turn left, and walk down this wide trail for a twenty-five-minute, gentle descent to Col de Voza, at 5424 ft. (1653 m.) and the Tramway du Mont Blanc station. Purchase a ticket to Nid d'Aigle, with a return to Bellevue. Try to take the 10:50 A.M. train, bringing you to the glacier at 11:20 A.M.

Arriving at the Bellevue station, it is a short walk up the meadow to your right to the cable car, which is in the building in front of a small restaurant. The cable car is closed for lunch between 12:30 and 1:30 P.M., so this might be a good time to picnic in the pleasant meadows until you catch the 1:30 P.M. lift down to les Houches. Purchase a one-way ticket for the short ride down the mountain. If you're lucky, the 1:30 P.M. Chamonix bus to les Bossons will be a few minutes late. If it's already departed, walk to your right along the road into the little village of les Houches to explore the shops while waiting for the 2:30 Chamonix bus. Tell the driver you wish to get off at les Bossons chairlift, and he'll let you off in the parking area.

Purchase a round-trip ticket for the exciting chairlift ride to the edge of the Bossons Glacier, dominating the entire Chamonix Valley. After visiting the glacier and returning to the parking area, you have two options, depending on the time and your attitude:

1. Walk down to the main auto road, crossing under the railroad tracks. Make a right turn on the path leading past les Pélèrins and Lacs des Gaillands, walking into Chamonix.
2. Wait for the Chamonix bus.

Walk #7

Le Tour Lift, Walk to Col de Balme to Col des Posettes to Charamillon Mid-Station (Optional Walk to le Tour)
Walking Easy Time: 2½ to 4 hours
Rating: Comfortable

The visit to Col de Balme is not only one of the highlights of a Chamonix visit, but it stands on its own as one of our favorite day hikes. The tiny, ancient hamlet of le Tour is situated at the end of the Chamonix Valley, surrounded by high, grassy meadows and framed by snow-covered peaks. *Easy Walkers* will leave Chamonix by public bus (or drive) for a twenty-minute ride to the le Tour Lift Station. The fifteen-minute trip to the top, at 7153 ft. (2180 m.), is interrupted only by a quick change at the mid-station from a six-person gondola to a four-place open chairlift.

The walk begins at the top station in the direction of Col de Balme to the Hotel Suisse, located on the Swiss border with France. Many walkers continue on to Switzerland, but today, you will hike along the perimeter of the "punchbowl" around le Tour, in the direction of Col des Posettes, and eventually back to the Charamillon Mid-Station, at 6070 ft. (1850 m.), with a final, optional descent to le Tour, at 4767 ft. (1453 m.). The views are stun-

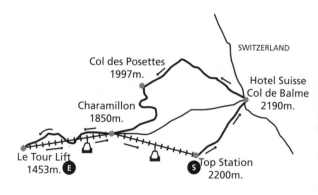

ning, and the Mont Blanc massif takes on a new perspective—on a clear day you'll be able to see throughout the Chamonix Valley.

Directions: Take a bus or drive to le Tour Lift Station (past Argentière) and buy a one-way ticket to the Col de Balme Top Station. The first stage of the lift is a continuously moving six-person gondola, and you transfer immediately at the mid-station to the four-seat chairlift for a final ascent to the top.

Start: After exiting the chairlift, follow COL DE BALME signs on a gently ascending path for a fifteen-minute walk to the hotel at the Swiss border, easily recognized by the friendly and familiar yellow signs directing hikers to various Swiss locations. Take enough time to view the panorama as it unfolds before you—this is one of the most beautiful sites on any walking itinerary. When ready, walk through the terrace and down to the right. Follow COL DES POSETTES signs. As you look to your left, you'll see your destination and the path you'll be taking. The comfortable trail winds around a grassy mountain, clearly marked before it descends toward the meadows below Col des Posettes. The snow-covered Mont Blanc massif towers over the Chamonix Valley in front of you, as you walk along a well-defined path around the perimeter of this mountain, with colorful wild flowers all around and cowbells clanging in the alps below. Reaching a wide path, note a group of signs taking you left in the direction of le Tour and the Charamillon Mid-Station. At the mid-station, the path continues to descend to le Tour, but if the one-hour descent of 1303 ft. (1453 m.) is too much for your knees today, take the gondola down.

Buses leave for Chamonix from le Tour Lift Station (where you were dropped off in the morning). Before you return, however, you might enjoy a stroll through the old hamlet of le Tour, cut off in the past from the rest of the Chamonix Valley by heavy snows and avalanches.

Walk #8

Lift and Excursion to l'Index, Walk la Flégère to Argentière
Walking Easy Time: 3 hours
Rating: Comfortable

After a visit by chairlift to l'Index, at 7825 ft. (2385 m.), to see fabulous views of the Aiguilles Rouges, you'll walk on a pleasant, descending trail from the Flégère Lift Station to the busy little village of Argentière. The trail is situated between the Grand Balcon Sud and the Petit Balcon Sud, site of another day walk. (See Walk #5.) *Easy Walkers* will leave from Chalet de la Flégère, at 6158 ft. (1877 m.), and finish the walk in Argentière, at 4102 ft. (1250 m.), with a bus trip back to Chamonix.

Directions: Take the bus to the lift at les Praz, or take the gentle, thirty-minute walk from Chamonix along the river, directly to the Flégère Lift Station at les Praz. If you decide to walk, leave Chamonix and walk down the little street in front of the hospital (av. de la Plage). It takes you over a small bridge across the Arve River. Turn left immediately, picking up a pleasant walking path leading to the lift station. Buy a lift ticket to l'Index with a return to la Flégère. Take the large cable car to la Flégère, and walk up to the chairlift that runs continuously to l'Index. When ready, return to la Flégère by chairlift.

Start: Pick up the trail in back of the restaurant, and after crossing under a small ski lift, take the right fork in the direction of Argentière. This walk is largely through the forest with little chance of distraction, except for two intervening paths on your left, one bringing climbers up to the Chalet des Chéserys. Continue on the main path, resisting another path climbing up the mountain. Continue down in the signed direction of ARGENTIÈRE, at 4101 ft. (1250 m.), entering directly into this little village. Before exploring the town, locate the bus stop on the main auto road in the village center for the ride back to Chamonix.

MEGÈVE

A charming village of 4900 inhabitants, Megève is built on narrow, cobblestone streets, with an imposing fourteenth-century church towering over its many ancient buildings. Although it's proudly traditional in terms of architecture and culture, one doesn't have to go far to find all the conveniences and luxuries of modern life. In fact, Megève is one of the more sophisticated mountain villages in the French Alps, with chic boutiques; a famous three-star, Michelin-rated restaurant; and sports, relaxation, and fitness opportunities everywhere. Lodgings range from luxury hotels to rental apartments and *gites*, simple farmhouse accommodations. The Megève Tourist Office is located in a remarkably beautiful, landmark building, just off the pedestrian street in the village center. At night, the small bridges over the river are attractively lit, and pedestrian streets and outdoor cafes are filled with vacationers enjoying an after-dinner snack.

Lovely Megève, in *Pays du Mont Blanc* (Mont Blanc Country), is one of fourteen villages and 400 hamlets in the shadow of the impressive 15,772-foot (4807-meter) Mont Blanc, bordered by Italy's Aosta Valley and the Valais canton of Switzerland. The origin of the name Megève can be found in the Celtic language: *mag* (village) and *eva* (water), referring to its position between two rivers.

There are over 90 miles (150 km) of hiking trails at all levels in the Megève area, many on mountain paths facing the Mont Blanc range, others winding past farms and barns or through shaded pine forests and flower-filled meadows. Megève's high valleys are covered with pine, larch, and willow trees, while the valley floor is lined with maple, ash, and birch. The scenery is a tranquil contrast of verdant valleys; colorful, flower-filled hillsides; and graceful, snow-capped mountains—home to chamois, ibex, and marmot.

Three major lifts are available in Megève in summer: Mont d'Arbois, rising to 6027 ft. (1837 m.), Rochebrune, rising to 5784 ft. (1763 m.), and Jaillet, ascending to 5200 ft. (1585 m.), all leading to a variety of scenic day-hikes, with stops at country inns and restaurants along the way. Local *navettes* or minibuses operate from the bus terminal, and they provide inexpensive and direct transportation in summer to lifts at the beginning or end of many *Walking Easy* hikes.

Megève is well located—only a short distance from the internationally famous resort of Chamonix (another *Easy Walking* base village)—and is surrounded by charming small villages and hamlets. Excursions to Chamonix, Annecy, Lake Geneva, and the Aosta Valley in Italy are easily accomplished. Megève hosts sports contests and music concerts, both classical and jazz, and offers many options for walking, sightseeing, or an evening stroll in town. Megève is an up-beat village: good food, interesting shops, comfortable accommodations, nice people, and most important for *Easy Walkers*—good hiking.

Transportation

By Plane - Geneva-Cointrin International Airport is 43 miles (70 km) from Megève. The airport has regular train service to Sallanches 7 miles (12 km) away, with a bus connection to Megève. In summer, there is one bus a day to and from the Geneva airport to Megève, but many car rental agencies are located at the airport.

By Train - The railroad station for TGV high-speed trains is in Sallanches. It's a thirty-minute bus ride from arriving trains to Megève.

By Car - Paris is 372 miles (600 km) from Megève. The most direct route is to drive from Paris to Mâcon on A6, picking up A40 around Bourg-en-Bresse, and staying on A40 around Geneva east toward Chamonix. At Sallanches, take N212 south into Megève. (For more explicit directions from Paris's Charles de Gaulle Airport, please see the Chamonix chapter's By Car section.)

A shorter route is from the Geneva airport. Pick up A40, following signs east to Chamonix. At Sallanches, note signs to Albertville/Megève on N212 south. Megève is only 45 miles (73 km) southeast of Geneva.

By Bus - The SAT *(Société Alpine Transporte Company)* operates local buses from the Megève bus station, located on main road N212, next to the sports center. They run to and from Combloux, Saint-Gervais, le Fayet, Sallanches, and Chamonix in one direction; and Praz sur Arly, Flumet, Ugine, Albertville, and Annecy in the opposite direction. Buses also operate to and from the Geneva airport.

Local Megève Bus Service (*Navettes*) - In summer, local buses start at the Megève Bus Station on Route N212, next to the Hotel Grange d'Arly and in front of the sports center, to Mont d'Arbois Cable Station and Cote 2000, with another line going to Rochebrune Cable Station. Check at the Tourist Office or bus station for current schedules and fares.

Favorite *Walking Easy* Hotel

Hotel Grange d'Arly

Three-Star; Owners - Familie Allard

10, rue des Allobroges, B.P. 68, 74120 Megève

Tel: 4 50 58 77 88, **Fax:** 4 50 93 07 13

E-mail: contact@grange-darly.com

Internet: www.grange-darly.com

Built about twenty years ago, this chalet-style hotel is attractively decorated in "country French," using natural woods, colorful print fabrics, and traditional Savoyarde furniture—both in its downstairs public rooms and its large, comfortable bedrooms, with modern bathrooms and outside balconies. Hotel Grange d'Arly is located away from the village center, near the bus terminal and sports center, yet only a quick, five-minute walk brings you into the village.

Its young owners, Christine and Jean-Marie Allard, take pains to make you feel very comfortable, as though you were visiting in their home instead of a full-service, twenty-four-room hotel. They speak English and can help you find everything and anything you may need on your visit to Megève.

Continental breakfast, with a basket of French bread, croissants, and pastry, can be taken in your room or downstairs in the sunny, attractive dining room. Dinner is also available to guests at a demi-pension rate—French home cooking at its best—an appetizer, the main course (such as coq au vin), cheese course, dessert and/or fresh fruit—a delicious ending to a day of walking or sightseeing around charming Megève.

Lifts in and Around Megève (open July and August)

Téléphérique de Rochebrune - This cable car rises to 5752 ft. (1753 m.) in about five minutes. (See Walks #2 and #7.)

Télécabine Mont d'Arbois - The gondolas rise to 5978 ft. (1822 m.), leaving every half hour. (See Walks #3 and #5.)

Télécabine du Jaillet - With gondolas rising to 5204 ft. (1586 m.), the top station provides fabulous views of the snow-covered Mont Blanc range, towering over the green hills around Megève. (See Walks #1 and #4.)

Excursions

The Megève Tourist Office is located in the restored *Maison des Frères* on the walking street in the center of Megève, rue Monseigneur-Conseil.

Fax: 4 50 93 03 09

E-mail: megeve@megeve.com

Internet: www.megeve.com

1. Megève - Originally built by Benedictine monks in 1085, **St-Jean-Baptiste Church** has a long and interesting history. The choir loft was raised at the end of the fourteenth century, the nave dates from 1692, and the gilded Virgin and Romanesque-style bell tower date from 1754.

Musical events include the **Megève Jazz Contest**, with international bands playing authentic New Orleans jazz; the International Musical Meetings, with classical concerts and master classes; the **Annual Megève Jazz Festival,** with New Orleans, be-bop, and modern jazz styles. There is a cycling tour from Megève to Mont Blanc, crossing five difficult passes, with a height difference of 11,766 ft. (3586 m.); and a large, colorful, **outdoor market** is held every Friday morning in the parking area in front of the Sports and Congress Centre

A former home, the **Megève Museum** is located at 66, rue Comte de Capré, with changing exhibits. Located at 88, rue du Vieux Marché in an old farmhouse, the **Haute Val d'Arly Museum** has exhibits depicting the local Savoie heritage.

2. Chamonix - See the Chamonix chapter for details.

Directions: By car - Take N212 north, following signs through St. Gervais to Chamonix. By bus - An early morning bus from Megève arrives in Chamonix in less than one hour. Or, you can take an SAT excursion bus to Chamonix and the Chamonix Valley.

3. Evian-les-Bains - See the Chamonix chapter, Excursion #2.

Directions: Follow N212 north to N205 into Cluses. Take D902 to Thonon and drive east on N5 to Evian. Return on a circle route by driving west on N5 to Thonon, then taking D903 to N206 to Annemosse. Pick up N205 to Sallanches and N212 into Megève.

4. Annecy - Annecy has been called "The Venice of the Alps" because of canals that cut through the old section of town. This "Jewel of the

Savoy Alps" is now a major urban center on Lac d'Annecy, but its old town is charming and well preserved, spanning the Thiou River as it leaves the lake. From one of its many bridges, note the **Palais de l'Ile,** a former prison, rising from the stream like the prow of a ship. Walk on **rue Ste-Claire,** a lovely old street with arcades and seventeenth-century gabled buildings. Visit **Musée Château Annecy,** former residence of the counts of Geneva and the dukes of Savoie-Nemours, now a museum of regional artifacts.

The lake itself can be seen best from avenue d'Albigny—enjoy this lovely body of water set in a glacial valley, surrounded by the Bauges massif to the south and gentle, rolling hills northwest toward Geneva. Walk around the popular lakefront and visit the **casino** if you are so inclined. If time permits, a dozen steamers leave Annecy for lake tours.

A noteworthy side excursion from Annecy is a visit to **les Gorges du Fier,** 6 miles (10 km) away. Take a train or bus from the train station for the short ride, getting off at Poisy. Follow signs for the mile walk to the gorge, where visitors make their way into the depths on platforms winding through rocks and torrents. An immense field of boulders greets you on exiting the chasm.

Directions: By car - Drive south on N212 to Aciéries, picking up N508 toward Ugine. Drive through Faverges and continue around the left side of the lake to Annecy. For a more exciting drive, at Flumet, pick up D909 and drive over the Col des Aravis. Stay on D909 around the lake to Annecy. By bus - An early morning bus from Megève arrives in Annecy in ninety minutes. Or, take an SAT excursion bus to Annecy.

5. Albertville - See Méribel chapter, Excursion #6.

Directions: By car - Take N212 southwest to Albertville. By bus - You can take an SAT excursion bus.

6. Geneva, Switzerland - See the Chamonix chapter, Excursion #14, for details.

Directions: By car - Take N212 north out of Megève, picking up the expressway to Geneva. By bus - SAT excursions can take you to and from Geneva.

7. Société Alpes Transporte - The SAT bus station and information office is located next to the Hotel Grange d'Arly, in front of the sports center, on the main route through town. This company runs bus excursions in summer.

Megève Walks

Recommended Map:

❖ Carte des Sentieres, Megève. (The Megève Tourist Office has marked the routes corresponding to the walking map simply and clearly, using easy-to-follow coding.)

Walk #1

Introductory Walk - Lift to le Jaillet, Walk to Chalet de la Vieille to Odier to Megève
Walking Easy Time: 2½ hours
Rating: Comfortable

This lovely ramble is a good introduction to walking in the heights around Megève. If you arrive in Megève in the morning, it's the kind of walk you might wish to take after settling into your hotel—a not particularly demanding or long one. You'll take the Jaillet gondola up to the top station and walk to Chalet de la Vieille on a lovely path with sensational views of the snow-covered Mont Blanc range, a stunning backdrop to the green, rolling hills around Megève. Along the way, you can visit a charming mountain restaurant with a sun-terrace overlooking the valley and Mont Blanc. At Chalet de la Vieille, you'll turn down the mountain to return to Megève through the suburban community of Odier.

Directions: Facing the bus station on the main road, walk to your right. Turn left up the hill and proceed past the Palais de Sport in the direction of le Jaillet. Make a right turn, following the LE JAILLET sign, with a picture of a gondola and walker. This short, uphill walk brings you to the lift entrance. Purchase a one-way ticket to the top. The modern, six-person gondolas move only on the hour and half hour for the seven-minute ride.

Start: Le Jaillet Top Station is at 5200 ft. (1585 m.). Walk ahead for only a minute to a sign that directs you right on path R3 MEGÈVE PAR BEAUREGARD. The wide, comfortable path descends gently under a ski lift, leading *Easy Walkers* to la Petite Ravine, a little mountain restaurant on the right, with marvelous views from its sun-terrace. Pause a while and enjoy the spectacular scenery of the snow-covered Mont Blanc range in the distance.

You might sample the homemade berry tortes, with the sound of cowbells clanging gently in the meadow. This seems to be a favorite spot of visiting French families.

When ready, continue ahead on R3. Do *not* turn down the mountain on R2 to la Fouettaz, but walk ahead on R3 in the direction of Beauregard and Chalet de la Vieille. Turn sharply right on a path signed CHALET DE LA VIEILLE, this short descent taking you to the old barn at the chalet. Walk left of the chalet, with a great view, and turn right at signed path O in the direction of Vauvray. This typical, narrow mountain path descends through forests and meadows, ending at an auto road with a small parking area. Turn right on this road, R1, in the direction of Megève, and continue to another small parking area marked LA FOUETTAZ. Look for the sign R in the parking area, leading to Odier. This mountain trail descends again, but it can be wet at times—walk carefully. You'll soon be in Odier. Turn left on the small road, meeting a major auto road where you turn right. Make your first right turn again and walk up the road. Turn left at an unmarked, grassy wagon path with an orange pump, winding through the meadow and coming out on another auto road. Turn left, then left again, and within a few minutes, you'll be at le Jaillet, where you started this morning. A quick walk past the sports center and the bus station brings you back to your hotel.

Walk #2

Lift to Rochebrune, Walk to l'Alpette to les Lanchettes to les Jardins to Javen to le Maz to Megève

Walking Easy Time: 3½ hours

Rating: Comfortable

Our walk today begins at the top station of the Rochebrune cable lift, a starting point for many area walks, as well as a jumping-off place for paragliders. You'll walk up to l'Alpette Restaurant, a rise of 355 ft. (108 m.), then continue gently downhill to the cut-off trail to les Lanchettes. This trail affords views of the Aiguille Chroche, the Tête de la Combaz, and Mont Joly, as well as part of the Mont Blanc massif. The remainder of the hike descends through Javen, with a visit to the tiny hamlet of le Maz for the final descent into the center of Megève. The walking is mostly downhill, except for the first thirty-five-minute ascent to l'Alpette from Rochebrune. If you haven't packed a picnic lunch, there are several restaurants along the way.

Directions:

Take a morning bus at the bus stop next to the Hotel Grange d'Arly for the ten-minute ride to the Rochebrune Lift Station. Or, if you wish, it is a twenty-minute walk through the village and up the hill to the cable station. Purchase a one-way ticket to Rochebrune, at 5755 ft. (1754 m.).

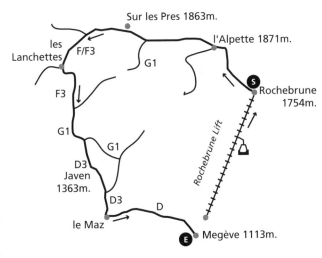

Start: Follow the G route to l'Alpette for a thirty-five-minute ascent, continuing around until you see a sign indicating the upcoming restaurant with a nice view from its sun-terrace.

When ready, walk back to the main path and follow the signs for F/G. In about thirty minutes, turn left on F/F3, descending toward LES LANCHETTES. Continue down on F3, which eventually turns into G1. Stay right, taking D3 in the direction of Javen, at 4472 ft. (1363 m.). As you descend, you pass over grassy meadows and through pine forests on a wide jeep trail. Occasionally, you'll come across a wire fence crossing the trail, placed there to keep the cows in the meadow. Unhook the wire, remembering to snap it back to reattach. The little mountain *altiport* is on your right, and the village of Megève is on the left. Make sure you remain on D3, and you'll soon approach an auto road. Turn right on this road and walk a few minutes until, on the right, note an old church with its lovely clock. This is the quaint farm hamlet of le Maz. Turn left on the road opposite the church, marked D on your map but not on the path, with a sign pointing to Megève. This path continues down, through farms and then forest, directly into the center of Megève.

Walk #3

Lift to Mont d'Arbois, Walk to Mont Joux to Hermance to le Planay to le Maz to Megève

Walking Easy Time: 4 hours

Rating: More challenging

This popular Mont d'Arbois hike is rated "more challenging," not because of any particular difficulty of the trail, but because of its long ascents and descents. The paths are easily found and well marked—Megève continues to do a particularly good job of keying trails to its walking map. Although there are numerous rest and restaurant stops on top of Mont d'Arbois, there are none on the descending trails between Pavillon du Mont Joly and Megève, so it might be a good idea to pack a picnic lunch and, of course, the ever-necessary bottle of water.

There will be immediate ascents and descents after leaving the lift, and the trail will head toward Mont Joly, rising from 5985 to 6496 ft. (1824 to 1980 m.), before descending to le Planay. *Note: For those of you who are interested in that ascent to Mont Joly, at 8285 ft. (2525 m.), the trail is well marked and well traveled.* The descent to le Planay passes through the ancient hamlet of Hermance, ducking in and out of shady forests and flower-filled meadows. At le Planay, a good picnic spot, you'll begin the return to Megève, with a short walk along the road and a final descent through the picturesque hamlet of le Maz.

Directions: Take a morning *navette* from the bus station in front of the sports center for the ten-minute ride to the Mont d'Arbois Lift Station. Purchase a one-way ticket to Mont d'Arbois. Take the gondola to the top station, at 5985 ft. (1824 m.), where you'll find a three-star hotel, restaurants, snack shops, and a souvenir store. The view is unobstructed in all directions, and you can look down the back side of Mont d'Arbois toward le Bettex and le Fayet.

Start: Turn right in the direction of the sign MONT JOUX - 1 HR. The path is wide, easy to follow, and marked B. Ski lifts can be seen in all directions—Megève is a popular ski resort in winter. The trail continues up to Mont Joux after passing the Chez la Tante restaurant on the right. Do *not* take path A1 down to le Planellet but continue in the direction of Mont Joly until you come to a path on your right marked C-HERMANCE. The path ahead continues up to Mont Joly, and *Easy Walkers* might wish to walk ahead to the Pavillon du Mont Joly for a spectacular view.

When ready, return back to the C-Hermance trail, signed LE PLANAY-

MEGÈVE PAR HERMANCE. It descends down the mountain from 6398 to 4593 ft. (1950 to 1400 m.), through Hermance, at 5994 ft. (1827 m.). If you are hiking in early summer, look up toward Mont Joly, and you'll see the famous "snow-duck" above you on the mountain. Local custom dictates that if the neck of the duck is broken (i.e., the snow has melted) by August 15th, the grain farmers will have a good harvest.

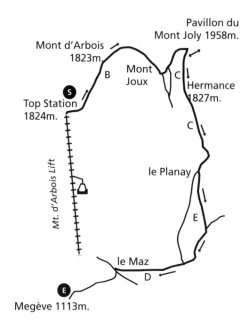

As you proceed, the trail changes from a wide, dirt path to a narrow, rocky, mountain trail and then reverts back again to a more comfortable path as it descends more rapidly toward le Planay. Make a right turn at the end of the trail on the path toward le Planay. After a few minutes of walking, you'll find a nice picnic spot on the left in a pine forest. When ready, turn left over a little stream, on path E1. This path ascends slightly, passing a flower-bedecked farmhouse on your right, as you enter a pretty, pine-needle-covered forest path. This part of the trail is level and cool and meets E, where you take a right turn down the hill on a trail with colorful wildflowers on both sides. Eventually, you'll walk through the meadow on a crushed-rock path and reach the road marked D on your map. Turn right on D, walking along the left side of the road, passing through wide, grassy meadows on each side, with Mont Joly at your back. After about twenty minutes, you'll reach another road. Turn left and, in the little hamlet of le Maz, opposite the old church with the pretty clock, turn right. This is path D on the map, but it's not marked at the trail. However, a sign points to Megève, and the trail leads directly into the main shopping street. The walk from le Maz to Megève is particularly pretty and takes about thirty minutes, first through the farms and then through the forest.

Walk #4

Lift to le Jaillet, Walk to Col de Jaillet to le Christomet to Megève
Walking Easy Time: 3 to 4 hours
Rating: More challenging

This more challenging part of today's hike has a considerable amount of uphill walking, taking *Easy Walkers* from 5200 to 5774 ft. (1585 to 1760 m.), with additional ascents and descents till you reach le Christomet, at 6070 ft. (1850 m.). The panoramic views from here are worth the extra effort. You'll return to Megève on a descending path, largely through the forest. This is a full day's excursion, and there are no restaurants or facilities between the le Jaillet Lift Station and Megève. Make sure you've packed a picnic lunch and water and taken your map. If possible, this walk should be taken after a dry period, as the walk down from le Christomet through the forest can be wet and slippery. *Note: Before reaching le Christomet, you can turn back on the same trail if you feel the ascent is too difficult. And remember, the views in the opposite direction are different and just as enthralling!*

Directions: Walk past the bus station, turning left up the street past the sports center, then turning right at the last street, following the sign to the le Jaillet gondola, which pictures a walker and a gondola. Purchase a one-way ticket for the seven-minute ride in the six-person gondola, leaving every thirty minutes on the hour and half hour.

Start: After exiting the gondola, follow the sign for the P route to COL DE JAILLET. Pass a path to the right marked R3, the site of another *Walking Easy* hike, and continue walking uphill on a path signed P. This is a popular, wide jeep road that ascends about 655 ft. (200 m.), before leveling off, just below Col de Jaillet, where the path meets S to the left, signed LE CHRISTOMET. There are many offshooting trails—resist them all—stay on the main path to this intersection with S, to le Christomet. You'll have walked through open meadows with a profusion of wild flowers, and through tall, cool forests, with some great views of Croisse Baulet. After making the left turn on path S in the direction of le Christomet, the trail ascends and descends and then rises more steeply to the le Christomet peak, at 6080 ft. (1853 m.). There are sensational views in all directions—enjoy the panorama.

When ready, continue to your left on path S, descending through the forest, splitting off on Z and X, all the way into Megève. This walk can be steep at times, and it is generally wet in the forest—take your time. Please return to Megève this way *only* if it has been dry recently. If not, you can return to the lift station at le Jaillet on the same trail on which you came and return to Megève by gondola.

Walk #5

Lift to Mont d'Arbois, Walk to le Bettex Lift, Lift Down to le Bettex, Walk to Plan Set to les Berthelets to Pont d'Arbon to Megève
Walking Easy Time: 3 hours
Rating: Comfortable

Although today's *Walking Easy* time is three hours, you should allow about six hours total time. This will allow ample time for lunch, two gondola lifts, bus transportation, resting, and scenery viewing. You'll leave by *navette* to the Mont d'Arbois Lift Station and, at the top, take a short walk to another lift for a gondola descent to le Bettex, where the walk begins. Most of the walk descends comfortably through the forest and meadows overlooking le Fayet and Combloux. Walkers should carry the local hiking map for this trek, as there are some unmarked entrances to trails and roads. There is a small section of paved-road walking before returning to Megève by way of Pont d'Arbon—however, the road is quiet and not heavily used. Pack a picnic lunch and water, as there are no restaurants between the Bettex lift station and the few hotels along the road to Megève.

Directions: Take a morning bus to Mont d'Arbois. (The long, uphill walk to the lift station is *not* advised.) The gondola operates on the hour and half hour. Take it to the top station.

Start: Exit at Mont d'Arbois, at 5985 ft. (1824 m.), and walk in the direction of Mont Joux for the short descent and ascent to le Bettex gondola entrance. Up ahead on the left, you'll see a chairlift that operates only in winter, and the Bettex gondola is adjacent to it. The sign from the road indicates TÉLÉCABINE DU BETTEX—15 MIN. This gondola serves skiers and walkers from the St-Gervais/le Fayet area, transporting them up the far side of Mont d'Arbois. It operates every half hour, at 15 minutes after and 15 minutes before the hour. Buy a one-way ticket for the ten-minute gondola ride down to the first stop at le Bettex.

At le Bettex, walk down the auto road, past a few shops, to a red arrow on the left side of the road. Turn left and follow the red arrow onto a small wagon path. After a few minutes, note a small ski lift and a red arrow pointing down the hill. Turn right and follow the trail down between a few houses to find the trail to the left marked L2, next to the auto road on your right. Turn left on L2. This delightful trail is a well-marked, fairly level path traversing cool forests and open, flower-filled meadows at about 4101 ft. (1250 m.).

Continue on L2, passing Plan Set, until you reach a four-way intersection marked L and L1. Continue on L1 through the forest, soon meeting another four-way intersection. Turn left on H1. This path remains in the pine forest and descends gently to H, with some pretty views overlooking the valley. The path spills into a small, *unmarked* auto road marked L only on your hiking map. Turn left on the road, Route du Petit Bois, which soon changes its name to les Poëx. Walk past the Hotel Princesse de Megève on the left. Continue to follow this road, passing les Berthelets, winding around to the right. Cross over major auto road N212 leading into Megève. Walk up on Chemin d'Arbon, passing Chalet de Vernay on the right. Cross the next, smaller auto road and continue ahead past an R painted on the old building on your left, passing a chalet and garden, also on the left. Turn left on a wagon path at a small, orange water pump. This path is signed CHEMIN D'ALLARD. Walk through the meadow, turning left at the first road, past the Summer Sledge and le Jaillet Lift Station. Cross the road leading to Albertville and walk down to the sports center, the bus station, and your hotel.

Walks #6

Option #6A - Le Leutaz to Chevan to le Leutaz
Walking Easy Time: 3 hours
Rating: Comfortable

Option #6B - Le Leutaz to Chevan to Refuge du Petit Tétraz (Crêt du Midi) to le Leutaz
Walking Easy Time: 5 hours
Rating: More challenging

Option #6C - Le Leutaz to Chevan to Praz sur Arly
Walking Easy Time: 3½ to 5 hours
Rating: More challenging

All of these walks begin at le Leutaz, a little less than 3 miles (4½ km) from central Megève. Unfortunately, there is no bus service to le Leutaz, and alternate transportation is necessary. Because Options #6A and #6B start in le Leutaz, you can use your car for transportation; there are parking facilities at the start of the walk. However, a taxi should be hired for transportation to Walk #6C.

Options #6A and #6B also bring you back to le Leutaz, and if your car has not been left in the parking area, there is no transportation available back to Megève except by taxi or a descending, 3-mile walk to the village on the road. We do *not* recommend walking up to le Leutaz, but the walk back is downhill. Option #6C brings you into Praz sur Arly, where you can take the bus back to Megève.

The walk from le Leutaz to all options is uphill and will take you from 4429 ft. (1350 m.) to 5414 ft. (1650 m.) at Chevan. However, the degree of ascent is comfortable. For those more aggressive *Easy Walkers*, the trail then continues uphill to 5873 ft. (1790 m.) to a *refuge* with a fabulous view, just below Crêt du Midi. Walkers who take option #6A or #6B, returning to le Leutaz along the same path, experience impressive views in the opposite direction, including the snow-covered peak of Mont Blanc peeking over the rolling green hills and tall pine forests around Megève.

Directions: Drive through Megève, following signs to Rochebrune Lift and le Leutaz, which are in the same direction. Le Leutaz is about 2½ miles (4 km) past the lift station. Park on the right side of the road opposite le Chaudron restaurant in le Leutaz.

Start: Walk ahead on the car road, which soon turns into a wide, dirt jeep road, used by those few people who drive up the mountain. This path is lettered H, but changes to H1 when the H path climbs up the mountain to the left. Continue on H1 until you come to a little wooden bridge on your right with a sign marked I, in the direction of Col de Véry and crêt du Midi. Turn right and walk over the bridge. As you ascend, there's a nice view into the valley on your right and of the mountains surrounding Megève. To your left and to the rear is the Rochebrune massif, which you will see clearly on your descent. At about 4790 ft. (1460 m.), note a little working farm and restaurant on your right—Alpages les Vetes—with a sun-terrace. The path continues to rise gently in the open, arriving at another small farmhouse, at 5112 ft. (1558 m.), a perfect spot for a picnic. There are tables for hikers to use for picnicking if they purchase drinks—fresh milk, soda, mineral water, etc.

The walk continues up to Chevan, at 5414 ft. (1650 m.), a scenic view-point marked on your map. This is the four-way intersection where *Easy Walkers* can choose their return options. A and B bring you back to le Leutaz. Option C is for those who did not leave a car at le Leutaz and wish to return to Megève by way of the bus at Praz sur Arly.

Option A: At the four-way intersection at Chevan, return to le Leutaz on the same path, this time with views of the snow-capped peak of Mont Blanc behind the green hills surrounding Megève.

Option B: For more aggressive walkers, the path straight ahead be-comes T2, going past the restaurant visible up ahead, in the direction of the Crêt du Midi, at 6201 ft. (1890 m.). You can rest at the *refuge* du Petit Té-traz, at 5850 ft. (1783 m.) before turning back on the same trail to le Leutaz. This is the extension for strong walkers.

Option C: At the four-way intersection, another trail turns down the mountain on the right, just a few feet past the intersection, and takes walkers directly to Praz sur Arly, on paths T2 and T1. From Praz sur Arly, take the bus back to Megève.

Walk #7

Le Leutaz to Chevan to Col de Véry to Pré Rosset to l'Alpette to Rochebrune Lift

Walking Easy Time: Allow a full day for this more demanding walk.

Rating: More challenging

For more experienced walkers, the following hike was suggested by M. André Seigneur, former director of the Megève Tourist Office. Due to time constraints, the authors did not have the opportunity to take this walk.

Directions: Hikers will need transportation to le Leutaz—available taxis can take you to this starting point. See Directions in Walk 6.

Start: The start of this walk is similar to Walk #6, taking you from le Leutaz on H and H1 to the turnoff, making a right turn on I over the little stream, and ascending to the viewpoint at Chevan.

However, at Chevan, make a sharp left turn at the four-way intersec-tion on path T4 to Col de Véry. Take path F along the ridge, staying left at la Croix de Pierre, at 6473 ft. (1973 m.), continuing on F to Pré Rosset, at 6188 ft. (1886 m.). Take G to l'Alpette, at 6139 ft. (1871 m.) and walk down the hill on G to the Rochebrune Lift Station, at 5755 ft. (1754 m.), for the ride down and the bus to Megève.

MORZINE

Quelle surprise! We weren't sure what to expect as we drove on winding mountain roads toward the Portes du Soleil—Gates to the Sun. However, it didn't take long—the Haute Savoie villages of Morzine and Avoriaz welcomed us with alluring country charm and serenity, belying the fact that they are part of one of the largest ski centers in the French Alps. Montreux, Geneva, and Lausanne, Switzerland, are within one to one and a half hours' easy drive, and nearby are medieval Yvoire and Thonon, two of the most beautiful villages in France.

Situated in the Chablais mountain range, halfway between Lake Geneva and Mont Blanc, Morzine cultivates a spirit that may be unique in the Alps. The local Morzinois have adapted to the new outdoor economy while maintaining their village's Savoyard identity. Architectural details reflect Chartreuse-style roofs with four sloping sides, and buildings are made of attractive stone, slate, and wood. Morzine is filled with comfortable hotels, has a particularly active Tourist Office, sophisticated shops, and restaurants serving creative, gourmet Savoyard cuisine.

Local hiking trails intertwine with ski pistes, offering over 180 miles (300 km) of marked paths. Lifts take hikers up to a myriad of walking opportunities—with typical mountain ascents and descents that most *Easy Walkers* will relish, and low-level walks through valleys and along streams that will appeal to young families and seniors alike.

Note: Morzine should be visited by Easy Walkers *during July and August, when lifts and hotels are open.*

Morzine and Avoriaz have a population of 3000 inhabitants, the altitude rising from 3300 ft. (1000 m.) in traditional Morzine to 5906 ft. (1800 m.) on the cliffs of its modern sister village of Avoriaz, first developed as a ski village in the 1960s. Since the middle of the eighteenth century, slate quarries brought revenue to this alpine region, contributing to the economic prosperity of Morzine, and in fact, five quarries are still in operation today.

The Morzine/Avoriaz area appeals to all sports enthusiasts, not only featuring summer hiking, but also with mountain biking, swimming, fishing, tennis, canyoning, rafting, and two major mountain golf courses. And, there is a special quality in this French, alpine air—gentle and relaxing. *Easy Walkers* will revel in this laid-back, charming resort and its easily accessible walking trails.

Transportation

By Plane - Geneva Airport is 47 miles (75 km) from Morzine. Car rental agencies are available at the airport.

By Car - After exiting the airport, follow signs to France. Pick up the A40 highway in the direction of Chamonix. Exit at Cluses Centre and follow signs to Morzine on D902.

By Bus - Area bus service is extremely limited in summer. We suggest renting a car.

Favorite *Walking Easy* Hotel

Hotel la Bergerie
Three-Star; Owner - Familie Marullaz
Route de Téléphérique, 74110 Morzine
Tel: 4 50 79 13 69, **Fax:** 4 50 75 95 71
E-mail: info@hotel-bergerie.com, **Internet:** www.hotel-bergerie.com

A most charming chalet-style hotel, situated on a quiet street minutes from the village center, la Bergerie represents a high standard in comfort and Savoyard decor. Caroline Marullaz is ever present, and *Easy Walkers* will feel at home in the warm environs of the hotel and its public sitting areas. We felt as though we were in our own living room as we looked out on the gardens, heated swimming pool, and comfortable lounges.

Although la Bergerie is listed as a bed-and-breakfast hotel, if you book with *demi-pension* or half-board, Caroline will arrange for dinner at the best restaurants in Morzine. With twenty-two rooms available, ask for a room with a balcony facing the garden. These are fully equipped with miniature kitchenettes—everything from a small refrigerator and stove to a tiny dishwasher!

Easy Walkers will appreciate the informal, homelike, yet country-elegant atmosphere of la Bergerie.

Excursions

The Morzine Tourist Information Office is located in the village center.
Fax: 4 50 79 03 48
E-mail: touristoffice@morzine-avoriaz.com
Internet: www.morzine-avoriaz.com

1. Chamonix - See Chamonix chapter.

    Directions: Follow local road D902 south to Cluses, where you pick up the A40 highway, following signs to Chamonix/Mont Blanc.

2. Yvoire - See Chamonix chapter, Excursion #4.

    Directions: Take local road D902 north, following signs to Yvoire.

3. Geneva, Switzerland - See Chamonix chapter, Excursion #14.

    Directions: Follow local D902 south to Cluses, where you pick up the A40 highway, following signs to Geneva.

4. Les Gorges du Pont du Diable - See Chamonix chapter, Excursion #3.

    Directions: Take local road 902 north to the gorges.

Morzine Walks

Recommended Maps

❖ IGN 3528 ET—Morzine Massif du Chablais (preferred)

❖ Carte des Sentiers—La Vallée d'Aulps Morzine-Avoriaz, les Gets

Walk #1

Introductory Walk around the Village of Morzine
Walking Easy Time: 1 to 2 hours
Rating: Comfortable

The purpose of this walk is to acquaint you with Morzine village and the location of the Super Morzine and le Pléney lifts. If you arrive in the afternoon, this would be a good time to explore the area. Visit the Office du Tourisme, well signed and situated in the center of the village. This is a very modern office, and a local village map of Morzine is available at no charge. The office provides a small public area with Internet availability. However, in order to access the Internet, it's necessary to use a French telephone card, available at *tabac* and *presse* shops, and the keyboard is French style and has a different letter configuration.

    Start: You can follow the village map or, leave the Tourist Office, going down the main street toward the church (*eglise*) for a visit. Then walk toward the sports center (*Palais des Sports Patinoire*), and if time permits, walk the *parcours* or fitness course, starting under the tall bridge above. There is a public elevator that can take you up to the Super Morzine lift near the village center. Walk through the village, locate the little supermarkets, note the restaurants and shops, and return to your hotel.

Note: There are usually only two afternoon buses to return to Morzine from les Gets. Make sure you have the bus schedule with you—available in the Morzine Tourist Office—if you plan on taking this option.

Walk #2

Lift to le Pléney Top Station, Walk to Golf des Gets to les Chavannes Area and Return

Walking Easy Time: 3 to 4 hours

Rating: Comfortable

The trail from le Pléney (also spelled le Plénay on some maps) is a typical mountain path, with many ascents and descents—none very challenging—but *Easy Walkers* may wish to take these changes slowly. You'll pass les Gets Golf Course, where golfers take these hills in stride—no carts allowed! The views are remarkable and a *table d'orientation* near the start of the hike will put names to the surrounding mountain peaks. You'll return on the same path to the top station of the Pléney lift.

Directions: From Hotel la Bergerie, turn left and walk up the street. Bear right at the top to le Pléney Télécabine. Buy a round trip ticket to le Pléney.

Start: After exiting the lift, walk up the wide path, passing the Viking Hotel on your left, following signs LE PLÉNEY and LES CHAVANNES. About ten minutes after you've started walking, a little trail ascends up the hill on your right for a few minutes to a table of orientation and panoramic views. When ready, walk ahead, returning to the main trail toward les Chavannes. Soon, the golf course will be on your right, and while the map indicates you are hiking at about 5086 ft. (1550 m.), there are quite a few ascents and descents along the trail. As you approach les Chavannes, you have a few options:

1. Continue down and around to the top of les Gets lift, at 4869 ft. (1484 m.). If the timing is right, take the Chavannes gondolas down to les Gets for a visit to the village with a short bus ride back to Morzine.

2. Walk straight ahead toward Tête des Crêtes, or even farther, for as long as you wish. Aggressive walkers can continue on a much longer hike, up to the table of orientation, at 5988 ft. (1825 m.), over-

looking Col de Joux Plane. With this second option, return to the top station of the Pléney lift on the same trail, making sure you arrive before the lift station closes.

Walk #3
Lift to Super Morzine Top Station, Walk to Avoriaz and Return
Walking Easy Time: 3 to 5 hours
Rating: Comfortable

Today you'll visit Avoriaz, walking from the top station of the Super Morzine lifts. After viewing the panorama from the table d'orientation at the top of the chairlift, you'll walk along the crest to Col de la Joux Verte, and then to the ski village of Avoriaz, with options returning to Morzine. This comfortable hike is mostly on a wide trail with the usual mountain ascents and descents and super panoramic views.

Directions: Follow village walking signs to the Super Morzine Lift Station and buy a round-trip ticket. Take the gondola to Mid-Station Zore and change for the four-person chairlift to the Super Morzine Top Station.

Start: On exiting the chairlift, note the sign to the right AVORIAZ PAR LA CRÊTE. Look for the little trail to the left up to the table of orientation. After viewing the panorama and naming the mountains, begin walking in the direction of Avoriaz on the crest trail as it gently descends down to the main trail. As you pass the closed ski lift, a signed trail descends somewhat steeply from 5761 ft. (1756 m.) to the observation point at Bélvèdere, at 5309 ft. (1618 m.), overlooking the valley and Lake Montriond. But remember, if you walk down to this observation point, you'll have to hike back up to the main trail to continue today's walk.

Just past this closed lift station the trail splits. Continue ahead on the main upper trail to Col de la Joux Verte, at 5775 ft. (1760 m.) and its restaurant. After a rest and a cool drink, look down the back

of the terrace of the restaurant, and you'll see two unsigned paths through the forest, leading up to Avoriaz, at 5992 ft. (1814 m.). As you leave the restaurant, walk *down* the road and enter the unsigned path to Avoriaz. The lower path will border the Avoriaz golf course and lead you directly into Avoriaz. At Avoriaz you have two options:

1. Return to the top station of the Super Morzine lift on the same trail, with fresh views of the remarkable panorama—about four hours round-trip. Take the lift down to Morzine.

2. At the far end of Avoriaz, take the lift down to les Prodains and catch one of the two afternoon buses to Morzine. *Note: If you are considering the bus option, make sure you pick up a schedule from the Tourist Office as buses on this route are very limited.* You can also walk back to Morzine from the bottom of the Prodains lift (if it is still early and you are in the mood for extra walking). Follow signs to Morzine on the hiking trail.

Walk #4

Les Gets Gondola du Mont Chéry to Mid-Station Bélvèdere, Walk to Mont Caly and Return (Optional Excursion to Top Station Mont Chéry)
Walking Easy Time: 2 hours
Rating: Comfortable

Today you'll take a short 3¾-mile (6-km) drive from Morzine to the neighboring village of les Gets and take the Mont Chéry lift for a lovely balcony walk on an extra-wide jeep road to Mont Caly. This comfortable trail offers spectacular views all the way to the snow-covered peak of Mont Blanc. There are two nice restaurants along the way, one at the mid-station and one at your destination at Mont Caly.

Directions: Follow signs in Morzine and drive to les Gets. Park in the center of town or at the signed Mont Chéry Télécabine Station. Buy a

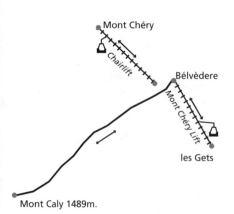

round-trip ticket to the top station at Mont Chéry. Take the gondola to the mid-station and change for the chairlift to the top. Check out the panorama at Mont Chéry and return on the chairlift to the mid-station.

Start: At the base of the chairlift, follow the sign to Mont Caly and walk up on the ascending, wide jeep path. After about fifteen to twenty minutes, you'll see a trail that buttonhooks to the right up the mountain in the directions of Mont Chéry. Do not take that trail. Instead, *Easy Walkers* will continue ahead on the wide trail to Mont Caly and its restaurant. Within the hour, you'll descend to the dross at Mont Caly and farther to the restaurant, if you wish. Return on the same trail to the mid-station and the descent by gondola to les Gets and your car.

Walk #5

Morzine to Cascade le Nyon and Return
Walking Easy Time: 2½ hours
Rating: Comfortable

Today's low-level, circular walk can be reserved for a cloudy day when you prefer to stay off the mountains. You will be traversing a pleasant, forest trail to the waterfall, a perfect spot for young family fun, then return to Morzine through the forest.

Start: Walk up to le Pléney Lift Station. Turn left, continuing down and around on the street to a trail that takes you off to the right, just before the river, signed CASCADE. This gentle walk is mostly through the forest with the river on your left. The trail eventually leads into the parking area at the Nyon Lift Station. Just before this parking area, take the trail to the right signed CASCADE DE NYON. At the waterfall, there are picnic opportunities and a play area for the children.

When ready, continue up and around, past the waterfall, crossing the auto road and walking just above the tiny hamlet of les Nantes. Walk under the Pléney lift, down to la Crusaz, and enter Morzine.

Walk #6

Lac des Mines d'Or to Col de Coux along the Chemin des Oiseaux Migrateurs and Return

Walking Easy Time: 4 hours
Rating: More challenging

Today's hike is on a spectacular, ascending trail from the parking area at Lac des Mines d'Or to Col de Coux. You'll rise from 4561 ft. (1390 m.) to 6300 ft. (1920 m.) on the Chemin des Oiseaux Migrateurs. As you ascend, look and listen for dozens of birds, and if you are lucky, you might spot an eagle or two! Return on the same trail to the lake and your car.

Directions: Drive down the hill in Morzine village, passing the church on route de la Mernaz, all the way to the parking signs at Lac des Mines d'Or.

Start: *Note: This trail ascends over 1640 ft. (500 m.), and* Easy Walkers *should be prepared for this rise in altitude.* Follow the sign ascending to Chalets de Fréterolle, at 5030 ft. (1533 m.). Shortly, pick up the Chemin des Oiseaux Migrateurs to Col de Coux. Hike only as far as you feel comfortable and return to the parking area on the same trail.

MÉRIBEL

When Glenn Miller's great orchestra of the 1930s and '40s played "String of Pearls," we doubt if they had the Méribel Valley in mind, but perhaps they should have. Thirteen small villages and hamlets are strung throughout this valley, recessed between two imposing mountain ranges. Nestled on a mountainside, Méribel is composed of four districts: Méribel Centre, Altiport, Belvédère, and Méribel-Mottaret, with altitudes rising to 5906 ft. (1800 m.) at Méribel-Mottaret, whose hotels and high-rise condominiums were built beneath the towering Aiguille du Fruit. Méribel's strict zoning code prescribes traditional alpine design, preserving a unity of style in the resort with Savoyard chalet architecture, using warmly shaded pine and rough-hewn stone.

Originally a tiny farming community, Méribel's winter sports possibilities were discovered by the British when their customary ski slopes in Austria were invaded by Germany in 1938. The four districts of Méribel are essentially new inventions for these winter sports enthusiasts, with few reminders of centuries gone by. Still, Méribel has a style, warmth, and charm that the neighboring ski megacenters of Courchevel and Val-Thorens forgot to consider in the rush to house their thousands of winter visitors. Méribel also recognizes that there can be life after ski season and provides the frequent and free summer *Méribus* to transport walkers between its districts and the lifts, and the Tourist Office closely supervises the hiking trails, their signs, and walking maps.

Méribel is the center of the *Trois Vallées* (the Three Valleys). The internationally famous ski resort of Courchevel lies in one adjacent valley, Val-Thorens, at 7546 ft. (2300 m.) the highest ski resort in Europe, in the other. The Trois Vallées is reputed to be the largest ski complex in the world, and with a single pass, skiers have access to all the ski lifts and runs in the area. The five resorts of the Trois Vallées—Méribel, Courchevel, Val-Thorens, les Menuires, la Tania—provide over 370 miles (600 km) of marked ski runs in winter, with 200 lifts. Over one thousand ski instructors work in this skiers paradise, which has the capacity to service over 250,000 skiers per hour!

The Vanoise National Park is bordered on the west by the Méribel Valley and includes a natural reserve with Lake Tuéda and Mont du Vallon, at 9686 ft. (2952 m.), where *Easy Walkers* will hike. Walking in the Méribel area is a pleasure; the trails have many ascents and descents, but most are within the range of *Easy Walkers.*

The French Alps

Transportation

By Plane - Geneva Cointrin Airport is located 75 miles (120 km) north of Méribel. It's more convenient to rent a car at the airport and drive to Méribel than to use train or bus connections.

By Train - Méribel is 12 miles (18 km) from the Moûtiers train station, which services TGV (high-speed) trains to and from Paris. During the summer, there are four buses a day to and from the Moûtiers train station to Méribel, with taxis also available.

By Car - From southern or western France, drive to Albertville, taking N90 southeast to Moûtiers where you follow signs to Méribel. From the north, drive to Albertville and take N90 southeast to Moûtiers, following above directions. Drive toward Méribel Centre, following signs to Altiport and then le Belvédère, if that is where your hotel is located.

From Geneva's Cointrin Airport, take superhighway A40 east, exiting at Sallanches, following signs to and driving through Megève and Albertville, where you follow earlier directions for the local road to Méribel.

From the Aosta Valley in Italy, drive on S26 and take it south over Col du Petit St. Bernard and the French border, past la Rosière to Bourg St-Maurice. Drive on N90 west toward Moûtiers, watching for the signs to Méribel.

Méribus (*Navette Vallée de Méribel*) - Free, scheduled shuttle buses run throughout the resort from 8:00 A.M. to 8:00 P.M., stopping at Altiport, Belvédère, Méribel Tourist Office, Bois d'Arbin, la Chaudanne, Lake

Tuéda, Méribel-Mottaret, and Mottaret-Hameau. The red dots on the village map in back of the *Bienvenue à Méribel—Welcome to Méribel* brochure indicate the bus stops. The Tourist Office can supply a bus schedule, and there is also one in the brochure.

Favorite *Walking Easy* Hotel

Hotel Allodis

Three-star; Owner - Familie Front

Le Belvédère, B.P. 43 F, 73550 Méribel

Tel: 4 79 00 56 00, **Fax:** 4 79 00 59 28

E-mail: allodis@wanadoo.fr, **Internet:** www.hotel-allodis.com

The Hotel Allodis is a three-star hotel with an excellent kitchen and a caring staff who will help to make your *Walking Easy* vacation in Méribel a belle expérience. The chalet hotel, designed and built in 1988 by a well-known local architect, is in le Belvédère, one of the highest areas in Méribel—situated against the ski runs and overlooking a marvelous panorama of mountains and forests. Although the road ends at the Hotel Allodis, a convenient Méribus stop is outside the front door, taking summer hikers to every section of the area.

Boasting modern amenities—indoor swimming pool, half-court tennis, sauna, fitness room, game room, and lovely gardens and sun-terrace—the Hotel Allodis was headquarters for CBS during the Albertville Winter Olympics. Its forty-three bedrooms and its public rooms are decorated in Savoie-contemporary style, making extensive use of traditional pine furniture and moldings, blending with contemporary fabrics and fixtures. In addition to the spacious bedrooms, all with balconies and views of the mountains, the hotel includes one large apartment and twenty-two mixed suites, some with lofts, fireplaces, and sitting rooms.

A typical French continental breakfast is served in the cheerful breakfast room. Dinner is a gastronomic experience, beginning with crisp Porthault linens, flowered Limoges/Porthault porcelain, and lovely flower arrangements. The demi-pension menu is artfully composed to increase the sensory experience—the taste and visual appeal of the chef's creations are outstanding. What a wonderful way to end a day of hiking in the mountains surrounding Méribel!

Lifts in and around Méribel

Note: The round-trip ticket cost is the same for all lifts. You're actually paying for the ascent; the descent is free. The Méripass Card is valid for six days and gives access to all Méribel, les Menuires, and Courchevel lifts, plus use of the Olympic Centre (swimming and ice skating). A photo ID is required. If you are staying in the area for only a few days, a one-day pass is a good option if you are taking the Courchevel walk and excursion. This pass allows one-day access to all lifts.

Télécabine de Tougnète - This gondola, rising up to 7874 ft. (2400 m.), runs several times a week in summer (at this printing: Monday through Thursday). It's located in la Chaudanne area near the ice rink. (See Walk #1.)

Directions: Take the Méribus and get off at the ice rink. It's a few minutes' walk up to the gondola station.

Télécabine Burgin-Saulire - This gondola rises to la Saulire peak, at 8859 ft. (2700 m.), usually on the days the Pas du Lac gondola is closed. It leaves from la Chaudanne area, next to the Tougnète cable station.

Directions: Take the Méribus and get off at the ice rink. Walk up to the station.

Télécabine du Pas du Lac - This gondola in the Méribel-Mottaret area rises to 8859 ft. (2700 m.) and usually runs on Monday, Tuesday, Thursday, and occasionally on Sunday. (See Walks #2 and #3.)

Directions: Take the Méribus to Méribel-Mottaret and exit at the lift station.

Olympic Gondolas - Located at the ice rink, these gondolas run continuously Tuesday, Wednesday, and Thursday, through les Allues to

> **Hint:** *Cable lifts around Méribel do not operate every day in the summer, so walkers should be very careful in selecting the day for a particular hike. We strongly suggest checking days and hours of operation with the Tourist Office before arrival.*

Brides les Baines.

Excursions

The Méribel Tourist Office is located in the center of the resort.

Fax: 4 79 00 59 61
E-mail: info@meribel.net
Internet: www.meribel.net

1. **Méribel Golf Course -** Magnificently set in its mountain environment, its fairways are lined with pine forests, and the clubhouse is an alpine chalet. You must buy a golf license to play on this course. Carts are available.

2. **Tuéda Natural Reserve -** Created in 1990, this nature area within the Vanoise National Park reaches from Lake Tuéda to the Gebroulaz Glacier via the Refuge des Saut. Along the banks of the Doron River, it comprises 2700 acres (1100 hectares) of natural beauty and unspoiled wilderness. A marked botanical trail will allow *Easy Walkers* to discover over eighty species of alpine flowers and plants, including the rare Cembro pine. (See Walks #4 and #5.)
   Directions: *Drive or take the Méribus to the large parking area outside the reserve in the Méribel-Mottaret area.*

3. **Vanoise National Park -** Situated between the upper valleys of the Tarentaise and Maurienne, this park's mountains and glaciers reach elevations from 4101 ft. (1250 m.) to 12,638 ft. (3852 m.) at the summit of the Grande Casse. The Vanoise and neighboring Gran Paradiso National Park in Italy together form the largest nature reserve in Western Europe. More than one thousand different varieties of flowers can be found in the park, which also boasts the largest herd of ibex in France and over 4500 chamois. Smaller animals include the hare and marmot, with bird species represented by golden eagles, ptarmigan, black grouse, and partridge. The Vanoise includes 310 miles (500 km) of marked trails (access into the park is only by foot), with an exceptional richness of protected flora and fauna. There is also a network of long hikes over mountain passes, with reserved lodging available in any of forty park *refuges*. Check in at the National Park counter in the Méribel Tourist Office for a slide show and reservations for organized trips into the park.

4. **Chamonix -** This world capital of mountaineering is dominated by the powerful majesty of Mont Blanc, the highest mountain in Europe—but

the town successfully combines boutiques, restaurants, hotels, and services of a large resort with the incomparable, awesome, natural surroundings of the French Alps. (See the Chamonix chapter for further details.)

Directions: Drive to Moûtiers, watching for signs for N90 to Albertville. In Albertville, pick up N212 north through Megève, then D909 into St-Gervais, following signs into Chamonix.

5. **Albertville -** Of interest here is the **XVI Winter Olympic Games Visitors Center**, an exhibition and information center where you can relive the atmosphere of the 1992 Winter Olympics. Note costumes from the opening and closing ceremonies, as well as photos and films. On a hill just above Albertville is the Medieval city of **Conflans,** with ancient, wrought-iron signs and twelfth- to thirteenth-century facades. Take time to look at the **castle** and walk on the old, winding streets of Conflans. Enter the town through a gateway, **la Porte de Savoie,** with remains of the town walls rebuilt in the fourteenth century still visible. Opposite the gate is **la Tour Ramus,** a fifteenth-century tower containing only a staircase. Walking further, note a little square with a **stone fountain,** designed in 1711 by an officer in the army of King Louis XIV of France. On rue Gabriel Pérouse, a little path leads to **la Place de la Petite Roche (Little Rock Square),** where strong arches still support the walls. The old shop district is located from here to the main square, **la Grande Place.** To the left, a short, steep flight of stairs leads to a **church,** built in the eighteenth century on the site of a church burned in 1632. Note the 1714 altarpiece and the Baroque pulpit. If you walk up the path at the church, the highest point in the area is at the ruins of the Red Castle or **le Château Rouge,** built in the fourteenth century, now in complete disrepair. Walk back and pass through **la Porte Tarine** or the Tarin Gate, used by ancient peoples coming from the Tarentaise region and from Italy—two brick arches can still be seen. If you return to la Grand Place, the main square where markets and fairs were held for centuries, note the **fountain** in the middle, designed in Baroque style in 1750. Also in the square is the Red House, **la Maison Rouge,** built in 1397 and now used as a museum of local history. In the Place de la Grande Roche is the **Saracen Tower,** built in the twelfth century. Wander in the maze of narrow, cobblestone streets where old houses have been converted to cafes and workshops.

Directions: *Take the road to Moûtiers, picking up N90 and following directions to Albertville and Conflans.*

6. **Courchevel -** The Saint-Bon Valley developed into one of the world's prime ski centers after World War I with the creation of Courchevel, and area planners decided to develop and expand winter sports to allow this area to compete at the same level as other great European ski resorts of the era: Davos, Cortina, etc. The Tovets mountainside, with north-facing slopes for consistent snow quality on a sun-filled plateau, was the stage for building the Courchevels. Each of the three areas—Courchevel 1300 (le Praz), Courchevel 1550, and Courchevel 1850—are referred to by the altitude in meters of each village.

In summer, cows in the mountain pastures around Courchevel still produce almost a thousand wheels of rich Beaufort cheese, the region's main natural resource, and local woodworkers still carve the Saint-Bon style of furniture—rustic, solid, and decorated with geometric patterns—mostly the famous pine of the Arolles. *Easy Walkers* might take the lift from Méribel to enjoy the magnificent views of the snow-capped peaks of the French Alps. From there, a cable car and gondola then descends to Courchevel 1850. (See Walks #2 and #3.)

Directions: *Drive to la Tania and follow signs to Courchevel.*

7. **Val d'Isère and Tignes -** See the Les Arcs/Bourg-Saint-Maurice chapter, Walk #6.

Directions: *Drive to Moûtiers and follow signs to N90 and Bourg-Saint-Maurice. Just past Bourg, turn right on D902 and head to Tignes and Val d'Isère.*

8. **Annecy -** See Megève chapter, Excursion #4.

Directions: *Drive to Moûtiers and follow signs to N90 and Albertville, where you pick up N212 going north. At Acieries, take N508 past Faverges, around the left side of the lake to Annecy.*

9. **Belleville Valley Towns -** The Vallée de Belleville is composed of twenty-four small alpine villages and two mega-ski resorts: **Val Thorens** and **Les Menuires.** Val-Thorens, at 7546 ft. (2300 m.), is the highest resort in Western Europe, and its summer scenery, without the dazzling snow cover of winter, can be stark and harsh because it lies above the

tree line. The **Val-Thorens Téléphérique de Caron** rises to 10,499 ft. (3200 m.). In Les Menuires, at 5955 ft. (1815 m.), the **Télécabine de la Masse, des Bruyères et du Mont de la Chambre** rises to 9351 ft. (2850 m.). **St-Martin-de-Belleville** is an authentic Savoie village nestled in the center of the valley, whose residents try to preserve the history and heritage of the past with festivals and fairs. Visit the ancient church in St.-Martin-de-Belleville and the Church of Notre Dame on the way to Les Menuires.

Directions: *Drive into Moûtiers and follow signs to the Belleville Valley, driving through the villages of St-Martin-de-Belleville, les Menuires, and finally, Val-Thorens.*

10. **Chambéry -** This beautiful city is called the historic capital of the Savoie region. From 1295 to 1536, it was the capital of a sovereign state stretching from Bern to Nice and Lyons to Turin, and its past lingers in the quaint, old streets of historic Old Town.

Walk along the pedestrian streets in the renovated old part of the city, near the famous **Elephant Fountain** or the **Carré Curial** shopping center, located in an old barracks dating from Napoleon's time. The **Musée Savoisien** contains archaeological treasures from prehistoric sites around Lake Bourget, the **Musée des Beaux-Arts** has one of the finest collections of Italian paintings in France, the **Musée des Charmettes** is the country house where Jean-Jacques Rousseau lived from 1732 to 1742, and the **Musée d'Histoire Naturelle** contains natural history exhibits.

Directions: *Drive into Moûtiers, following signs to Albertville on N90. Stay on N90 and pick up the A430 expressway, then A43 and A41 into Chambéry.*

11. **Aix-les-Bains and Lac du Bourget -** Aix is the second-largest town in the Savoie and the most-fashionable and largest spa in eastern France, stretching down to the shores of Lake Bourget, the largest natural lake in France. Stroll in Aix's charming Old Town district and among its gardens. Many traces of the town's ancient past have been preserved: the **Roman Arch of Campanus,** the **Roman baths,** the **Temple of Diana,** and the **Archaeological Museum,** with fine Roman remains and statuary. Visit the **Musée Faure,** containing sculptures by Rodin and a fine

collection of Impressionist paintings, and stop by the **aquarium** and **Maison du Lac** on the waterfront. Boat trips on the lake take you to the **Savières Canal** or **Hautecombe Abbey,** founded in 1101 by the Benedictine monks, where the princes of Savoie are entombed. If you are driving around the lake, visit the eleventh-century priory at **le Bourget-du-Lac**, and drive through the famous **Chautagne vineyards** or to **Mont Revard** for breathtaking views of the lake.

Directions: Drive into Moûtiers, following N90 toward Albertville, where you pick up A430 south. Then take A43 and A41 past Chambéry into Aix.

12. Bus Tours - The Transavoie Bus Company runs excursions from Brides to many interesting villages and areas if you prefer not to drive. They include **Annecy, Beaufort, Chamonix, Chartreuse, Hautecombe, Megève, Mont Blanc, Pralognan, Val d'Isere, Vercors,** and **Yvoire/Geneva.** Check at the Tourist Office for days of departure, length of trips, and costs.

Méribel Walks

Recommended Maps:
> ❖ Cartes IGN—#3534 OT—Les Trois Vallées Modane

Walk #1

Méribel Lift to Tougnète Top Station, Walk to Méribel-Mottaret
Walking Easy Time: 2 to 3 hours
Rating: Comfortable

You'll see the best view of the Méribel Valley from the peak station of the Tougnète gondola lift. Try to make this excursion when the weather is clear, keeping in mind that this lift does not operate every day. Restaurants at the lift stations may not be open in summer, so it might be advisable to pack a picnic lunch. You'll leave from la Chaudanne, a minute or two south of Méribel Centre, near the Olympic Ice Arena, for a gondola ride to the Tougnète Top Station, at 7973 ft. (2430 m.), and fabulous views of the Méribel area and the adjacent valley.

On one of our visits to the Tougnète peak, the internationally famous

Tour de France bicycle race was ending one of its sections in Val-Thorens in the adjacent valley, and hundreds of people were walking and biking down into this high mountain village to watch the bikers finish their arduous day! From this vantage point, you'll be able to better understand the importance of ski development in the Méribel Valley. This was the site of the downhill skiing events at the 1992 Winter Olympics, and this mountain range is the center of the Trois Vallées, providing winter skiing for 250,000 skiers per hour. *Easy Walkers* have many walking options from the top Tougnète station, but today, you'll descend on a jeep road near the Tougnète peak and walk past the mid-station for the gentle walk to Méribel-Mottaret and a Méribus return to your hotel.

Directions: Take the free Méribus to the Olympic Ice Rink at la Chaudanne and walk a few minutes to the Tougnète lift. Buy a one-way ticket to the top, taking the two-section gondola to the peak.

Start: After exiting the gondola and enjoying the views, walk on the jeep road down on your right past the restaurant. Take the right fork, *not* going ahead to Pas de Cherferie. Walk on a zigzagging path. Stay to the left at the first intersection. Continue on the jeep road in the direction of Méribel and the mid-station. Just above the mid-station, continue on the road below the restaurant as it descends, following the sign MOTTARET to the right. Walk along the mountain toward the Chalets du Méribel-Mottaret, where you have two options:

1. Turn left and walk down to a large parking area and another Méribus stop.

2. Walking ahead takes you up on a route above Lake Tuéda, where you can then turn down a zigzagging path to the end of the lake and walk back along the lake to the parking area and the Méribus stop—a walk extension.

Walk #2

Pas du Lac or Burgin-Saulire Lift to la Saulire, Lift Down to Courchevel 1850, Walk to Méribel/Altiport

Walking Easy Time: 2½ to 3½ hours

Rating: Comfortable

Note: Before attempting this walk, check with the Tourist Office to see if all lifts are operating on the same day! Reserve the better part of a clear day for a series of high-mountain lifts to the internationally famous ski resort of Courchevel 1850. You might want to pack a picnic lunch for today's excursion, although there are some limited restaurant options in Courchevel. You'll take a lift from Méribel-Mottaret to the peak station of la Saulire for an exciting 360-degree panorama of the surrounding peaks. After descending to Courchevel on a giant, 160-passenger cable car, you'll transfer to a gondola for the final descent to Courchevel 1850, the beginning of today's walk. Courchevel 1850 is a modern ski center, built in the 1950s to service winter sports enthusiasts. It's a mix of concrete condominiums, apartments, and hotels, many closed in summer.

Directions: Take the Méribus to whichever lift is open to la Saulire. (Check with the Tourist Office.) *Note: If you haven't bought a six-day Méripass, purchase a one-day lift pass, entitling you to unlimited lifts in the area for the day.* Take the lift to the top station, remaining in the car as you pass through the mid-station. Exit at la Saulire, at 8859 ft. (2700 m.), and enjoy the incredible vista of snow-covered peaks and the highest glacier in the Vanoise, *La Grande Casse.*

When ready, walk up to your left to the Courchevel-la Saulire Lift Station for the descent to the mid-station on the giant cable car. At the mid-station, change to a gondola for the short ride to Courchevel 1850.

Start: Turn left on leaving the lift building, passing several large hotels, and descend on the wide auto road to its termination at a paved circle and ski lift. Take the *unmarked* gravel path left in the direction of the forest, where the path narrows to a comfortable wagon path. A sign indicates the path is for cross-country skiing, and while it says not for

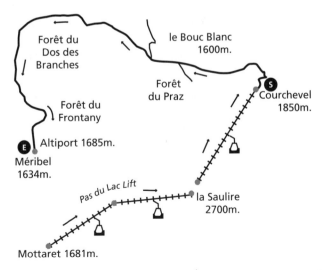

walking, those directions are for winter only. For the remainder of this walk, stay on the main path in the direction of Méribel.

In a few minutes, another sign indicates the path to Plantrey and Bouc-Blanc, with another not-so-timely warning, Be careful, you are crossing a major alpine run, give way to the skiers! Little chance of skiers now, so continue ahead. Note the superb views of small villages and hamlets dotting the valley and mountains on the right; there are side paths that can tempt you into the forest, but remain on the major trail. After a while, signs confirm your direction to Méribel.

It's interesting to note that you'll be walking through three forests on your way from Courchevel to Méribel/Altiport. The first is Forêt du Praz, and it takes about forty-five minutes to exit this forest on to an open meadow lined with wild flowers. Continue ahead, meeting a signed junction for le Bouc-Blanc and a trail going up to the left to Lac Bleu, but forge ahead on the main path, following the sign for Méribel.

You now enter the second forest, Forêt du Dos des Branches, where the road eventually divides. Follow the path up to the left, ascending easily in the direction of Méribel. This trail is now blazed regularly with yellow dots. The golf course at Altiport appears through the trees on the right, and although it's possible to take a steep mountain path to Altiport on the left, do *not* take that trail, but remain on the main path, following additional ALTIPORT signs all the way to a paved auto road.

Here, *Easy Walkers* have two options to catch the Méribus back to their hotel:

1. Turn left and walk up the paved road to reach Altiport, the Altiport Hotel, the golf course, and the bus stop in the parking area in front of the hotel.

2. Make a right turn and walk down to the restaurant le Blanchot and another bus stop (*arret navette*). Check the bus schedule, and if there is time, enjoy the sun-terrace of this restaurant, overlooking the golf course.

Walk #3

Pas du Lac or Burgin-Saulire Lift to la Saulire, Lift Down to Courchevel Mid-Station, Walk to Courchevel 1850, Lift to la Saulire, Walk to Méribel-Mottaret

Walking Easy Time: 2½ to 4 hours
Rating: Comfortable

Note: There are a few conditions you should think about before setting off. First, confirm with the Tourist Office that the Saulire and Courchevel lifts are operating on the same day. Second, you may not wish to visit Courchevel again if you are planning to take Walk #2. And of course, the weather should be sunny and clear, as we recommend for all high-level excursions. Today's walk utilizes a combination of lift systems, interspersed with downhill walking. It also affords *Easy Walkers* the opportunity of viewing the Méribel Valley, Méribel-Mottaret, and Courchevel 1850.

You'll take the Pas du Lac or Burgin-Saulire lift from Méribel-Mottaret to the peak of la Saulire, at 8859 ft. (2700 m.). Here are fabulous views over Courchevel and the Vanoise National Park, including Mont du Vallon, at 9686 ft. (2952 m.), towered over by the Aiguille de Péclet, at 11,684 ft. (3561 m.), looking down on the famous ski resort of Val-Thorens. In the other direction, the Glacier de la Vanoise is bordered by the Aiguille du Fruit, at 10,010 ft. (3051 m.), and below them lies the internationally renowned ski resort of Courchevel 1850—today's destination.

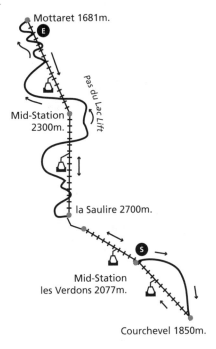

From the peak at la Saulire, you'll descend to the Courchevel Mid-Station and walk down to Courchevel 1850. After visiting this resort, you'll return to la Saulire, using the gondola and cable car. *Easy Walkers* now have the option of walking back to Méribel-Mottaret, a descent of 3281 ft. (over 1000 m.), on a well-graded, open, jeep road, or taking the lift down to the mid-station for the gentle walk to Méribel-Mottaret.

Directions: Take the Méribus, getting off at the lift station in Méribel-Mottaret. *Note: Purchase a one-day Méribel lift pass if you haven't bought a six-day Méripass.* Take the lift to la Saulire Top Station and its spectacular panorama. Walk up to the Courchevel cable car station and take the large cable car to les Verdons, at 6815 ft. (2077 m.)—the Courchevel Mid-Station.

Start: Exit the mid-station and walk to your left on a well-graded path, passing your first right turn and walking down past and under two ski lifts to the bend in the road. Here, a forest trail takes you ahead into Courchevel 1850. If you wish, however, you can stay on the road as it zigzags to the little lake and golf course on your right, continuing to walk into Courchevel from there. Courchevel 1850 is not a particularly pretty village in summer, but you might enjoy having lunch or browsing through the shops in town. This village was built to accommodate the tens of thousands of winter visitors who come to the area for outstanding skiing.

When ready, take the Verdons gondola back to the mid-station and change for the cable car up to la Saulire, where *Easy Walkers* have two options:

1. Descend to Méribel-Mottaret by walking down the wide jeep trail, past the Pas du Lac Mid-Station. Turn left at the fork in the road, zigzagging down to Méribal-Mottaret and the main road. This is a descent of a little over 3281 ft. (1000 m.), and you should stop occasionally and rest your knees.

2. Take the lift down to the Pas du Lac Mid-Station and walk to Méribel-Mottaret from there. The descent from the mid-station is only 1969 ft. (600 m.). Access to the path down to Méribel-Mottaret is to the left as you exit the mid-station. Make your first left at the fork in the road, continuing down on the wide jeep trail, through open meadows ablaze with flowers in summer, with the wooden chalets of Méribel-Mottaret and the Olympic ski slopes on the opposite side of the valley visible at all times.

With either option, at the main road take the Méribus to the stop closest to your hotel.

Walk #4

Méribel-Mottaret into the Vanoise National Park to Mont Vallon and Return
Walking Easy Time: 6 hours
Rating: More challenging

Note: There are limited facilities and no food is available on today's hike, so pack a picnic lunch and, of course, plenty of water. A more challenging, full-day's excursion is in store for *Easy Walkers* today.

The walk to Mont Vallon is rated "more challenging," but it is within the range of those in good physical shape. There is *no* difficult or perilous hiking involved, but the altitude increases from 5591 to 7051 ft. (1704 to 2149 m.)—a rise of 1460 ft. (445 m.)—on a wide jeep road. The return is a delightful descent along the same path. This is the only route available to reach Mont Vallon, and it takes three to four hours. Yet, this is one of the most popular hikes in the Vanoise National Park and on a clear day many walkers take this hike.

The Vanoise was developed to preserve and protect the upper valleys of the Tarentaise region. It encompasses many mountains over 9843 ft. (3000 m.) and numerous glaciers. Preserves within the park are reserved for the protection of nature without the intrusion of civilization, except for the mountain *refuges*. In winter, skiers enjoy the natural environment, but they must leave the reserve at the end of the day. The walk back is along the same path, passing Lake Tuéda, for the return to Méribel-Mottaret.

Directions: Take a morning Méribus for the ride to the Mottaret-Lake Tuéda parking area. Of course, if you have your own car, there is plenty of available parking at the entrance to the Tuéda Preserve. Follow the signs to Méribel-Mottaret and Lac de Tuéda for the short drive from Méribel.

Start: Walk through the parking area and on to the wide plain, passing to the right side of Lake Tuéda. At the end of the little lake, a trail ascends to the right, passing a small dairy farm where local cheeses are sold. You'll ascend from 5591 ft. (1704 m.) at the lake to 5906 ft. (1800 m.) to reach the main path going directly to Mont Vallon. This path is well marked with signs to Mont Vallon, and it climbs up to the lift station, at 7051 ft. (2149 m.). Take the ascent slowly and rest as often as needed.

When ready, walk back along the same trail, this time descending pleasantly, with views of Lake Tuéda. Walk to the parking area for the bus or your car back to the hotel.

Walk #5

Pas du Lac Lift to Mid-Station, Walk to Chalet du Fruit to Lake Tuéda to Méribel-Mottaret (with Possible Extension to Refuge du Saut)

Walking Easy Time: 3½ to 6 hours

Rating: More challenging

Today's more aggressive hike begins from the mid-station of the Pas du Lac Lift in Méribel-Mottaret and enters the Tuéda Reserve in the Vanoise National Park in the direction of Refuge du Saut. *Easy Walkers* have the option of descending down and around to Chalet du Fruit, at 6004 ft. (1830 m.), or taking the extension past Chalet de la Plagne all the way to Refuge du Saut, at 6956 ft. (2120 m.). You'll return on the same trail, then descend to Chalet du Fruit, down through Plan de Tuéda, past the lake, into Méribel-Mottaret. It's possible to take this hike starting from the lake, ascending past Chalet du Fruit and hiking on to the *refuge*, but the climb up to the chalet may be a bit steep, although it can be handled if done slowly. At any rate, we have suggested taking it from the mid-station of the Pas du Lac lift, avoiding the climb past the Chalet du Fruit. Pack your lunch and water, of course.

Directions: Take the Méribus to the Pas du Lac Lift Station in Méribel-Mottaret. Buy a ticket to the mid-station and exit there.

Start: Turn left as you exit the mid-station and walk on the jeep road, descending down the mountain. Walk under the gondolas, then under one ski lift down to a second ski lift, where the trail continues into the meadows and up to the left. This is where you depart from the road, following the sign REFUGE DU SAUT. Do *not* walk down the road to Méribel-Mottaret, as you did in Walk #3. This trail continues up through the meadows and forest until it meets the wider path descending to Chalet du Fruit. You now have a few options:

1. If you choose to take the extended hike to Refuge du Saut, continue down the road for a minute or two, following the sign to the left, past the Chalet de la Plagne, up to the Refuge du Saut, at 6961 ft. (2126 m.). If you take this extension, remember, you can reverse your direction at any time.

2. If you choose not to take the extension, continue down the road, taking the rather steep but manageable descent, past Chalet du Fruit into the Plan de Tuéda. Walk past the lake to the parking area and the Méribus.

Walk #6

Les Allues to le Villaret to Hauteville to Villarnard to Hauteville to les Allues
Walking Easy Time: 3½ to 4½ hours
Rating: Comfortable

Our walk today begins in the lower Méribel Valley in its main village of les Allues, 4 miles (6 km) from Méribel. You can use the Olympic Gondolas from Méribel to les Allues instead of driving. The word *allues* dates back to the thirteenth century, when the inhabitants of the area were exempted from local taxes, becoming known as freeholders, or *allodis* in the old French language. The church in this village dates back to the seventeenth century and is dedicated to St. Martin, patron saint of the village.

You'll descend on a narrow path, over a rushing stream, to the stone remains of an ancient mill. There is the option to continue up to le Villaret and take the quiet, country road to Hauteville, or to ascend to Hauteville through the forest on a steeper path. A forest path then takes you around the mountain, ascending and descending to the hamlet of Villarnard. You will return along the same path, but once on the road at Hauteville, you can stay on this quiet road all the way back to les Allues. This can be a picnic lunch day, as there are few restaurants between the beginning and end of the hike.

Directions: Although it is possible to drive to les Allues, we recommend using the Olympic Gondolas (if they are in operation the day of this walk) from la Chaudanne/Méribel to les Allues. If you drive from Méribel to les Allues, park in any available spot in the area of the church.

Start: If you arrive on the Olympic Gondolas, follow the forest path ahead, making a right turn at the sign to le Batchu. If you arrive by car, walk back to the main road on the little auto road on which you entered les Allues, passing the tennis court on your left. Cross the road and walk a minute to your right to the LE VILLARET and HAUTEVILLE signs. Follow the descending path on the left, down through a small suburban area. Continue descending under the Olympic Gondolas, heading toward the rushing water below, and cross on a small wooden bridge. After crossing the bridge, note the stone remains of an old mill. A sign a few feet ahead directs you to the right to le Villaret. This path takes you up through woods and meadows to the hamlet of le Villaret, at 3855 ft. (1175 m.), and a paved country road. Make a left turn on the road in the direction of Hauteville.

It's also possible, from the point after the bridge crossing, to take a short cut by walking to your left to Hauteville on a rocky, descending trail—but walkers who choose this trail will then have to find an *unsigned,* steep path on their right, rising up the mountain into the forest. This trail meets the country auto road before Hauteville.

At 3967 ft. (1209 m.) in Hauteville, the road ends. Take the left path through the woods in the direction of Villarnard. The path rolls around and down the mountain to the hamlet of Villarnard, at 3393 ft. (1034 m.). Return on the same path to Hauteville and take the quiet, country road through le Villaret, all the way down to les Allues and your car or the Olympic Gondolas.

Walk #7

Tougnète Lift to Top Station, Ridge Walk to Pas de Cherferie to Col de la Lune to les Allues

Walking Easy Time: 5 to 6 hours

Rating: More challenging

Directions: Take the Méribus to the Olympic Ice Rink at la Chaudanne and walk a few minutes to the Tougnète lift. Buy a ticket to the top.

Start: Exiting at the top station of the Tougnète lift, 7973 ft. (2430 m.), descend gently along the ridge of the Cherferie to Pas de Cherferie and then ascend, either by road or by mountain trail, to le Verdet, at 7527 ft. (2294 m.). Continue along the Sentier des Crêtes to Col de la Lune, at 5857 ft. (1785 m.), for the descent to les Allues, at 3708 ft. (1130 m.) by way of the refuge at la Traie. Take the Olympic Gondolas back to Méribel, remembering that the gondolas close at 5:00 P.M.

It's possible to cut this walk short at Pas de Cherferie. Instead of climbing up to les Crêtes, take the descending jeep road back to the mid-station of Tougnète, where you can ride down to Méribel by lift.

LES ARCS/BOURG-SAINT-MAURICE

A typical village in the heart of the French Savoie Alps, Bourg-Saint-Maurice and its high neighbor Les Arcs can provide *Easy Walkers* with a stimulating, outdoor vacation. You'll discover the natural as well as the cultural resources and treasures of these strategically located country villages, with all the necessary resort amenities, but where herds of cattle are still led to graze each summer in high, alpine pastures.

The Upper Tarentaise region of the Savoie Alps is the setting for the charming village of Bourg-Saint-Maurice, at 2658 ft. (810 m.), and its mountain neighbors of Les Arcs 1600, 1800, and 2000. Situated at the crossroads of some of the world's best winter skiing and summer hiking, Les Arcs and Bourg-Saint-Maurice are easily accessible by car and offer *Easy Walkers* a variety of trails for day-hiking.

The traditions of old Savoie are still in evidence. Baroque churches with ancient frescoes and local museums with old costumes and artifacts are evidence of a rich inheritance. Each summer Saturday morning, farmers, bakers, and cheese and sausage makers from the surrounding countryside set up a traditional country market in Bourg-Saint-Maurice. You walk through streets and alleys crowded with local vendors presenting the best foods and wines of the region—baskets of freshly picked peaches, tomatoes, lettuce, and melons; wheels of Savoyard cheeses in all shapes, sizes, and aromas; loaves of country breads; local fresh fish packed in ice; honey, from combs to cakes; and dozens of varieties of local *saucisson* (sausage). To this enticing mixture of sights and aromas, add the usual proliferation of T-shirt and apparel stands.

Les Arcs is linked to Bourg by an "umbilical cord": a funicular providing quick, comfortable transportation between the two areas. While Bourg-Saint-Maurice provides the traditional and commercial impetus, Les Arcs brings thousands of visitors to the region for summer and winter sporting activities. Les Arcs was the scene of a major downhill ski event of the 1992 Winter Albertville Olympics, with proud evidences everywhere of that honor. The mountain includes three distinct areas, each designated by its altitude—Arc 1600 (meters), Arc 1800, and Arc 2000. The first hotel in Arc 1600 opened in 1968, followed by rapid hotel and apartment development at Arc 1800 and Arc 2000. Arc 1800 is the largest complex within Les Arcs, with three sections, Charvet, Villard, and Charmettoger. Access to Arc 1600 by the ultramodern funicular was introduced in 1989, and a free bus system shuttles visitors back and forth between the funicular and the Arc villages.

Vacationers can leave Paris in the morning by express train to Bourg-Saint-Maurice, take a bus or funicular to Arc 1600, the shuttle bus to the Arc of their choice, and be in their room in time for dinner, without the hassle of driving! The transportation system and a reasonably priced, all-inclusive discount card (offering holders unlimited use of all operating lifts and the funicular), allows *Easy Walkers* to stay either in the more traditional village of Bourg-Saint-Maurice or up on the mountain in one of Les Arcs, site of *Walking Easy* in this area.

Yes, Les Arcs was constructed for skiers, but walkers can take advantage of its lifts and trails—some lifts operating every day, and others operating three to five days a week. You'll have the opportunity of rising to 10,499 ft. (3200 m.) at the Aiguille Rouge, with impressive views of the snow-covered Mont Blanc range to the north. Walks can begin and end at the same Arc station or at other Arc stations, but there is always a bus to take you back to your desired location.

You'll also have the opportunity of taking an excursion to the internationally famous ski resorts of Tignes and Val d'Isère, to Chamonix, to the medieval city of Conflans at Albertville, or to the "Venice of the Savoy Alps," the lovely lake town of Annecy.

Les Arcs/Bourg-Saint-Maurice are enjoyable *Walking Easy* base villages, and few Americans have discovered these summer, alpine treasures.

Transportation

By Plane - The international airport in Geneva, Switzerland, is 93 miles (150 km) to the north. Car rentals are available at the airport.

By Train - From Paris, a combination of high-speed (TGV) and local train can bring you to Bourg-Saint-Maurice from Paris in about five hours.

By Car - Les Arcs/Bourg-Saint-Maurice is easily accessible. To drive from Geneva, pick up superhighway A40 south of Geneva, driving east to Sallanches, where you follow signs to Albertville, taking N212 past Megève to Albertville. Pick up N90 southeast and drive past Moûtiers into Bourg-Saint-Maurice. If your hotel is in Les Arcs, drive past the railroad station and follow the signs to Les Arcs. Once on the mountain, the signs will direct you to Arc 1600, Arc 1800, or Arc 2000.

Northwestern Italy is traversed through the Aosta Valley and the road over the Col du Petit St. Bernard. While there is train and bus service in this area, you'll probably want the convenience of a car.

Local Bus Service - There is regular bus service from the railroad station at Bourg-Saint-Maurice to Arc 1600 and Arc 1800. A free shuttle bus (*navette*) runs on a regular schedule from the funicular station at Arc 1600 to Arc 1800 and Arc 2000 and return. Many of these buses are timed to meet the funicular, so a schedule, available at the Tourist Office, is essential.

Favorite *Walking Easy* Hotel

Gran Hotel Mercure Coralia
Three-Star; part of the Mercure/Accor hotel chain
Arc 1800, Charmettoger, 73700 Les Arcs
Tel: 4 79 07 65 00, **Fax:** 4 79 07 64 08
E-mail: H1669@accor-hotels.com

This modern hotel, located on the mountain in the village of Charmettoger at Arc 1800, is the newest hotel in Les Arcs. A large hotel with eighty-one rooms, all equipped with modern private facilities, balconies, and minibars, it offers superb views of the surrounding mountains. This is a full-service, quality hotel with evening entertainment, bar, reception rooms, full restaurant with a terrace—and all the know-how of the Mercure chain. Their demi-pension summer prices are very attractive, and because most of the walking is on the mountain in the three Les Arcs areas, this hotel offers *Easy Walkers* a viable alternative to staying down in Bourg-Saint-Maurice. Another bonus is the cooler evenings, because this hotel is situated 3300 ft. (1000 m.) higher than Bourg in the valley.

Lifts in Les Arcs (operate in July and August only)

Funiculaire Bourg-St-Maurice rises from Bourg, at 2658 ft. (810 m.), to Arc 1600, at 5250 ft. (1600 m.). It operates every day from 8:30 A.M. to 7:30 P.M. and leaves in both directions on the hour and half hour.

From Arc 1600, a continuously moving chairlift, the **Télésiège Débrayable de la Cachette**, accesses the Arpette plateau and rises from 5292 to 7087 ft. (1613 to 2160 m.). (See Walk #4.)

From Arc 1800, the **Télécabine Transarc** gondola runs every day in summer and rises from 5617 ft. to 8367 ft. (1712 to 2550 m.), with an intermediate stop. (See Walks #1, #4, and #5.)

Hint: A seven-day pass allowing unlimited access to the funicular and all lifts is a good buy for Easy Walkers, *especially if your hotel is down in Bourg-Saint-Maurice, and you take the funicular up and back for walks in the Les Arcs area.*

From Arc 2000, the **Télécabine du Varet** is the mid-station for access to the Aiguille Rouge.

The cable cars of the **Téléphérique de l'Aiguille Rouge** then rise from 8760 to 10,585 ft. (2670 to 3226 m.). You should allow about two hours for the ascent, descent, and viewing at the Aiguille Rouge; weather conditions should be clear and dry for this trip. It's usually not very cold at the top, but sunscreen and sunglasses are a must. (See Walk #2.)

The **Télésiège Débrayable des Plagnettes** rises from 7153 ft. (2180 m.) at Arc 2000 to 8367 ft. (2550 m.), near the top station of the Transarc gondola lift coming from Arc 1800.

Excursions

The Bourg-Saint-Maurice Office du Tourisme is across the street from the railroad station on place de la Gare and in Arc 1800.

Fax: 4 79 07 45 96

E-mail: lesarcs@lesarcs.com

Internet: www.lesarcs.com

1. **Bourg-Saint-Maurice Area -** The **Musée du Costume** in Hauteville-Gondon, about 1 mile from Bourg, features ancient, regional costumes of the Haute-Tarentaise area. **Minéraux-Faune de l'Alpe** at 82, ave. Maréchal-Leclerc, Bourg-Saint-Maurice, highlights twenty years of discoveries by Joseph Canova, *cristallier*. **La Maison des Artisans de Séez** is located two miles from Bourg at Place de l'Église in the village of Séez.

Hint: The gondolas, cable cars, and chairlifts in the Les Arcs area all operate on different schedules; most are not open every day. When planning your daily walks and excursions, make sure you consult the Les Arcs lift schedule, available at the Tourist Information Office.

The museum displays the work of local Savoy artisans. You can also visit the **Centrale Hydro-Electrique de Malgovert** in Séez, which has audio-visual exhibits on power in the Haute-Tarentaise Valley.

2. **Tignes** - Tignes is a modern village. Its oldest buildings were built only forty-five years ago, with the construction of a large hydroelectric dam, when the old village of Tignes was destroyed and rebuilt 1000 ft. (305 m.) higher, next to a small lake. The world's largest fresco is painted on the wall of the dam—representing the strength of the ancient world and the energy of the modern world. Tignes offers summer skiing, lake water sports, and the highest eighteen-hole golf course in Europe. (See Walk #6.)

   Directions: By car - Take N90 northeast out of Bourg, following signs on D902 southeast 15 miles (24 km) into Tignes. By bus - The early morning bus from Bourg arrives in Tignes-le-Lac in forty-five minutes.

3. **Val d'Isère** - Although skiing plays a central role in Val d'Isère's winter life, summer brings hikers and sightseers to this mountain village. Ascend on the cable car to **Rocher de Bellevarde** for outstanding views of the upper Tarentaise region and the Vanoise National Park. (See Walk #6.) On the way to Val-d'Isère, stop to view the hydroelectric dam at Tignes, with the largest fresco in the world painted on its wall.

   Directions: By car - Drive on N90 through Séez to D902 southeast, past Tignes, for the 25-mile (40-km) drive. By bus - The early morning bus arrives in Val d'Isère in about an hour.

4. **Annecy** - See the Megève chapter, Excursion #4.

   Directions: Follow N90 through Moûtiers into Albertville. Outside of Albertville, pick up N212 north to N508, taking you around the lake to Annecy. To return, you can drive around the other side of the lake on D909 before picking up N508 and then reversing directions to Albertville and Bourg/Les Arcs.

5. **Courchevel** - See the Méribel chapter, Excursion #7.

   Directions: Take N90 out of Bourg toward Moûtiers. Follow signs to Courchevel and drive south on the winding, local road to the Courchevels.

6. **Albertville** - See the Méribel chapter, Excursion #6.

   Directions: By car - Take N90 west into Albertville, where you follow signs to the medieval city of Conflans and/or the Olympic site.

7. **Belleville Valley -** See the Méribel chapter, Excursion #10.

   Directions: *Take N90 west, following signs in Moûtiers to Vallée de Belleville, picking up local road D915 south through St-Martin-de-Belleville, les Menuires, and finally, Val-Thorens.*

8. **Chamonix -** This world capital of mountaineering is dominated by the powerful majesty of Mont Blanc, the highest mountain in Europe—but the town successfully combines boutiques, restaurants, hotels, and services of a large resort with its incomparable, awesome, natural surroundings of the Mont Blanc massif. (See the Chamonix chapter.)

   Directions: *From Bourg, drive on N90 northeast, crossing the Italian border, following signs to Courmayeur, Italy, and the Mont Blanc Tunnel. Drive through the tunnel, which brings you outside of Chamonix.*

9. **Courmayeur, Italy -** Only 37 miles (60 km) northeast of Bourg/Les Arcs, Courmayeur is a well-known summer and winter resort at the foot of Mont Blanc. (See Chamonix chapter, Excursion #7.)

   Directions: *Follow D90 northeast, driving over the Italian border and Col du Petit St. Bernard. Pick up S26 into Courmayeur.*

10. **Peisey-Nancroix -** Visit **la Chapelle des Vernettes**, dating from 1722 and built at an altitude of 5906 ft. (1800 m.). Note its beautiful cupola and magnificent old polychrome, recently restored.

    Directions: *Take N90 driving southwest out of Bourg, following directions to Peisey.*

11. **Hauteville-Gondon -** The Baroque **Eglise d'Hauteville-Gondon** dates from 1694, while the **Eglise de Peisey** was built even earlier, in 1685. Visit the **Costume Museum** for exhibits of how people dressed in years gone by in the Haute-Tarentaise area.

    Directions: *Take the narrow, winding local road south, following directions into Hauteville.*

12. **Gran Paradiso National Park, Italy -** See the Chamonix chapter, Excursion #8.

    Directions: *Take N90 east over the Italian border, which becomes S26 in Italy. Turn east on S26 toward Aosta, into the Aosta Valley. Make a right turn at Aymavilles, about 4 miles (6 km) west of Aosta, climbing into the Val di Cagne. Twelve miles (20 km) up into the valley is the vil-*

lage of Cogne, at 5033 ft. (1534 m.), a good place to stop and enjoy the beauty and solitude of the park.

13. Aosta, Italy - See the Chamonix chapter, Excursion #13.
   Directions: Drive on N90 east over the Italian border, becoming S26 in Italy. Turn east on S26 into Aosta.

14. Chambéry - The capital of the Duchy of Savoy from the thirteenth to the seventeenth centuries, Chambéry is an appealing, small city of handsome arcades, squares, and shopping streets. Its famous **Fontaine des Éléphants (Elephants Fountain)** is situated in the center of town, and it commemorates a trip to India made by a local hero. At the other end of the Boulevard de la Colonne from the Elephants Fountain is the Tourist Office. **Château des Ducs de Savoie,** built in the fourteenth century, located in the southwest corner of Old Town, was the residence of former dukes, and it towers over the city. Guided tours to the château are mandatory—check with the Tourist Office for information. *Easy Walkers* might enjoy climbing the 200 steps of **Round Tower** for a terrific view of the city.
   Directions: By car - Take N90 through Moûtiers and Albertville. In Albertville, take A430 south, leading to A43 into Chambéry. By train - An early morning train arrives in Chambéry in less than two hours.

15. Aix-les-Bains - Only 10 miles (16 km) north of Chambéry, one of France's largest and most fashionable spa towns is set on the eastern shores of Lac du Bourget, at the foot of the Alps. The Tourist Office on place Maurice-Mollard can provide you with information about the hot-water springs, which are said to help arthritis. This is a pretty town, with colorful gardens, a race course, casinos, and a golf course, as well as a beach for swimming on the lake.
   If there is time, take a four-hour boat ride on the lake, including a visit to the **Abbaye de Hautecombe** in Chindrieux, the mausoleum of many of the nobility of the House of Savoy, built on a cliff jutting into the lake. Check with the Tourist Office for boat schedules. **Musée Faure** boasts an interesting collection of modern art, including Rodin sculptures.
   Directions: Follow N90 through Moûtiers and Albertville. Then take A430 to A43 past Chambéry, taking the local road into Aix.

16. Great Saint Bernard Pass and Hospice, Switzerland - See Chamonix chapter, Excursion #15.

Directions: Take N90 northeast over the Col du Petit St. Bernard and the Italian border, where the road changes to S26. Continue north till the road splits and take S26 into Aosta. Drive north on S27 but do not drive through the Saint Bernard Tunnel—take the old, winding road, right over the Swiss border to the hospice.

17. Bus Excursions - Transports Martin, located in the railroad station, runs bus excursions from Bourg-Saint-Maurice to the following places: **Aix-les-Bains** and **Abbaye de Hautecombe; Annecy** and **Musée du Château; Chamonix, Tunnel du Mont Blanc** and **Courmayeur; Lac de Tignes; Val d'Isère; Col de l'Iseran** and **Bonneval-sur-Arc; la Rosière; Hauteville** and **the Musée du Costume Savoyard; Albertville, Conflans,** and **Beaufort; Aosta; Tour du Parc National de la Vanoise** and **Tour du Mont Blanc.**

Les Arcs Walks

Recommended Maps:

❖ Sentiers de Moyenne Montagne in Haute-Les Arcs, Bourg-Saint-Maurice

❖ Cartes des Promenades à Pied—et V.T.T.—Les Arcs, Bourg-Saint-Maurice

---

Hint: *Walking in the Les Arcs/Bourg-Saint-Maurice area requires a transportation strategy. Many walks begin and end at the different Les Arcs stations, where you can take advantage of the free bus system between Arc 1600, Arc 1800, and Arc 2000. If you are staying in Bourg, you'll travel up to Arc 1600 by the funicular in back of the train station and then take the free bus to any one of the Arc stations. It's also possible to drive to the Arcs. However, the authors found it best to use available public transportation, leaving the car at your base village—either Bourg-Saint-Maurice or Les Arcs. As most of the following walks begin at one of the Arc villages, you might choose to stay at a hotel on the mountain, driving down to Bourg for the colorful Saturday morning market or for sightseeing.*

Directions to all walks begin in one of the Arcs. If you are departing from Bourg-Saint-Maurice by funicular to arrive at the start of a hike: Follow the funiculaire signs on the main auto road in the center of the village near the railroad station, bringing you to a large parking area. Park your car and follow the sign reading FUNICULAIRE ACCESS at the far end of the parking area. A covered passageway takes you over the railroad tracks to the funicular, leaving Bourg for Arc 1600 (and Arc 1600 for Bourg) on the hour and half hour. After leaving the Arc 1600 station, turn left to catch the bus to either Arc 1800 or Arc 2000. We strongly suggest you pick up a current Les Arcs funicular and bus timetable at the Tourist Office when you arrive in town.

Walk #1

Transarc Lift Arc 1800, Walk Top Station to Col de la Chal to Lac Marloup to Arc 2000
Walking Easy Time: 3 hours
Rating: Comfortable

Today's walk should be taken on a clear day for best views of the incredible panorama presented from the trails. You'll take the Transarc Télécabine from Arc 1800 to the 8531-foot (2600-meter) top station. The walk begins here, descending gently to Col de la Chal, at 8061 ft. (2457 m.), and continuing to tiny Lac Marloup on wide, open paths. Lac Marloup is surrounded by grassy plateaus that offer terrific opportunities for picnicking, scenery viewing and picture taking. After passing Lac Marloup, you'll see the gondolas rising toward the Aiguille Rouge, at 10,588 ft. (3227 m.), surrounded on three sides by glaciers. If you look carefully up at the mountain to your right, you'll be able to see the protruding receiving station for the cable car that rises up from the mid-station to the peak. The walk ends at Arc 2000, as you descend the mountain on a wide, comfortable, popular path. There's a restaurant with a sun-terrace at the Transarc Top Station, but nothing else is available until you reach your destination at Arc 2000, where you'll take the shuttle bus to Arc 1600 and another bus to the funicular or Arc 1800 and your hotel.

Directions: If you are staying in Arc 1800, walk up to the Transarc 1800 gondola. If you are at a hotel in Bourg, take the funicular to Arc 1600 and the free bus to Arc 1800. If you haven't purchased a seven-day pass, buy a one-way ticket to the top station. Take the Arc 1800 Transarc Télécabine, staying on the gondola to the top station. This location is the start of many walks in the Les Arcs region.

Start: Walk ahead, following COL DE LA CHAL, ARC 2000 and LAC MARLOUP (sometimes spelled "Marlou") signs. Descend to a large, grassy plateau at Col de la Chal, and a wide, dirt path. At a signed intersection, follow signs to LAC MARLOUP. Pass two teeny-tiny lakes before reaching Lac Marloup, its blue waters reflecting the mountains and hillsides around it. Photographers will have opportunities to record the mountain panorama, including imposing Mont Blanc in the distance, and there are many picnic opportunities around the lake.

When ready, continue on the path, and you'll soon be able to see the gondolas operating up to the modern cable car station high on your right. A cable car leaves that mid-station, ascending to the Aiguille Rouge, at 10,588 ft. (3227 m.), a *Walking Easy* excursion on another day. Continue ahead on the path until you arrive at a sharp left turn, down the mountain, around Plan de l'Homme.

This path circles down and around, with the chalets of Arc 2000 in view. Walk down the steps at the end of the shops and cafes, which brings you to the bus stop for Arc 1600. Here, you either change to the funicular to go down to Bourg or to the bus to Arc 1800 and your hotel.

Walk #2

Excursion to Aiguille Rouge, Walk Aiguille Rouge Lift Mid-Station to Lac Marloup to Transarc Top Station

Walking Easy Time: 2 hours

Rating: Comfortable

Today's walk is not long and doesn't require an early start. It does, however, require a bright, clear day. You'll leave from Arc 2000 on a lift, rising to the mid-station at 8695 ft. (2650 m.), transferring to a cable car that ascends to the Aiguille Rouge, at 10,588 ft. (3227 m.). A quick climb through a small snowfield to the ridge reveals unparalleled panoramic views of the surrounding glaciers, Mont Pourri in the Vanoise National Park, and the dominating Mont Blanc range to the north.

Easy Walkers will return to the mid-station by cable car to begin today's walk, descending easily on a nicely graded, zigzagging path under the Aiguille Rouge to the main walking path. The walk finishes with a pass by Lac Marloup, at 8203 ft. (2500 m.) (as in Walk #1), and a walk up to the top station of the Transarc gondola to return to Arc 1800.

Directions: If you are staying at Arc 1800, take the free bus to Arc 1600 and change for the bus to Arc 2000. If you are staying in Bourg, from the top funicular station, take the bus to Arc 2000.

After leaving the bus at Arc 2000, walk up the steps and through the Arc 2000 sports center. Continue past the small shops to a wide dirt path ahead, following signed directions to TÉLÉCABINE DU VARET. On your left, notice the markings of the 1992 Winter Olympics—the torch, the flags, and the downhill ski runs—as you pass under several ski lifts not operating in summer. Look high to the left—you can see the Aiguille Rouge cable station protruding over the mountain—your destination. During the comfortable eighteen-minute chairlift ride to the mid-station, look to your right to the Transarc Top Station, where you'll walk after your excursion to the Aiguille Rouge.

On exiting the lift, note the sign for AIGUILLE ROUGE. Enter the cable car, which leaves every twenty minutes for the five-minute ascent to the top station, at 10,588 ft. (3227 m.).

Start: After exiting the cable car, walk carefully to the peak over the little snow and rock field. Just below the Aiguille Rouge and down to your left is the Glacier du Varet, at 10,171

ft. (3100 m.). To the right and in front of towering 11,086-foot (3779-meter) Mont Pourri are two glaciers: Grand Col and Geay. The area to the right, including Mont Pourri, is in the Vanoise National Park, which becomes Gran Paradiso Park at the Italian border. To the north looms the *grand-père* of them all—the peaks of the Mont Blanc range. Take enough time to absorb the scene around you.

Return to the mid-station by cable car and follow the sign reading SORTIE, walking back down the steps you climbed earlier. Turn right on the dirt jeep road and follow the wide, well-graded, zigzag path down to the main trail. Here, turn left and descend gently to the small, clear reflecting lake—Marloup—sitting in the midst of a grassy plateau. Once again, there are great views of Mont Blanc and many picnic opportunities here. Continue on the path as it descends easily to Col de la Chal, in the direction of the top station of the Transarc gondola visible ahead. The wide path then rises until you reach a restaurant with a sun-terrace and the Transarc lift station. Take the lift down to Arc 1800.

Walk #3

Arc 2000 to Arc 1600
Walking Easy Time: 3 hours
Rating: Comfortable

Arc 2000 is the starting point for a walk through the forest and along the Chemin du Canal to Arc 1600. This gentle descent of 1312 ft. (400 m.) is on a wide path shared with mountain bikers. The path, lined with tall, bright purple flowers in summer, is mostly through the shady forest and is blazed all the way.

Directions: Take the bus to Arc 2000.

Start: After leaving the bus, walk up the steps and through the sports fields of Arc 2000, noting the Olympic torch and flags on the left. Continue ahead until you see a sign, PRÉ ST. ESPRIT, and follow the path down to the right. Just before the Varet gondolas, turn down a narrow, descending, mountain trail marked V.T.T./PIETON #5 toward the rapidly running stream. As you continue to walk, snow-capped Mont Blanc will be in full view to the north. Turn left at the intersection, walking on a wide dirt path for about 50 meters to the closed Bois de l'Ours chairlift and a group of signs pointing to ARC 1600 and PRÉ ST. ESPRIT to your right. Follow this wide path all the way to Arc 1600, with few diversions. If you are unsure of a marking, follow the bike signs. You'll pass a little road that takes you down to Pré St. Esprit, with its restaurant and sun-terrace. If you don't want a snack, remain on the main path, staying out of the way of bikers. The path sometimes meets the road, but continue walking on the yellow-blazed main trail that has directional signs for bicyclists.

At an intersection, follow the sign ARC 1600, bringing you to the Hotel Beguin. Walk on the road to the right, buttonhooking to a lower road to the left, quickly noting the blaze and bicycle sign taking you sharply down on a narrow trail through the forest. This trail ends shortly at another paved road. Follow the blaze and sign to the right and enter the forest again on a descending path leading to another road and Arc 1600. Turn left and immediately enter the gravel path to the right, turning right again to the funicular or to the shuttle bus to other Les Arcs stations.

Walk #4

Transarc 1800 Lift to Mid-Station, Walk to l'Arpette to Arc 1600 (Optional Excursion on Cachette Chairlift)
Walking Easy Time: 2½ hours
Rating: Comfortable

This walk begins at the mid-station of the Arc 1800 Transarc gondola, descending easily to Arc 1600 along the middle balcony of the mountain, offering continuous views of the Mont Blanc range. There are additional views of Bourg-Saint-Maurice dominating the valley below, as well as the three villages of Arc 1800: Charmettoger, les Villards, and Charvet. You'll also walk under a half-dozen closed ski lifts that serve winter sports enthusiasts.

A delightful restaurant is along this path, with lovely views of the valley. The walk continues on the Chemin des Sources, past the tennis complex above Arc 1600. Because this is an easy, half-day excursion, you might wish to take the Cachette chairlift at Arc 1600 to the station below le Signal des Têtes, at 7054 ft. (2150 m.). This station provides a somewhat higher view over the area you just walked and can be the starting point for a more demanding hike around the peak. Take the lift back down to Arc 1600 for the return.

Directions: At Arc 1800, walk up the steps to the Transarc gondola and disembark at mid-station.

Start: Walk out of the station and turn to your right under the Transarc lift. The walk begins with a comfortable, fifteen-minute ascent on a wide path, with views of the Arc 1800 eighteen-hole golf course down on the left. You'll soon arrive at a modern, terraced, wooden chalet, with flags of the l'Arpette restaurant below on the left. Follow the road around and down to the left, continuing as it zigzags back and forth under the chairlift (closed for the summer).

As you proceed, note Arc 1800 down to the left, and Bourg-Saint-Maurice sitting in the valley below. The road forks down to the left to Arc 1800, but continue ahead in the signed direction of ARC 1600. This path is blazed yellow and goes in and out of forested areas and meadows filled with tall, purple flowers, continuing to descend toward Arc 1600. Walk under the operating ski lift, one you might choose to take later to visit le Signal des Têtes. At the intersection ahead, turn left toward the tennis courts and right again on the main path, as the path splits left for skiers. Keep the tennis courts on your right as you descend. At another intersection, follow the sign for Arc 1600 going to the left, to the small auto road. Turn right on the road, walk past the Hotel Beguin, and turn left again on the lower auto road. Note the yellow blaze and bicycle sign, pointing down a narrow, forest path (it's only steep for a few seconds). This trail meets an auto road. Follow the yellow blaze to the right and turn again into the forest, to an Arc 1600 paved road. Turn left, then immediately right on to the gravel path. Here you have two options:

1. Take the Cachette chairlift straight ahead for an excursion to le Signal des Têtes.

2. Turn right and take the shuttle bus to other Les Arcs stations. For those who are staying in Les Arcs, this might be a good time to take the funicular down and visit Bourg-Saint-Maurice.

Walk #5

Arc 1800 Transarc Lift to Mid-Station, Walk to Bergerie du Rey through Forêt de Plan Peisey to la Maitaz to Arc 1800

Walking Easy Time: 2½ hours

Rating: Comfortable

This walk was recommended to the authors by other hikers staying at the hotel.

Directions: Depart from Arc 1800 on the Transarc gondola to the mid-station.

Start: After exiting the gondola at the mid-station, take the path down in the direction of Bergerie du Rey marked #6, all the way to Arc 1800.

Walk #6

Excursion to Tignes and Val d'Isère

Walking Easy Time: ¾ hour to ?

Rating: Gentle to more challenging

Because the internationally famous ski centers of Val d'Isère and Tignes are so close to Bourg-Saint-Maurice/Les Arcs, we think it's interesting to pay them both a visit, for sightseeing as well as walking.

Directions: Leave Bourg-Saint-Maurice on N90, the main road, following signs to Tignes and Val d'Isère. Drive through the little village of Séez and climb on #902 through Saint-Foy, past the reservoir at Tignes, all the way to Val d'Isère, at 6037 ft. (1840 m.). Val d'Isère is bordered by peaks up to 11,155 ft. (3400 m.) and serves as the entrance to a mountain pass close to Italy, the Col de l'Iseran, at 9088 ft. (2770 m.). At Val d'Isère, you might wish to ascend on the cable car to Rocher de Bellevarde for views of the Upper Tarentaise region and the Vanoise National Park. There is an optional drive between Val d'Isère and Tignes. Watch for the signs to Lake Saut, the road leaving the main road along the large lake and ascending up to Lake Saut, at 7546 ft. (2300 m.), with its convenient parking area. There are great views from here, and some gentle walking is available.

Drive back toward Tignes and park at the area overlooking the large dam on your left, for views of a remarkable sight: The largest fresco in the world is painted on the wall of the dam, representing the strength of the ancient world and the energy of the modern one. Continue driving over the dam, following signs to Tignes-le-Lac, at 6890 ft. (2100 m.). Park close to the lake, right before the open mountain tunnel.

Start: Just behind you on the hill are signs describing walks in this area, but first you can enjoy a gentle, forty-five-minute walk on the path around the lake. Returning to the hiking signs, stronger walkers might wish to ascend to Col du Palet, at 8705 ft. (2653 m.), a rise of 1837 ft. (560 m.). Going and coming on the same path to the Col du Palet will take about four hours. However, you might hike until you are ready to return on the same trail. Pick up your car and return to the main road for the drive back to Bourg/Les Arcs.

EMBRUN

You have the best of French sporting and cultural worlds around the *Walking Easy* base village of Embrun—a secret jewel of the French Alps—waiting to be discovered. One can't help but sense its prestigious past when walking through this town, with its colorful, narrow streets lined with boutiques and charming cafes. A portion of Embrun's heritage is revealed in a walk from the centrally located Tourist Office to the finest cathedral in the southern Alps, dating back to the end of the twelfth century. The fountains, arched doorways, and stone sculptures on Embrun's cobblestone streets reflect its architectural importance. The Embrun Tourist Office is situated at the head of Embrun's walking streets in the extraordinary and historically important Gothic Chapels of an ancient convent, with recently restored fifteenth- and sixteenth-century frescoes.

The village of Embrun is the nucleus of activities within l'Embrunais and the gateway to the wilderness of the Parc Nature Régional du Queyras and the famous peaks of Parc National des Ecrins. Embrun has the distinct advantage of being close to a multitude of activities—from water sports on Lake Serre-Ponçon to the myriad of walks in mountains and meadows and in the ski resorts of les Orres and Réallon. As you expand the perimeter around Embrun, the high peaks and glaciers of la Meije, at 13,068 ft. (3983 m.), in the Ecrins Park; the natural beauty of the Queyras Park; the setting of Saint-Véran, Europe's highest village; the fabulous, desertlike mountain crossing over Col d'Izoard, 7874 ft. (2400 m.), ringed by dramatic peaks; and ancient Briançon, one of the highest towns in Europe, at 4334 ft. (1321 m.), are all easily reached.

One of the more important resort villages in the Hautes-Alpes, Embrun sits high on a rocky terrace overlooking the Durance River near Lake Serre-Ponçon, the largest human-made lake in Europe. Once a "cathedral city," Embrun now attracts large numbers of water-sport enthusiasts, walkers, and campers during the high season of July and especially August, bringing tourism dollars into what used to be a disadvantaged valley. The 20-mile-long lake, which spreads over 75,000 acres, was formed when the Durance River's bed was dammed in the 1950s. It's interesting to note that the small village of Savines all but disappeared under the water as the dam was completed; the little Chapel of St-Michel perched on top of a hill in the middle of the lake is the only visible remains of the original village. The lake, surrounding mountains, and neighboring villages make the Embrunais (the area around Embrun) an attractive and unusual *Walking Easy* destination.

Located southeast of Grenoble, Embrun is close to the Italian border, yet not far from Marseilles and the French Riviera. This region is a mix of Dauphinois and Provençal—fields of lavender alpine flowers with Mediterranean sunshine warming the fresh, cool mountain air. The Hautes-Alpes has a population of only 150,000 in 2180 square miles (5643 sq. km). Altitudes rise from 1640 ft. (500 m.) at Buëch, to 13,458 ft. (4102 m.) on the Barre des Ecrins. In remote Hautes-Alpes villages, *Easy Walkers* may still hear dialects whose roots trace back to the archaic Oc language of southern France. Look for ancient sundials as you travel through the Hautes-Alpes—through Pays de Buëch, the Queyras, the Valloise, and the Briançon areas. Created to keep time for the villagers, these unique artistic and cultural timepieces have survived since the eighteenth century. (See Walk #6 for details about the sundials in Saint-Véran.)

Embrun boasts beautiful surroundings—old, fortified ramparts high above the valley; a majestic cathedral; ancient buildings—complemented by meadows, farms, and sleepy country hamlets of the Embrunais. You'll be astonished at the charm and vitality of this off-the-beaten-path village and its area's *Walking Easy* trails.

Transportation

By Plane - From the United States, flying into Nice via Paris entails the shortest drive to Embrun. Geneva is a full-day's drive, but if you are flying into Paris, plan on spending at least one night on the road.

By Train - Two main rail lines, one from Paris and one from Marseilles, provide daily service to Briançon by way of Gap. These trains are scheduled into the Gare S.N.C.F. à Embrun, the station at Embrun.

By Car - From Nice by car, take N202 north and then west to N85 to Digne-les-Bains, picking up D900B. At the lake, take the right fork of D900 a short distance, following signs around the lake to Embrun.

From Geneva, take A40 east, picking up superhighway A41 to bypass Annecy. Continue on A41 south to Grenoble. Pick up N85 south into Gap and N94 east into Embrun. N85 is the famous Route Napoléon. This scenic road runs from the Mediterranean Sea at Golfe-Juan to Grenoble, following the route taken by Napoléon on his return from Elba in 1832. It's marked on its entire length by the flying eagle symbol, inspired by

Napoléon's remark, "The eagle will fly from steeple to steeple until he reaches the towers of Notre-Dame." In Gap, pick up N94 east into Embrun.

Coming from the Briançon area to the north, take N94 south into Embrun.

Note: While in Embrun, it will be necessary to use a car for transportation from your lodgings to and from walks and sightseeing explorations.

Favorite *Walking Easy* Hotels

Hotel les Peupliers

Two-Star; Owner - Jacques and Françoise Bellot
05202 Baratier; **Tel:** 4 92 43 03 47, **Fax:** 4 92 43 41 49
E-mail: jfbellot@aol.com, **Internet:** www.hotel-les-peupliers.com/

The Hotel les Peupliers is situated in the heart of the Hautes-Alpes, two kilometers from Embrun, just outside the tiny village center of Baratier. This gem of a two-star hotel has three-star ambience, and its new young owners cater personally to the needs of their guests. The food is delicious country cuisine and the views from the balconies are outstanding, as this hotel is perched on a hillside overlooking their outdoor pool, snow-capped mountains, and Lake Sere-Ponçon—when making reservations, ask for a room with balcony.

Hotel Les Bartavelles

Three-Star; Owner - Nancy Jaume and Christophe Pernin
05200 Crots/Embrun, **Tel:** 4 92 43 20 69, **Fax:** 4 92 43 11 92
E-mail: info@bartavelles.com, **Internet:** www.bartavelles.com

Les Bartavelles is a few kilometers from Embrun and sits on a grassy meadow near the village of Crots. There are well-maintained tennis courts and an outdoor swimming pool, making this hotel a comfortable family resort in a park-like setting. Its new young owners recently renovated les Bartavelles's rooms—providing central air conditioning and easy Internet access—making this a comfortable hotel for *Easy Walkers.*

Lifts around Embrun

Les Orres - During the summer, three chairlifts operate in les Orres: Pré-longis, rising to 6316 ft. (1925 m.), operating every day; Fontaines, rising to 7901 ft. (2408 m.), open four days a week; and Pousterle, rising to 8301 ft. (2530 m.), open the days Fontaines is closed. Fontaines and Pousterle operate from the top of the Prélongis station. (See Walk #4.) *Note: Check with the Tourist Office for current schedules of the Les Orres lifts.*

Télésiège de Réallon - *Note: Check with the Tourist Office for schedule changes.* This double chairlift operates Monday, Tuesday, and Friday in summer—from des Aurans to the mid-station and Chabrières to the top at Belvédère, at 7010 ft. (2135 m.). The top station provides spectacular views of the nearby, needle-like Aiguilles de Chabrières. (See Walk #3.)

Excursions

The historic Office de Tourisme de L'Embrun, headed by its interesting and charming director Mme. Claude Chowanietz, is on place Général Dosse.

Fax: 4 92 43 54 06
E-mail: ot.embrun@laposte.fr
Internet: www.ot-embrun.fr/

1. **Embrun -** Watching over the Durance River, the old city of Embrun received its Celtic name from its high, rock position: *ebr* meaning water, and *dunum* meaning heights. (See Walk #1.)

2. **Boscodon Abbey (Abbaye de Boscodon) -** The twelfth-century Boscodon Abbey is 2 miles from Lake Serre-Ponçon and 400 feet (122 meters) above the valley. It's the largest abbey in the region, built by the hermit monks of the Order of Chalais. Extensive renovations are taking place, but the abbey church with its austere lines and somber beauty can be visited every day. An English brochure is available at a nominal cost. (See Walk #2.)

   Directions: Drive past Crots in the direction of Savines-les-Lacs, turning at the Boscodon sign and following the road into the hills.

3. **Montdauphin -** Acting on orders from King Louis XIV, famous military engineer Vauban ordered the **Fort of Montdauphin** to be built above

Guillestre. Wander through narrow streets and visit the artisan shops, constructed of the pink stone peculiar to this area. Nearby, facing Mont Dauphin on the steep rocky slopes above the Durance, an impressive, open-air stalactite formed above a natural basin—called the **Petrified Fountain of Réotier.**

Directions: Take N94 north out of Embrun past Guillestre. Follow local signs to Montdauphin.

4. **Briançon -** One of the highest towns in Europe, at 4351 ft. (1326 m.), at the crossroads of five valleys and near the Italian border, Briançon's landscape is dominated by its ancient fortifications. The first walls were built in the Middle Ages, then added to by the military engineer Vauban, turning Briançon into a heavily fortified town. Briançon's narrow streets in the Old Quarter (or **Ville Haute**) are filled with small stores and cafes, while the **Church of the Cordelier** entices art lovers with ancient paintings and frescoes. The twin-towered **Eglise Notre-Dame** boasts a lovely view of the surrounding countryside, and the blue-and-white front of the **Pope's House** is a reminder that Italy is not too far away.

Directions: Take N94 north of Embrun to Briançon and follow signs reading VAUBAN-BRIANÇON. Park at the Champs de Mars, and enter by the Pignerold Gate.

5. **Gap -** Situated in a pleasant, glacial valley only 16 miles (26 km) from Embrun, Gap's economy is supported by farms on the surrounding hillsides—it's one of the most prosperous areas in the southern French Alps. Visit the **cathedral** and the **museum,** with its archaeological collection. Outside of town, the **Château de Tallard,** once owned by knights of the Order of Malta, is perched on a rocky outcropping. Note also that this town's Roman origins are still intact and very much in evidence.

The Gap Tourist Office has put together a *Randonée Pedestres* packet that includes instructions for over twenty day-walks, mostly blazed and at all levels of difficulty. Unfortunately, everything is printed in French. If you bone up on your high school French and check the easy-to-follow maps, you might enjoy walking in the Gapençais. It's always a good idea to carry the IGN map of the area—#3338 *Gap*—as well.

Directions: Cross Lake Serre-Ponçon at Savines-le-Lac on 94 west in the direction of Chorges, and then drive into Gap.

6. **La Meije -** A two-stage cable car, the **Télépherique des Glaciers de la Meije-la Grave,** takes you from the tiny village of **la Grave,** with its traditional architecture, up to 10,500 ft. (3200 m.), and unsurpassed views of the 13,065-foot (3982-meter) **la Meije** and the Ecrins glaciers. In the heart of the Haute Romanche, la Grave, Villar d'Arène, and hamlets at even higher levels at the foot of la Meije offer stunning views of the mountain and its glaciers. In summer, the impressive glaciers form a fascinating backdrop to the colorful meadow flowers.

   Directions: Take N94 north of Embrun toward Briançon, then N91 west to la Grave.

7. **Queyras Regional Nature Reserve and Villages -** A vast, almost forgotten area, this 250 square miles of open alpine country has trails leading through larch woods to higher elevations of pine and grazing sheep amid wild flowers and berries—a visual feast and a photographer's delight. Abriès, Aiguilles, Arvieux, Ceillac, Château-Ville-Vielle, Molines, Ristolas, Saint-Véran—these villages in the highest valley in the Hautes-Alpes have enjoyed a reputation for wood craftsmanship since the sixteenth-century, when villagers began carving objects during the long winter months. Don't miss the shops of modern-day craftspeople.

   At 6693 ft. (2040 m.), Saint-Véran, called "the village where the cocks peck at the stars," is the highest community in Europe. It's one of the main tourist attractions of the Queyras, notably for its distinctive, old architecture: wooden buildings decorated with sundials and long galleries where crops are dried. (See Walk #6.)

8. **Parc National des Ecrins -** Founded in 1973, Ecrins is the largest national park in France, covering over 350 square miles (91,800 hectares). Its unspoiled land includes the famous Massif des Ecrins, which reaches its high point at the Barre des Ecrins. Bounded by the Romanch, Durance, and Drac Valleys, the park covers the whole spectrum of spectacular mountain scenery and lies at altitudes between 2625 and 13,459 ft. (800 and 4102 m.). Within the Ecrins' mountain ranges are impressive glaciers and a network of smaller glaciers and mountain lakes. The flora is typical of alpine landscapes and includes several rare species among its 2000 types of flowers. The park's fauna includes most alpine species, such as chamois, marmots, and ermines; 110 different types of birds; and numerous species of insects and invertebrates little

known to the public. There are about 400 miles of constantly monitored marked trails in the park, and the saying in the park is that you'll meet more chamois than people on the trails! Only one gate marks the entrance into the park, which is along the narrow road winding through the Vallée du Guil. The Park House is at Vallouise, and it offers numerous activities, including exhibitions, lectures, discussions, videos, and workshops. *Easy Walkers* can follow the signed path around the house, a walk in a type of open-air museum, discovering a different way to look at nature.

   Directions: *Take N94 north of Embrun toward Briançon. At l'Argentière-la-Bessé, turn left onto D994 and follow signs to the Park House Information Center at Vallouise.*

9. Les Demoiselles Coiffée - Sometimes called "fairy chimneys," they are one of the strangest sites in the Hautes-Alpes (the authors also encountered these rare geological formations in the Italian Alps: the Earth Pyramids of Segonzana). Stony columns of crumbly, alluvial deposits support enormous rocks at their tops.

   Directions: *Drive through Savines-le-Lac on D954, turning before the lake in the direction of Barcelonnette. There is a parking area and signs pointing in the direction of the columns, also visible from sections of the road. You can also see some of these formations on the ascent to Saint-Véran. (See Walk #6.)*

10. Lac de Serre-Ponçon - This body of water is the largest human-made lake in Europe, with 20 miles of crystal-clear water for swimming, fishing, sailing, waterskiing, canoeing, and rowing. **Chapelle Saint-Michel** on its tiny island in the lake is the only remnant of the old, drowned village of Savines—the resort village of Savines-le-Lac was built nearby on the shore of the new lake. The green surrounding mountains contrast pleasantly with the bright blue of the lake, dotted with small sailing boats and windsurfers.

11. Barcelonette - The streets of Barcelonette were laid out in 1213. Many of its ancient buildings are painted in warm colors to counteract the glare of snow and were designed with large projections to protect them from heavy area snowfalls. The "Barcelonettes," or "Mexicans," were local townspeople who made fortunes in textile trade with Mexico in the 1800's. When they returned to Barcelonette, they built homes that can still be seen on the outskirts of town.

An interesting side excursion from Barcelonette is the 6-mile (10-km) drive northwest on a very winding, bumpy road to the **Bordoux Torrent (Riou Bordoux)** of the Ubaye Valley, considered by geologists to be a textbook example of erosion in a glacial landscape.

Directions: Take D954 south through Savines-le-Lac. Turn left before the bridge, following signs to Barcelonnette.

12. **Digne-les-Bains -** The capital of the "Lavender Alps," or the Alpes de Haute-Provence, Digne is the perfect place to relax in shaded parks and enjoy flowered fountains. Note the old alpine facades of the buildings, combined with local Provençal charm, and stroll along walking-only streets to shop and relax in the outdoor cafes.

Directions: Take 900B past Lake Serre Ponçon and pick up N85 south and then east to Digne.

Embrun Walks

Recommended Maps:
- ❖ IGN 3615—3438 ET Top 25—Embrun, Les Orres, Lac de Serre-Ponçon
- ❖ IGN 3437—ET Top 25—Orcières-Merlette
- ❖ IGN 3637—Mont Viso, St-Véran, Aiguilles

Walk #1

Introductory Walk—In and around Embrun
Walking Easy Time: 3 hours
Rating: Comfortable

Park your car in the center of Embrun. Walk along the main auto road in the direction of the lake to arrive at a shopping area at the foot of the village. Walk through the parking area and pick up the Moulineaux path, going under the rocky terrace. At the crossroads, turn left, walking along the small, country car road under the rock, with tiny farms on the left and right, until you reach another intersection. Turn left and follow the car road up to town.

This might be a good time to spend the rest of the afternoon acquainting yourself with this fascinating town. The best way to begin is at the Office de Tourisme on place Général Dosse, located in a little square off the main pedestrian shopping street. The Tourist Office headquarters is situated in four chapels of the ancient convent of Les Cordeliers, consecrated in 1447; the frescoes in these Gothic chapels have been recently restored. Pay the Tourist Office a visit and spend a few minutes admiring the treasures of this ancient building.

The ancient city of Embrun, high above the Durance River on its sheer rock cliffs, was named because of its location—from the Celtic *ebr* meaning water and *dunum*, height. During the Roman Empire, Embrun was the capital of the Alps region, and until the French Revolution, a fortified military town. Embrun was also called the "Lourdes of the Middle Ages," as thousands of people made pilgrimages to its famous Gothic cathedral to seek cures for their ailments. From the Tourist Office, walk to rue Clovis Hugues, noting building #29, with seven arcades and a twelfth-century sculptured lion. At the top of the street on place St. Marcellin, beneath a one hundred-year-old tree, is a marble fountain made of stone from Queyras. Walk on to rue Caffe, with its overhanging houses, and turn right into rue Neuve—on the front of two houses here are eighteenth-century armorial bearings and inscriptions from the sixteenth century.

On place Dongois, with its ancient fountain, turn right into rue Isnel to reach sixteenth-century place de la Marie. From this square, walk down rue Clovis Hugues as far as Place de la Mazelière and note an old tower, a medieval figure on a wall, and a fountain monument to those who died in the War of 1870. Walk along rue de la Liberté to the former Hôtel of Governers, with its Gothic wooden door. Note also the lion casting its shadow over the entrance. At the bottom of rue de la Liberté, turn left into rue Emile Guigues and walk to the cathedral bell tower at the end of the street. On your right, you'll pass a former Jesuit College that was turned into a prison in 1803 and later into army barracks. Its immense door (now closed off) dates from the eighteenth century. When you arrive at the cathedral, walk around before entering and observe the sculpted heads of fantastic animals, as well as masks under the cornices and two large, stone lions. The Cathedral of Embrun, dating from the end of the twelfth century, reflects the transition from Norman to Gothic styles—huge, somber, yet elegant—with its austere interior accentuating the magnificent stained-glass windows. The knave of the cathedral has four vaulted bays on ribbed transept crossings, and the side aisles, with semicircular vaults, are sepa-

rated from the nave by pointed archways. Note the high altar in polychrome marble dating from the eighteenth century, the carved wooden
stalls, the great organ, and, of course, the majestic Rose Window. During
the summer months, the cathedral is also used for classical concerts.

Diagonally across from the cathedral sits the Tour Brune or Brown
Tower, dating back to the thirteenth century. A watchtower and prison, this
was the ancient keep of archbishops. From the back of the cathedral, you
can walk up through the park. Turn left on any number of streets to reach
the main shopping area.

Walk #2

**Baratier to Champ de Lare to l'Osselin to le Poet to Baratier (Excursion to Ab-
baye de Boscoden)**
Walking Easy Time: 2½ hours
Rating: Comfortable

The Baratier walk is a circular route and brings you from the little village of
Baratier, at 2874 ft. (876 m.), up to Champ de Lare at 3681 ft. (1122 m.).
You'll be walking along a country wagon road for a comfortable ascent,
with views over the lake and the Embrunais. A steeper, uphill climb will
bring you to a peaceful country lane, past old farms at Champ de Lare and
l'Osselin. The walk from Champ de Lare back to Baratier is downhill all the
way, through the hamlet of le Poet. The part of the walk ascending to
Champ de Lare is more demanding, but the views of the lake and the Embrunais make the climb worth the effort.

There are no facilities or restaurants along the way (except at the beginning and end of the walk), so you may want to put lunch in your backpack along with your usual water. If you take this walk in the morning, the
rest of the day can be spent enjoying an excursion to Boscodon Abbey.

Directions: Follow signs into Baratier. Parking is usually available in
the tiny village center in front of the Post Office.

Start: From the center of Baratier, across from the little restaurant,
walk up the hill on rue de Pouzenc. (If you face the post office, the street
is in back of you.) The path is marked occasionally with bike signs for #16
and #22 and is a small, paved country road. Continue walking on this road,
bearing to your right, although you might wish to explore the old, narrow
streets of the village first. You'll begin to see blue-and-yellow blazes on
trees, poles, or fences as you continue to gently ascend on this road, with

views of the lake and the Embrunais below on your right. Passing barns and houses, ahead on the Chemin de Verdun and passing the Verdun estate. After a short while, a sign directs you more steeply up to your left in the direction of CHAMP DE LARE and L'OSSELIN. At this point, the road also goes to the right past barns and houses, but this is private property, and although your map may show a small walking path through the meadow, do *not* attempt to walk on it. You may be warned off by an irate farmer and his equally irate, barking dogs.

The trail up to the left begins to ascend steeply; take this ascent slowly, knowing that the view from the top of the hill makes the effort worthwhile.

When you reach the road at the top, turn right, passing the working farm Champ de Lare and, within a few minutes, l'Osselin with its campground. The barns are old, and the green mountains in the background provide a lovely contrast to the sun-drenched fields of grain. Continue around and down on this road, resisting a little, signed path to les Vernées. Stay on the quiet, comfortable, country auto road as it zigzags down the mountain to the little hamlet of le Poet.

Hint: Near the top of this climb, use the two little cut-offs on the right to ease your level of ascent.

Turn right at the four-way intersection signed BARATIER, passing le Mélèze, a chalet on your right. This is a wide, rocky, jeep path, ending at a paved road. Turn left on the road and *voilà*, on the right is the charming sun-terrace of the Hotel Peupliers, a pleasant spot to enjoy lunch or a cool drink.

Continue down the road and make a right turn at the first intersection. Walk into the village center of Baratier and to your car. Considering lunch, resting, and scenery viewing, you should be back in Baratier about four hours after you began today's walk. This might be a good time to visit the Abbaye de Boscodon, completing a gratifying day in the Embrunais. Leave Baratier as you entered this morning, following D40 to the main highway and circle. Drive three-quarters around the circle toward Crots and pick up N94. Shortly, signs direct you to the left turn to the Abbaye de Boscodon. Follow that road up to the abbey. This popular attraction is usually crowded, and parking can be difficult. There is a second parking area around the circle and to the right.

The abbaye was built by monks 350 years before the discovery of America and is undergoing ongoing restoration, as it did in the fifteenth, seventeenth, and eighteenth centuries. Active local and religious groups

are in charge of the restoration, while promoting numerous cultural activities at the site. Ninety-minute tours are given in various languages (French,
German, Italian, and English). Please check with the Tourist Office for the
current schedule. The abbey is open to visitors every day.

Walk #3

**Réallon Station Chairlift to Top and Return, Walk Réallon to Fortress Ruins to
   le Villard to Réallon**
Walking Easy Time: 2 hours
Rating: Comfortable

Plan on a full day as you explore the Réallon region of the Embrunais. The
morning will be spent taking a thirty-minute drive to the Télésiège de
Réallon for a double chairlift ride to the peak and a view of Lake Serre-
Ponçon and its surrounding mountains. *Note: This chairlift is not open
every day. Check with the Tourist Office before beginning today's excursion.* While it's possible to walk down on a wide mountain-bike path, we
recommend you take the lift back down, as there is another treat in store
for you at the tiny village of Réallon. You'll be able to see the ruins of the
twelfth-century fortress above Réallon on your left as you descend on the
chairlift, and if you look closely, you'll also see the mountain path you'll
take later in today's hike.

It will be necessary to drive from the Réallon Lift Station to the *village*
of Réallon to begin today's walk. The first part of the walk to the fortress,
an ascent of 656 ft. (200 m.), is a forty-five-minute steady climb. The trail
down is part of a "Grand Randonée" route, cutting through hillside
meadows to reach a quiet, country mountain road for the walk back to
Réallon. We suggest you take the chairlift portion of today's excursion and
walk in the morning, hiking to the fortress afterward.

Directions: The drive to the Réallon chairlift station is along the far
side of the lake and affords new viewing perspectives. Take D94, the main
road from Embrun to Savines-le-Lac, cross the bridge (Pont-de-Savines),
and make a right turn in the direction of Réallon. Watch for signs for a
quick left turn up a mountain road. As you climb this narrow, winding road,
you'll split off to the left in the direction of the large sign to RÉALLON STA-
TION. (Later in the day, you'll drive up the right fork toward the village of
Réallon.) It takes about thirty minutes from Crots to reach the large parking

area in front of the lift station. Walk to the lift station and purchase a round-trip ticket to the peak.

Take the fifteen-minute chairlift ride to the mid-station, with its restaurant and sun-terrace. Walk to the second lift station for another fifteen-minute ascent to 6933 ft. (2113 m.). The short walk up to the jagged peak affords exciting close-up views of the "needles" of the Aiguilles de Chabrières.

When ready, return to the Réallon base station for the drive to Réallon Village. Take the auto road down, just as you came up, and make a left turn on the signed fork in the road to Réallon, driving through the picturesque hamlet of les Rousses. The road is narrow and winding, so take it slowly. After entering Réallon, drive through the town until you see signs on the right reading PARKING (with an arrow to the right) and RUINE. Make a sharp right turn up the hill until you reach a parking area at the top of the village. The church steeple will be to your right. *Note: If you are using Embrun Map #3838, the village of Réallon is printed on the border of the map above Station de Réallon. Please note that the walk itself is on another map, and you should have #3437 "Orcière-Merlette" with you also.*

Start: Walk to the back of the parking area, heading left for a minute. Turn right at the signs directing you to the fort and *ruine*. This rocky, mountain path ascends fairly steeply to the ruins—clearly in view in front of you. The climb looks tougher than it is; just take it slowly, and you'll reach 5233 ft. (1595 m.) within forty-five minutes. A sign indicates that you are at the ruins of a twelfth-century fortress—a great place to explore and enjoy a picnic lunch.

When ready, retrace your steps, heading back for a few minutes on the white and red blazed path. However, take the first right turn and walk along the mountainside. The trail narrows as it descends easily along the hillside, with waist-high purple flowers in the surrounding meadows. This trail is somewhat rocky in spots but easily traversed. The map identifies it as "GR 50-Tour du Haut Dauphinée." You can see the hamlet of le Villard down on the left. At a descending, rocky stream bed, turn left and walk down the rocky wagon path to the road at le Villard. Turn left again and walk back on the rarely used road to Réallon and your car.

Walk #4

Les Orres Lift to Top Station, (Optional Walk to Petit Vallon and along the Ridge), Walk to Les Orres
Walking Easy Time: 3 to 5 hours
Rating: Comfortable

Today's hike at les Orres gives *Easy Walkers* a fresh perspective of the Embrunais and could be considered more challenging if you go on to take the ridge walk. You'll drive to the lift station at Les Orres, a large ski complex that services 7000 skiers a day in winter. With the development of Lake Serre-Ponçon, summer visitors are also using the ski facilities, keeping the lifts busy and the trails open.

You'll take one of several lifts up to either 7874 or 8202 ft. (2400 or 2500 m.), depending which chairlift is open, and take an optional walk up to the peak at 8859 ft. (2700 m.). The paths are wide and easy to find, and an hour's ascent brings you up to the ridge. After exploring the high ridge area between Petit Vallon and Grand Vallon, you can return to Les Orres by using one of several options. Allow the better part of the day for this hike and excursion, including travel, lunch, rest, and photography. There are restaurants with sun-terraces at the base and mid-stations of the chairlifts.

Directions: Turn off the main road from Embrun at the Baratier/Les Orres traffic circle, driving in the direction of Les Orres Station (*not* the town of les Orres), on an ascending, winding, mountain road, with lovely views across the valley and back to the lake.

You 'll soon arrive at Les Orres Station, easily recognized by the myriad of high-rise apartments, typical of French ski villages built in the 1950s and 60s. As you enter Les Orres Station, take your first available parking spot. Walk through the center of the village, following the signs reading REMONTÉE MÉCANIQUE, to the Pré Longis Télésiège, open every day in summer. Buy a ticket to the top station, good for any of the chairlifts in this area. The return is free of charge.

Take the Pré Longis chairlift to the mid-station at 6316 ft. (1925 m.) and exit to one of the two second-station chairlifts that are open that day—either Fontaines or Pousterie. Fontaines will take you to 7819 ft.

Hint: *Europeans love to take these mountain roads at breakneck speed. If you wish to sightsee, park on one of the wider, inside shoulders, but while driving, keep your eyes on the road and your rearview mirror.*

(2383 m.), while Pousterie rises to 8304 ft. (2531 m.). *Note: Check with the les Orres Tourist Office or at the lift station to see which of the mid-station chair-lifts are running.* There are trails to the top ridge visible from both stations.

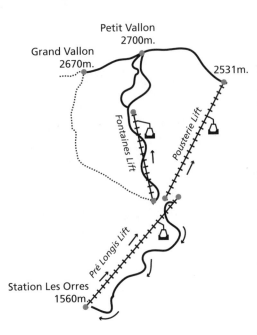

Start: The climb from either lift station takes about an hour to reach le Petit Vallon at 8859 ft. (2700 m.), for a remarkable panorama of Haute-Alpes peaks. At the top, you can walk further toward Grand Vallon, at 8760 ft. (2670 m.). This trail is safe, somewhat rocky, and with the usual ascents and descents. Bikers descend from the peak on a variety of trails, but *Easy Walkers* have the following options:

1. Return by chairlift to the mid-station and take the wide path down to the base station for an easy descent.
2. Follow the biker's path from the top at le Petit Vallon. Walk down to the mid-station and then the bottom.

There's a restaurant with a sun-terrace at the mid-station, but as you walk up to the lift, there's also a shaded picnic table under the trees to your left.

Walk #5

Les Pinées to la Cascade to les Pinées
Walking Easy Time: 3½ hours
Rating: Comfortable

Note: Use the Orcière-Merlette Map #3437 for this walk. Today, *Easy Walkers* have the opportunity of walking in a forest region north of Embrun, close to the village of Châteauroux, to view la Pisse Cascade, a lovely waterfall. This hike is different than many others in the area because it is on a narrow, sheltered forest trail for most of the way and is fairly level till just before the waterfall. The path is blazed orange, easy to find, and winds under tall pine trees in the cool forest. Your walk will begin at les Pinées after driving from Châteauroux on a narrow, one-lane country road, and it will take about two hours to reach the waterfall, where you return by the same route. There are no restaurants or facilities along the trail except for the restaurant at the parking area at les Pinées.

Directions: Drive north from Embrun on main road N94. Make a left turn at the sign for CHATEAUROUX-DES-ALPES and another left turn at a small intersection in the center of the village. At the statue of the soldier, follow GITE AUBERGE LES PINÉES. You'll be driving on a small, winding country road that changes to a bumpy, gravel, one-lane road, ascending to 4265 ft. (1300 m.) at les Pinées. Several side roads take you off to campgrounds and tiny hamlets, but stay on the ascending road and follow the signs GITE AUBERGE to reach the parking area next to the inn (*auberge*).

Start: On the other side of the inn is a blazed sign directing you to CASCADE DE LA PISSE. Walk up the wide gravel path until you come to a tiny stream. Follow the trail to the right in the direction of LA CASCADE, with the canal on your left. This mostly level trail is clearly defined. The path soon goes along a small pipeline in the forest that brings water down the mountain, and there are occasional leaks, so the trail can be very muddy in spots. Other signs confirm your direction to la Cascade, and after about fifty minutes, the path descends sharply down to the right, signed again LA CASCADE. Turn left across the stream, taking the path on the right. It's steep for a bit but levels out and meets the road to the waterfall. To return, follow the same path back to the parking area at les Pinées and retrace your car route to your hotel.

Walk #6

An Excursion in the Queyras—A Walk around and about Abriès (Excursions to Saint-Véran and Château Queyras)
Walking Easy Time: 2 to 3 hours
Rating: Comfortable

Plan a full day for today's walk and excursion, because there's a special treat in store for *Easy Walkers* today. The Parc Natural Régional du Queyras was first designated in 1977 to preserve the character, rural heritage, and natural beauty within 250 square miles of high mountains, interspersed with broad, grassy meadows, farms, small villages, and hiking trails. But the pur-

Hint: *Today's excursion is split amongst several maps. We recommend using the following Michelin driving maps: #245 - Provence, Côte d'Azur; and #244 - Rhône-Alps; and the following hiking map: IGN #3637 - Mont Viso, St-Véran, Aiguilles.*

pose of our visit today is not only to walk, but also to give you the opportunity to experience the simple grandeur that pervades this natural treasure. You'll travel by car from Embrun, bypassing Guillestre, continuing on a narrow, twisting, mountain road through the remarkably beautiful Gorge du Guil. High, jagged cliffs frame the racing Guil River below; rafters come from all over the world to ride the Guil rapids. As you enter the heart of the Queyras, after driving through a few natural mountain tunnels, the auto road broadens and rises to 4446 ft. (1355 m.) at imposing Château-Queyras—which you'll visit on the way back.

Ahead are the villages of Ville-Vieille, Aiguilles—the commercial center of the Queyras—and Abriès. After your hike, you'll return to the village of Ville-Vieille, which you drove through earlier, and proceed to Saint-Véran, at 6726 ft. (2050 m.), the highest community in Europe. After visiting Saint-Véran, a stop at Fort Queyras will complete this exciting day before your return to Embrun.

Directions: Drive north from Embrun on N94, turning right on D902 in the direction of Guillestre. Continue on 902 until you branch to the right to Château-Queyras, Aiguilles, and Abriès. (D902 branches to the left to Col d'Izoard, climbing on a high, serpentine mountain road toward Briançon. This route was made famous by the bikers of the Tour de France.) Aiguilles is a small village, at 4777 ft. (1456 m.), with a tiny shopping district teeming with French and Italian backpackers (the Italian border is quite close) and the local Tourist Office. It's a good place to pick up a picnic lunch if you didn't do so earlier. From Aiguilles, continue on D947 into Abriès, where your walk along the hillside through the Forêt de Marassan begins. Continue on D947 into Abries. Cross the Torrent de Bouchet (still driving on D947), and as you approach the last group of buildings, make a right turn and park near the Guil River.

Start: Walk across the river and turn right on the path, passing a shrine. Proceed through the Marassan Forest in the direction of Aiguilles. There is a left turn on the trail that rises up the mountain, but you'll continue ahead along the hillside, walking as far as you feel comfortable (remembering the forthcoming excursions to St-Véran and Fort Queyras). The return along the same path provides outstanding views of the high peaks along the Italian border, very close to Abriès. In fact, if you were to walk past Ristolas instead of turning left to return to Abriès, you could pick up trail GR58 and cross Col Lacroix into Italy!

However, drive back from Abriès as you came on D947, and at Ville-Vieille turn left on D5 to St-Véran. The Demoiselles Coiffée or Coiffeured Ladies were formed when rocks of various sizes became imbedded in loose, alluvial deposits and, over the centuries, were topped by a single, large stone block. They form one of the strangest sights in the Hautes-Alpes, and you can see some of them on the ascent to Saint-Véran. Drive up to the high parking area outside Saint-Véran, park, and walk through the village, the main tourist attraction of the Queyras. A rare, preserved village, the streets of Saint-Véran are bordered by ancient houses, many decorated with sundials painted in the early nineteenth century. In fact, there are fifteen different sundials preserved in Saint-Véran. The architecture in Saint-Véran is distinctive—simple structures of wood and stone, with complementary roof lines, framed by open meadows and hills.

When ready to leave, return by way of Ville-Vieille on D5, turning left on D947 to Château-Queyras. Park at the top of the hill, just below the château. It's fun to wander through the dungeons, along parapets, and into army barracks, while crossing drawbridges. Walk through impressively engineered Fort/Château Queyras, but remember, it's easy to get lost in this cavernous building, so it's best to follow the little guide given to you upon entering.

On the way back to Embrun, if there's time, you might wish to pay a visit to Mont Dauphin/Guillestre. Follow signs to Mont Dauphin, built on steep, rocky slopes above Guillestre and the Durance River. Acting on order from King Louis XIV, famous French military engineer Vauban planned to control the country between the Guil and Durance Rivers and ordered the fort built in the eighteenth century.

Return to Embrun by reversing directions on the same roads.

PARIS EXPRESSED

"Paris Expressed" is written expressly for *Easy Walkers* who wish to spend a few days exploring Paris before or after their alpine walking vacation, using Paris airports for arrival and/or departure. It is not intended to be a thorough guide to the City of Light but rather a "hot list" of important sightseeing attractions.

Most *Walking Easy* readers visit France to walk in the Alps. However, you might wish to add a few extra days to your itinerary for walking in this extraordinarily beautiful and exciting city. If you have only one or two nights to spend in Paris, it might be easier (and cheaper) to stay at one of the new, modern hotels at the airport, using quick public transportation to and from Paris. Of course, if your itinerary permits more time in Paris, you'll probably want to stay in the city. It's recommended that you purchase one of the many available Paris travel guides to supplement the following information and suggested walking itineraries.

Paris Expressed Transportation

Arriving By Plane - Roissy/Charles de Gaulle Airport is 15 miles (25 km) northeast of Paris. **Roissybus** operates every fifteen minutes for the forty-five- to sixty-minute ride between the airport and the Opera House on rue Scribe (in central Paris). The bus runs from 5:45 A.M. to 11:00 P.M. The **Air France Shuttle Bus** departs every fifteen to twenty minutes between 5:40 A.M. and 11:00 P.M. and operates between the airport and Métro stops at Port Maillot and Charles de Gaulle Etoile (Arc de Triomphe). The ride takes between forty-five and sixty minutes. **Roissyrail** operates between the airport and central Paris every fifteen minutes, with fast RER trains heading to important change stops at Gare du Nord, Châtelet-les-Halles (near the Louvre Museum), and Notre-Dame Cathedral, among many others.

Orly Airport is 8 miles (13 km) south of Paris. Public transportation from Orly to the city includes a **free shuttle bus** leaving every fifteen minutes for the nearby Métro and RER train station where it is a thirty-five-minute RER ride to the center of Paris. The **Air France Bus,** with departures every twelve minutes between 5:45 A.M. and 11:00 P.M., leaves from Orly and makes the trip to Gare des Invalides in about thirty minutes.

Arriving By Train - There are six major train stations in Paris; buses operate between the stations and each has a Métro stop linking it with the rest of the city. Taxis are always available. These stations and their surrounding areas are not in the best parts of the city, so be alert. **Gare St-Lazare** services northwest France, such as Normandy; **Gare du Nord** is the arrival point for European trains from the north, such as London, Holland, etc.; **Gare Montparnasse** is the arrival point for trains from western France; **Gare de Lyon** handles the southeast, with trains from the Riviera, **Gare de l'Est** is the destination for trains from the east, such as Alsace, Zurich, Luxembourg, and Austria; and finally the **Gare d'Austerlitz** services the southwest, such as the Loire Valley and further into Spain.

Hint: Taxis are available at either airport for a more expensive ride into the city, but they will take you right to your hotel. Always take a metered cab from the cab line; do not take a meterless taxi.

Arriving by Car - Driving in Paris is not recommended—parking is limited and traffic is horrendous. We suggest that if you arrive by car, park it in a garage for your stay and take public transportation.

Paris Transportation

By Métro - The subway trains operate between 5:30 A.M. and 1:15 A.M., are efficient, easy to use, fast, and fairly safe (warnings have been issued for pickpockets, however). Each station provides a directional map, and many stations now have maps with lighted route indicators—just press the button for your final destination. Within city limits, the same tickets can be used for the Métro, RER trains, and buses. At the station entrance, insert your ticket into the turnstile and walk through. Remember, tickets are sometimes checked at exits and on trains and/or platforms.

In addition to a one-ticket purchase, you also have the option of buying the following money-saving passes:

Carnet - A ten-ticket packet.

Paris-Visite Pass - This is probably the most economical pass for *Easy Walkers*. It is good for three or five days and allows *unlimited* travel on the Paris Métro, bus systems, and RER trains. These passes are sold at main Métro stations and at the Tourist Office on the Champs-Elysées. **Carte Mobilis** allows unlimited travel on all bus, subway, and RER lines during a one-day period. It is sold at any Métro station.

Carte Orange is good for seven days and allows unlimited travel on the subway and buses. You'll need a small photo of yourself (1 inch wide by 1¼ inch long).

By Bus: Many first-time visitors to Paris opt to take a get-acquainted bus tour before striking out on their own. Terrific for sightseeing, regular buses run from 7:00 A.M. to about 8:30 P.M. You can use your Métro tickets or passes on the bus line; however, buses charge by distance, and the Métro does not. You can pick up an RATP bus map at the tourist office.

By Tourist Bus (Balabus) - If you are in Paris for the first time **on Sunday or a public holiday, from noon to 9:00 P.M., April 15 to September only** and want an overview of the city (without commentary), you can take the orange and white Balabus. The Balabus takes you to the main tourist sites of Paris, with bus stops marked Balabus Bb. They run in both directions between the Grande Arche de La Défense and Gare de Lyon. For a get-acquainted, two-hour tour of Paris with commentary, on a double decker bus, you might try **Cityrama**. The buses don't stop at any attractions for a visit, but the tour will give you a feel of the city, and you can then go back in depth on your own.

By Taxi - If the *libre* sign is lit, the cab is available. Do **not** take cabs without meters unless you agree on a fare first. Fares increase at night and weekends, and a 15 percent tip is customary.

By Boat - The **Batobus** operates on the Seine River from May to September every thirty minutes from 10:00 A.M. to 7:00 P.M., stopping at locations near the Eiffel Tower, the Louvre, Notre-Dame, etc. Look for signs on the quays. You can enjoy many of the best views of Notre-Dame and the bridges and areas along the river on **Bateaux-Mouche** cruises on the Seine. The tours leave every day, every thirty minutes, between 10:00 A.M. and 11:30 P.M., from the right bank of the Seine next to Pont de l'Alma, Métro stop: Alma-Marceau. The trip lasts about seventy-five minutes.

Paris Expressed Walks

The main Paris Tourist Information Office (Office du Tourisme) is located at 127 Champs-Elysées (George V Métro stop) and is open daily from 9:00 A.M. to 8:00 P.M., April to October. *Easy Walkers* should pick up a city map, a public transportation map, brochures with current museum hours and costs, and *Paris Information*, a tourist magazine written in English.

> **Hint:** *To save money on museum visits, buy a Carte Musée et Monuments at the first museum you visit. It will get you into seventy-one museums and attractions in Paris and allow you to bypass the lines at admission windows because you just show the card as you enter. There are one- , three- , and five-day passes.*

Walk #1

Place de l'Opera to rue de la Paix to place Vendôme to place de la Concorde to Musée de l'Orangerie to Tuileries Gardens to the Louvre Museum to Notre-Dame Cathedral

Walk or take the Métro (*Opéra stop*) to **place de l'Opéra.** Walk away from this Rococo opera house and turn right on the fashionable shopping street rue de la Paix, to **place Vendôme,** one of the loveliest squares in Paris. Designed in the seventeenth century, it's now a walking-only area. Its arcade shops contain jewelers, perfumers, banks, the Ministry of Justice, and the Ritz Hotel. Walk through Vendôme and pick up rue Castiglione to rue Rivoli, crossing over Rivoli straight ahead to enter the **Jardin des Tuileries (Tuileries Gardens)**—one of the finest examples of French formal gardens, designed by the man who planned the gardens at Versailles—laid out in geometric shapes with shrubbery, flower beds, statues, and fountains.

A right turn brings you to **Jeu de Paume,** a gallery of contemporary art facing place de la Concorde, in the northeast corner of the Tuileries. Turn right on the main walking path in the gardens to arrive at the **Louvre Museum** entrance, **la Pyramide,** designed by I. M. Pei. The entrance to the Louvre is through this controversial 71-foot-high glass pyramid, housing a collection of shops, restaurants, and automatic ticket machines. The two most famous ladies of the Louvre Museum, the *Venus de Milo* and Leonardo da Vinci's *Mona Lisa*, draw the crowds, but familiar masterpieces are commonplace in this treasure trove. The museum is divided into seven departments: Asian antiquities; Egyptian antiquities; Greek, Roman, and Etruscan antiquities; sculpture; painting, prints and drawings; and objets d'art. Many days are needed to fully appreciate one of the world's largest museums! Guided tours in English covering the highlights of the Louvre are available. Check for information and purchase tickets at the window marked *Acceul des Groupes*, located inside the Pei pyramid. Check the Louvre's Web site at www.louvre.fr for current data on hours and exhibits.

Exit the Louvre on to the banks of the Seine and walk along the river, crossing at its oldest bridge, **Pont Neuf.** The Seine forks here to form **Ile de la Cité,** actually the birthplace of Paris—about 250 B.C. Turn left as soon as you cross the first fork of the river and walk ahead to the **Conciergerie,** the remains of the former royal palace, used as a prison during the French Revolution. It is open daily from 10:00 A.M. to 6:30 P.M. In back of the Conciergerie is **Sainte-Chapelle** and the **Palais de Justice.** The Gothic architecture of Sainte Chapelle was originally conceived to house the sacred crown of thorns and other holy relics sent from Constantinople in the thirteenth century. Note the brilliant, stained-glass windows, with miniature scenes of biblical life, and the graceful 247-foot church spire.

Exiting the church, walk ahead into place du Parvis de Notre Dame. Distances from Paris to all parts of France are measured from a plaque in the center of this square. **Cathédrale Notre-Dame de Paris** is located on the front of the square on this island in the Seine, rich in history and historical monuments. To better appreciate one of the world's finest examples of Gothic architecture, first walk around the entire building. The foundations for the cathedral were laid in 1163, and it took more than 200 years to build, with sculptured portals, graceful columns, splendid stained-glass windows (best viewed at sunset), choir screens, altars, paintings, and sculptures. Victor Hugo immortalized the cathedral in *The Hunchback of Notre Dame*, and to visit the famous gargoyles, you can walk up the steps leading to 225-foot-high, twin square towers—flat on top. Perhaps you can visualize Quasimodo peering from behind one of those grimy, grotesque stone sculptures! Walk through the garden in back of the cathedral to the end of Île de la Cité for a view of the **Memorial des Martyrs Français de la Déportation,** in memory of French martyrs of the underground resistance of World War II who were sent to concentration camps.

Between Notre-Dame and the Church of Sainte-Chapelle is the Cité Métro stop with its art deco entrance.

Walk #2

Eiffel Tower to École Militaire to Hôtel des Invalides (Napoléon's Tomb) to Rodin Museum to Petit Palais (Museum of Fine Arts of Paris) to Grand Palais to Champs-Elysées

Walk or take the Métro (Bir-Hakeim or Trocadéro stop) to **le Tour Eiffel (Eiffel Tower).** This symbol of the Paris skyline, built in 1889, is one of the most recognizable structures in the world. The tower is 1056 ft. (322 m.) high, and on a clear day, the incredible views from the top span a radius of over 40 miles. The elevator to the first landing provides views of the rooftops of Paris, and access to a movie, museum, restaurants, and bar; the second landing gives you a view of the city, with Le Juiles Verne Restaurant; the third stage boasts an incredible panorama of Paris, with its monuments and the surrounding countryside. The Tower is open daily from 9:30 A.M. to 11:00 P.M. After leaving the Eiffel Tower, walk through **Champ de Mars** park, with trees, gardens, reflecting pool, and fountains, to **École Militaire,** established in 1751 by King Louis XV for needy officers-in-training—now a defense study center. Facing the school and just beyond it is the main **UNESCO** building, erected in 1958 and decorated with frescoes by Picasso, mobiles by Calder, murals by Miró, Japanese gardens by Noguchi, and sculptures by Henry Moore.

Turn left past UNESCO on ave. de Ségur, and walk ahead to place Vauban and straight ahead to **les Invalides** and **Napoléon's Tomb.** This vast building was built by Louis XIV as a refuge for disabled soldiers; it contains 10 miles of corridors under its golden dome. The royal Church of the Dôme, part of the complex, houses the Tomb of Napoléon. Also part of les Invalides is an **Army Museum** containing weapons, uniforms, and equipment.

Passing Eglise du Dôme and the Court of Honor, you can detour to the **Musée National Auguste Rodin,** located in an eighteenth-century Paris home, the Hôtel Biron at 77 rue de Varenne. Many of Rodin's sculptures are placed throughout the elegant gardens. To reach the Rodin Museum, turn right on place des Invalides, right on boulevard des Invalides and left on rue de Varennes. The museum is on the right. Walk back and cross place des Invalides, now walking on ave. W. Churchill, crossing the Seine on **Pont Alexandre III.** On the right is the **Petit Palais-Museum of Fine Arts of Paris,** containing exhibits of Paris history along with early paintings and sculpture. Across from the Petit Palais is the **Grand Palais,** built for the 1900 World Exposition. It's now the home of the **Paris Science Museum** and **Planetarium**.

There is a Métro stop (*place Clemenceau)* where ave. W. Churchill meets the Champs-Elysées.

Walk #3

Arc de Triomphe to the Champs-Elysées to place de la Concorde to Madeleine Church to place de l'Opera

Walk or take the Métro (Charles-de-Gaulle/Etoile stop) to the **Arc de Triomphe,** the largest and probably the most famous triumphal arch in the world—163 feet high and 147 feet wide—located at the western end of the Champs Elysées. It was commissioned by Napoléon to commemorate his victories, and beneath the Arc is the Tomb of the Unknown Soldier and the Eternal Flame. The view of Paris from the top is extraordinary, and you can take the elevator or climb the stairs.

Twelve broad avenues, including the Champs-Elysées, radiate from the Arc like spokes on a wheel. To reach the Arc and/or the Champs Elysées, use the underground passage—do **not** attempt to cross the busy square on city streets! Walk on the **Champs Elysées** from the Arc de Triomphe and place de l'Étoile, past Rond-Point. Mark Twain wrote that the Champs-Elysées was the liveliest street in the world. Today, you'll find high-priced sidewalk cafés, tourist stores, and even fast-food hamburger places. However, the broad, tree-lined boulevard stretches for 2 miles and is still a great place for window shopping or people watching.

Turn left on ave. de Marigny and right on rue du Faubourg St. Honoré, passing the **Palais de l'Elysée,** residence of the president of France. This street is noted for the chic boutiques of high fashion designers. Turn left on rue Royale and walk to place de la Madeleine and the **Church of the Madeleine,** built in 1806 by Napoléon to honor his fighting men. Note the 34-foot-high bronze doors depicting the Ten Commandments. At the front of place de la Madeleine, turn diagonally right and enter blvd. de la Madeleine, strolling onto one of the grand boulevards of Paris, and then entering place de l'Opera. If you turn right on to rue de la Paix, you can enjoy some expensive Paris shopping, but if you turn left and walk 2 blocks, you'll find the department stores Galeries Lafayette and Printemps. The imposing Rococo Paris **Opera House** is located to the left on the square. Its ornate interior, including a famous Chagall dome, is open daily. The nearest Métro stops to the Opera House are: Opera (in the square) or R.E.R. Auber (on rue Auber, past the American Express office).

Optional Paris Expressed Sightseeing Attractions

1. **Centre National d'Art et de Culture Georges Pompidou -** place Georges-Pompidou - Named for the French president who decided to create a cultural center, the innovative, skeletal, outer structure sits in the middle of a large, pedestrians-only area and now draws more visitors than the Eiffel Tower! The center is made up of the **Musée d'Art Moderne (National Museum of Modern Art)** and its collection of

twentieth century modern art masterpieces; the **Public Information Library,** with free access to over one million books, periodicals, etc.; the **Institute for Research and Coordination of Acoustics/Music,** primarily for musicians and composers; and the **Center for Industrial Design.**

Métro stop: Rambuteau, Hôtel-de-Ville.

2. **Musée d'Orsay -** 1, rue de Bellechasse - A former train station has been transformed into a great museum of nineteenth-century art, and its Impressionist section continues to draw large crowds. Don't miss the incredible paintings by van Gogh displayed on the top floor—just one section of its eighty different galleries with furniture, photography, objets d'art and, of course, its celebrated paintings.

Métro stop: Solférino.

3. **Basilique du Sacré-Coeur -** place St-Pierre - The Montmarte section of Paris, location of Sacré-Coeur, was the artists' area of Paris in the late-nineteenth and early-twentieth centuries, its night scenes immortalized in the paintings of Toulouse-Lautrec. The shining white-domed church, located on the highest of the seven hills of Paris, was built in the late 1800s. Its interior is in rich Byzantine style; the view from its dome extends almost 35 miles in every direction. The basilica, dome, and crypt are open daily.

Métro stop: Abbesses or Anvers. Take the elevator to the street and follow funiculaire signs. The funicular rises up to the church.

4. **Les Forum des Halles -** The central market of Paris was razed in 1969, and eighty acres of trendy shops, theaters, galleries, and restaurants, mostly underground, have been built in a contemporary steel-and-glass structure near Orly Airport. For many people, a bowl of traditional French onion soup at a Les Halles restaurant is the only way to end a night on the town.

Métro stop: Les Halles.

5. **Musée Picasso -** Hôtel Salé, 5, rue de Thorigny - The Hôtel Salé is a seventeenth-century mansion located in the oldest area of Paris, and it houses the greatest Picasso collection in the world, as well as Picasso's own collection of works by other famous artists.

Métro stop: St-Paul or Chemin-Vert.

Hint: *Spectacular views of Paris can be seen from the Arc de Triomphe (walk up 284 steps to the top or take the elevator for the highest views over Paris), the Eiffel Tower (on a clear day it provides a 50-mile panorama of the city and its suburbs and is the most popular viewing spot in Paris), the Basilique du Sacré-Coeur (at dawn or sunset, the terrace here is the place to be), Notre-Dame (the top of the towers not only boast thrilling, close-up views of the cathedral, but excellent views of the Île de la Cité and all of Paris), and Centre Georges Pompidou (note the fabulous panorama from the landing at the top of the escalator).*

Paris Expressed Excursions

Most sightseeing areas around Paris can be reached by train, but because of time constraints, a car might be a more viable travel option, enabling *Easy Walkers* to visit more areas in a shorter period of time.

1. Versailles - The opulent palace of Versailles, one of the greatest monuments to lavish living (its cost nearly bankrupted France!), is 13 miles (21 km) southwest of Paris. Construction was started in 1661 and progressed over fifty years. In the mid-nineteenth century, after Napoléon's victories, Versailles was converted to a museum "dedicated to the glory of France."

Versailles is composed of three main areas: the **palace** with its six magnificent **Grands Appartements;** the **gardens;** and the **Trianons**. The most famous room in the palace is probably the **Hall of Mirrors,** 236 feet long, with seventeen large windows and reflecting mirrors. The **gardens** of Versailles cover 250 acres, originally with 1400 fountains. A walk across the gardens brings you to the palaces of the **Grand Trianon** and **Petit Trianon.** Between the Trianon palaces is a **carriage museum**, with coaches from the eighteenth and nineteenth centuries. The apartments, chapel, and Hall of Mirrors can be visited without a guide. Other areas may be seen with a guide on specific days. Fireworks and illuminated fountains can be seen on many summer evenings. Check with the Paris Tourist Office for current information, dates, and prices.

Directions: By car - Take route N10 to Versailles and park in front of the palace on place d'Armes. By Métro - Exit at Pont de Sèvres station and transfer to bus #171, stopping near the palace gates. By train - Take RER line C5, leaving every fifteen minutes from Paris to Versailles Rive Gauche. Turn right when you exit the station and walk to the palace, or take a shuttle bus.

2. Fountainebleau - The Palace of Fountainebleau, called by Napoléon the "house of the centuries," lies 37 miles (60 km) south of Paris. It was originally used as a hunting resort in the wooded forest and, under François I, grew into a royal palace. Some of the more outstanding rooms in the palace are the Gallery of François I, the ballroom, and the Napoléonic rooms. You can enjoy most of the palace on your own, but the Napoléonic rooms are open by guided tour only. Outside the palace, walk through the gardens and around the carp pond.

Directions: By car - Follow A6 out of Paris toward Lyon, exiting at Fountainebleau. By train and bus - Trains leave from Gare de Lyon in Paris and take thirty-five minutes to one hour. The station is outside of town in Avon—a local bus makes the 2-mile drive to the château every fifteen minutes Monday to Saturday and every thirty minutes on Sunday.

3. Chartres - Sixty miles (97 km) southwest of Paris, the medieval **Cathédrale de Notre-Dame de Chartres,** third-largest cathedral in the world, has become known as the "stone testament of the Middle Ages." Its architecture, sculpture, and most of all, its stained glass give us a new appreciation of art forms of long ago. Even before entering the cathedral, there are the Romanesque sculptures of the Royal Portal, which reportedly mesmerized Rodin for hours. The nave is broader than any in France, its arches rising to 122 feet. The Clocher Vieux (Old Tower Steeple) dates back to the twelfth century, and the Clocher Neuf (New Tower) is from 1134. The Royal Portal was added in the twelfth century, and inside the church is a famous choir screen, created between the sixteenth and eighteenth centuries. However, it is the extraordinary stained-glass windows that seem to transfix most visitors; like a kaleidoscope, they never look the same as the sun moves across the sky. The crypt, third largest in the world and the oldest part of the cathedral, was built from the ninth to the eleventh centuries. A walk through the Episcopal Gardens will give you yet another perspective on this remarkable place.

Directions: By car - Take A10/A11 southwest and follow signs to Le Mans and Chartres. By train - Trains run to Chartres from the Gare Montparnasse and take less than an hour.

FAVORITE ACCOMMODATIONS
INDEX—BY TOWN

France

Baratier: Hotel les Peupliers, 195

Chamonix–Mont Blanc: Hotel La Sapinière, 114

Crots/Embrun: Hotel Les Bartavelles, 195

Les Arcs: Gran Hotel Mercure Coralia, 179

Megève: Hotel Grange d'Arly, 138

Méribel: Hotel Allodis, 161

Morzine: Hotel la Bergerie, 152

Italy

Alleghe: Sporthotel Europa, 66

Cortina d'Ampezzo: Hotel Aquila, 32

Merano/Südtirol: Hotel Bavaria, 50

Merano/Südtirol: Hotel Castel Rundegg, 51

Merano/Südtirol: Hotel Palma, 50

Selva/Gardena: Hotel Malleier, 13

Vigo di Fassa: Hotel Cima Dodici, 81

INDEX

A

Abbaye de Boscoden, 196, 202
Abriès, 208
Agordo, 67
Aiguille du Midi, 128
Aiguille Rouge, 186
Aix-les-Bains, 166, 183
Albergo Miralago, 94
Albertville, 140, 164, 181
Algund, 58
Algunder Waalweg, 58
Alleghe, 65–78
Allues, les, 175, 176
Alpe di Siusi/Seiser Alm, 14, 22
Alta Via di Fassa, 92
Alte Via Dolomiti, 73
Annecy, 117, 139, 165, 181
Aosta, 120, 183
Arc 1600, 188
Arc 1800, 191
Arc 2000, 185, 188
Arc de Triomphe, 216
Arcs, les/Bourg-Saint-Maurice, 177–92
Argentière, 134
Auronzo, 39
Avoriaz, 155

B

Bái de Dónes, 45
Baratier, 202
Barcelonette, 199
Barre des Ecrins, 198
Bellevue, 131
Belluno, 37, 68
Belleville Valley, 165, 182
Belvedere, 34, 92
Bélvèdere, 156

Bergerie du Rey, 191
Berthelets, les, 147
Bettex, le, 147
Bindelweg/Viel del Pan, 92
Bolzano/Bozen, 16, 53, 83
Boscodon Abbey, 196
Bossons Glacier, les, 131
Bossons, les/Planards, les, 115
Bourg-Saint-Maurice, 177–92
Bressanone/Brixen, 16, 36, 55, 85
Brévent, le, 115, 126
Briançon, 197
Brogles, 25
Brunico/Bruneck, 36
Burgin-Saulire, 162, 168

C

Cabin Alpina, 46, 47
Campitello, 83, 87
Canale d'Agordo, 77
Canazei, 69, 83, 92, 94
Cascade le Nyon, 157
Cascade, la, 207
Chalet de la Vieille, 141
Chalet du Fruit, 174
Chambéry, 166, 183
Chamonix, 112–35, 139, 153, 163, 182
Champ de Lare, 202
Champs-Elysées, 215, 216
Charamillon, 133
Chartres, 220
Chavannes, les, 154
Chemin des Oiseaux Migrateurs, 158
Chevan, 148, 150
Chiusa/Klausen, 36, 56

Christomet, le, 146
Ciampedie, 88, 92
Ciampinoi, 14, 18
Cinque Torri, 33, 45
Città di Carpi, 44
Città di Fiume, 73
Clark, 21
Col de Balme, 133
Col de Coux, 158
Col de la Chal, 185
Col de la Lune, 176
Col de Varda, 44
Col de Véry, 150
Col de Voza, 131
Col dei Baldi, 70
Col Drusciè, 40
Col Raiser, 14, 23, 26
Col Rodella, 87
Col Tondo, 33, 42
Col des Posettes, 133
Coldai, 70
Comici, 18
Concorde, la, 214
Cortina d'Ampezzo, 18, 29–47,
    68, 84
Cortina, 33, 40–44
Corvara, 16
Courchevel, 165, 168, 181
Courmayeur, 119, 182
Cristallo, 33

D
Dantercepies, 14, 21
Demoiselles Coiffée, les, 199
Digne-les-Bains, 200
Dobbiaco/Toblach, 34
Dorf Tirol, 61, 62

E
École Militaire, 215
Egna/Neumarkt, 84
Eiffel Tower, 215
Embrun, 193–210

Evian-les-Bains, 116, 139
Evionnaz, 119

F
Falcade, 67, 85
Falier, 78
Faloria, 42
Falzeben, 59
Flégère, la, 115, 126, 134
Fociade, 94
Forchiade, 76
Forêt de Plan Peisey, 191
Forst, 62
Fortress Ruins, 204
Fountainebleau, 220
Friedrich August, 87

G
Gamsblut, 23
Gap, 197
Gardeccia, 88
Gardena Valley, 11
Geneva, 120, 139, 153
Gets, les, 154, 156
Ghetto, The, 100
Glorenza/Glurns, 56
Gorges du Pont du Diable, les,
    117, 153
Grand Palais, 215

H
Hafling, 59
Hans-Friedenweg, 63
Hauteville-Gondon, 175, 182
Helbronner, 128
Hermance, 144
Hochmut, 61, 63
Hôtel des Invalides, 215
Houches, les, 131

I
Ifinger, 59

J
Jaillet, le, 138, 141, 146
Jardins, les, 142
Javen, 142
Jëndertal, 22

L
l'Arpette, 189
l'Osselin, 202
Lac Bleu, 128
Lac de Serre-Ponçon, 199
Lac des Mines d'Or, 158
Lac du Bourget, 166
Lac Marloup, 185–86
Lagazuoi, 33, 46
Lago di Alleghe, 70
Lago di Carezza, 90
Lago di Fedaia, 72, 92
Lago Ghedina, 40
Lake Misurina, 37, 44
Lake Tuéda, 174
l'Alpette, 142, 150
Lana, 62
Lanchettes, les, 142
Larzonei, 86
Lausanne, 118
Lavaredo, 39
Leiter Alm, 63
Leutaz, le, 148, 150
Lienz, 37
l'Index, 134
Longfallhof, 62
Louvre Museum, the, 214

M
Madeleine Church, 216
Maitaz, la, 191
Malga Ciapela, 78
Malga del Sasso Piatto, 87
Malga Prendera, 73
Marlinger Waalweg, 62
Marmolada, 92
Marmolada Glacier, 72

Martigny, 119
Masarè, 76
Maz, le, 142
Mazzin, 82
Megève, 117, 136–50
Meije, la, 198
Mer de Glace, 115, 124
Meraner Hütte, 59
Merano/Meran, 18, 48–64, 84
Méribel, 159–76
Merlet, 127
Micheluzzi/Duron, 87
Miétres, 33, 42
Moena, 82, 94
Mont Caly, 156
Mont Chéry, 156
Mont d'Arbois, 138, 144, 147
Mont Joux, 144
Mont Vallon, 173
Montdauphin, 196
Monte Pana, 20
Montreux, 118
Monument Christomannos, 90
Morzine, 151–58
Mottaret, 171–74
Musée de l'Orangerie, 214

N
Negritella, 92
Nid d'Aigle, 131
Notre-Dame Cathedral, 214

O
Odier, 141
Orres, les, 206
Ortisei/St. Ulrich, 15, 22, 23,
    27, 58, 85

P
Paolina, 90
Paris, 211–20
Pas de Cherferie, 176
Pas du Lac, 162, 168, 174

Passeggiata, 38
Passo Gardena, 21
Passo San Pellegrino, 94
Passo Sella, 18
Pecol, 92
Peisey-Nancroix, 182
Pera di Sopra, 88
Petit Balcon Sud, 127
Petit Palais, 215
Petit Tetraz, 148
Petit Vallon, 206
Piazza di San Marco, 97
Piazza Roma, 95
Pieve di Cadore, 34, 69
Piffing, 59
Pinées, les, 207
Place de l'Opera, 214, 216
Plan, 21
Plan da Tieja, 23
Plan de Gralba, 18
Plan de L'Aiguille, 124
Planay, le, 144
Planpraz, 126
Pléney, le, 154
Pocol, 34
Poet, le, 202
Pont d'Arbon, 147
Ponte Gardena/Waidbruck, 17
Pozza di Fassa, 82
Prarion, 131
Praz sur Arly, 148
Praz, les, 126, 129
Pré Rosset, 150
Puez-Geisler Park, 17

Q
Queyras, the, 208

R
Raschötz, 14
Réallon, 204
Regensburgerhütte/Rifugio
   Firenze, 27

Ridge Walk, 176
Riffian, 53
Ristorante Rio Gere, 42
Rochebrune, 138, 142, 150
Rodin Museum, 215
Rosengarten, 90
Rovereto, 84
Rue de la Paix, 214

S
Saint-Véran, 208
Sala, 76
Saltria, 22
San Candido/Innichen, 35
San Giovanni di Fassa, 83
San Marco, 97
Sandro Pertini, 87
Saulire, la, 171
Schenna/Scena, 53, 64
Schloss Brunnenburg, 61
Schloss Tirol, 61
Scoiattoli, 45
Scotoni, 46
Seceda, 14, 25–27
Selva di Cadore, 68
Selva/Wolkenstein, 11–28
Sesto/Sexten, 35
Soraga, 82
St. Jakob, 23
Staulanza, 75–76

T
Tappeiner Weg, 58
Tignes, 165, 181, 191
Tines, les, 130
Tiroler Kreuz, 61
Tofana di Mezzo, 33, 40
Tondi di Faloria, 33
Tougnète, 162, 167, 176
Tre Cime Locatelli/Drei Zinnen
   Hütte, 39
Trento, 54, 84
Tuileries Gardens, 214

V
Vajolet, 88
Val d'Isère, 165, 181, 191
Val di Fassa, 82, 94
Val di Garès, 77
Vallonga, 86
Vallunga/Langental, 28
Vanoise National Park, 173
Vellau, 63
Vendôme, 214
Venezia, 75
Venice, 17, 69, 95–100
Verona, 56

Versailles, 219
Vigo Catinaccio, 88, 92
Vigo di Fassa, 79–94
Villard, le, 204
Villaret, le, 175
Villarnard, 175
Vipiteno/Sterzing, 55

Y
Yvoire, 117, 153

Z
Zermatt, 122

ABOUT THE AUTHORS

Chet and Carolee Lipton became enchanted with the incredible alpine trail system during their travels abroad, and they've been walking it ever since. The Liptons authored the *Walking Easy* series to fill a need for user-friendly, day-walk hiking guides for active adults and young families.

The Liptons return to the Alps each summer to research new base villages, summer day-walks, and hotels for the *Walking Easy* books, including *Walking Easy in the Italian and French Alps* and *Walking Easy in the Swiss and Austrian Alps.*

You can contact Chet and Carolee by E-mail at walkingez@aol.com or on the Internet at www.walkingeasy.com.

Help Us Keep This Guide
Up to Date

Every effort has been made by the author and editors to make this guide as accurate and useful as possible. However, many changes can occur after a guide is published—establishments close, phone numbers change, hiking trails are rerouted, facilities come under new management, etc.

We would love to hear from you concerning your experiences with this guide and how you feel it could be improved and be kept up to date. While we may not be able to respond to all comments and suggestions, we'll take them to heart and we'll make certain to share them with the author. Please send your comments and suggestions to the following address:

The Globe Pequot Press
Reader Response/Editorial Department
P.O. Box 480
Guilford, CT 06437

Or you may e-mail us at: editorial@globe–pequot.com

Thanks for your input, and happy travels!